Normative Theories of the Media

THE HISTORY OF COMMUNICATION

Robert W. McChesney and
John C. Nerone, editors

*A list of books in the series appears
at the end of this book.*

Normative Theories of the Media

JOURNALISM IN DEMOCRATIC SOCIETIES

Clifford G. Christians • Theodore L. Glasser
Denis McQuail • Kaarle Nordenstreng
Robert A. White

UNIVERSITY OF ILLINOIS PRESS
Urbana and Chicago

© 2009 by the Board of Trustees
of the University of Illinois
All rights reserved
Manufactured in the United States of America
1 2 3 4 5 C P 5 4 3 2 1
∞ This book is printed on acid-free paper.

Library of Congress Cataloging-in-Publication Data
Normative theories of the media : journalism in
democratic societies / Clifford G. Christians [et al.].
p.   cm. — (The history of communication)
Includes bibliographical references and index.
ISBN 978-0-252-03423-7 (cloth : alk. paper)
ISBN 978-0-252-07618-3 (pbk. : alk. paper)
1. Journalism—Political aspects. 2. Journalism—
Social aspects. 3. Democracy. 4. Press and politics.
5. Freedom of the press.
PN4751.N67   2009
070.4—dc22   2008049081

Contents

Prospects

Preface

The question of the role of journalism in a democratic society is so central that even students and practitioners of communication are used to taking it for granted. Yet, today, both journalism and democracy are challenged by great changes, ranging from information technology to the global economy. All of this is an invitation to examine critically the media's place and task in society—in particular in societies where democracy is understood not only as a political system but as a culture. At issue is not only what *is* the role of journalism in society but above all what this role *should be.* Such a perspective of the media's mission in democracy leads us to a normative level—beyond factual landscapes toward values and objectives.

This book is inspired by two interrelated aims: one practical and the other theoretical. The practical motivation grows out of the fact that the field of journalism and mass communication has an ongoing need for more theoretical treatments of media and society in general, and journalism and democracy in particular. The best known book in this category, *Four Theories of the Press,* by Fred Siebert, Theodore Peterson, and Wilbur Schramm (1956), is badly outdated and without obvious successors (see the reviews by Merrill [2002] and Nerone [2002]). What is needed is an approach that has much of the same didactic clarity, but with foundations in normative and political theory that can deal more adequately with basic questions, such as: What is and what should be the media's role in a democratic society? How do we classify media systems and journalistic traditions? These questions are more and more burning in the contemporary world, where earlier Cold War divisions are replaced by new divides.

The theoretical motivation for this book is to respond to the intellectual challenge posed by scholars who are concerned with professional ethics, with a more responsible performance of the media industries, and with a more adequate education of journalists. The academic study of journalism and mass communication has become established over the past fifty years. But it still remains inadequate for describing and explaining the media's role and task in society—in short, in providing us with normative theory. And this intellectual challenge is becoming more and more acute in a world where cultures are clashing and media are converging.

The authors of this book found each other working on these points more than two decades ago. By the early 1980s, one of us (McQuail) had written a chapter on normative theories of the press in his introductory textbook, while another one (Nordenstreng) had made ambitious plans to rewrite the *Four Theories*. It was in the middle of the 1980s that we really focused on the topic, brought together in platforms of the Association for Education in Journalism (AEJ, later AEJMC), International Communication Association(ICA), and International Association for Media and Communication Research (IAMCR). Fueling this collegial process was Christians's work in Illinois on theories of media ethics, Glasser's work in Minnesota on theories of democracy and the media, and White's work in England on democratization and communication.

An initial inspiration for all of us came from the debate on the New World Information and Communication Order (NWICO), which was largely about the normative role media were supposed to perform in society—something lost in the big power politics waged around the United Nations and UNESCO. A common concern was that the framework of *Four Theories* was not sufficiently open to the whole range of value traditions and sociopolitical philosophies underlying public communication throughout the world. The typology of *Four Theories,* and the variations it inspired, almost invariably favored the industrialized Western powers and tended to institutionalize and justify the great imbalances of the present global order of communication.

Formal and informal meetings between us evolved in the spring of 1993 into this book project, the basic concept of which was outlined at a lake outside Tampere under the sponsorship of the Academy of Finland. Our intention was to look for a fresh approach to normative theories of the media—not just to revise and complement *Four Theories*. A new beginning was natural because another team project, *Last Rights* (Nerone 1995; see also Nerone 2004), with its excellent critical analysis that revealed the biases of *Four Theories,* opened the way for a new framework. Accordingly, we are continuing the project from where *Last Rights* left it. We admit that normative theories are culturally bound constructs or paradigms rather than actually existing systems. Indeed, the point made by Altschull's seventh "law of journalism" is well taken: "Press practices always differ from press theory" (1995, 441). But we recognize the need for normative theories as cognitive maps for media professionals—despite suggestions that in these postmodern times they might be obsolete (Nerone 1995, 184).

A theory is here understood to be a reasoned explanation of why particular actions lead to certain outcomes. Our premise is that there are two types of "theories of the press": first, those *prescribing* the *normative tasks* for the media in society, and second those *describing* the *factual role* of the media in society. The latter approaches the issue from the "objective" angle of media sociology, while the former deals with the "subjective," culturally related values held by various actors about the mission of the media. Normative theory, in our view, attempts to explain why a certain organization of public discourse leads to better collective decisions and eventually to an improved quality of life. For instance, if the norms of public debate in a given country insist that all participate, including the poor, then one might argue that the country ought to have a more just system of education. Thus the media–society relationship can be articulated at two levels, real or descriptive and ideal or normative, although the difference between these is far from crystal clear.

Journalism education has typically separated these two levels by placing the sociological approach into the category of scientific studies, whereas the normative approach usually has been taught together with media law and ethics as something that is value bound and part and parcel of professional practice. Normative approaches to the media among professionals have usually been taken for granted without questioning their foundations. Thus the prevailing professional and philosophical assumptions have remained unchallenged and even legitimized by theories of the press.

Our work is inspired by the idea of raising professional consciousness within the media world, including media scholarship. Normative theories may serve not only as a defense of political philosophies but can also be made to sensitize media policymakers and professionals to acknowledge their own unstated premises—by exposing discrepancies between philosophical rationales and actual operations. Thus normative theories are justified, not as affirmative instruments to strengthen the prevailing ideology—typically the case of *Four Theories*—but as instruments of emancipation from the status quo. In this respect, normative theories support media autonomy and self-regulation. Likewise, normative theories are foundational for serious press criticism, as aptly demonstrated by Wendy Wyatt (2007).

At the same time, however, we take seriously the challenge posed by the two types of theories: ideal and real, normative and sociological. After reviewing past attempts toward theories of the press, one is no longer sure whether they cover the ideal or the real level. Obviously a new beginning must cover both. There is considerable confusion regarding the concept of normativity and therefore we attempt to clarify what is a normative theory and its role in contemporary journalism.

Today this project is especially challenging, as new media and new types of messages enter the field, affecting the nature of journalism in a computer-mediated information system. This information society is characterized by globalization, with simultaneous tendencies for localization. Furthermore, a fundamental soul-searching is occurring among social scientists, with classics of sociology experiencing a revival in the information society and communitarianism gaining momentum in the heartlands of liberalism.

In this context we were faced with much more than a theory of professional ethics, which has typically been the locus of discussion of normative foundations. We were led to reflect on a general normative approach to public communication that integrates issues ranging from personal ethics to professional codes, industry guidelines, national policies, and finally, moral philosophies. As this book has evolved in our discussion, it has become more an attempt to outline a *methodology* of thinking about establishing norms. This methodology builds on and in some way summarizes the very extensive recent debate on normative theory in communication and the role of the media in a democratic society.

The new beginning does not aim at a universally valid typology. Thus we do not wish to replace the original four theories with an alternative set or to add or subtract "theories" from the quartet. The constructs offered in the first place by Siebert, Peterson, and Schramm were not theories in a proper sense but rather descriptions of four types of media systems, with guiding principles of their operation and legitimation. John Nerone, the editor of *Last Rights,* pointed out that he and his collaborating authors decided they were "not in a position to write a new *Four Theories,* that to do so would require hammering out a consensual scheme among scholars with very different beliefs and priorities" (2002, 136). We could say exactly the same thing. We simply wish to shed light on fundamental issues concerning the relation between media and society in a way that will assist the diagnosis of problems (that undoubtedly exist) and promote reform (certainly needed) based on clear principles of public communication and democracy.

Our project deliberately limits itself to what might be called democratic theories. We recognize, however, that there are many ways of organizing democracy and no particular society can claim to represent the democratic ideal. Building the framework on models of democracy rather than models of communication also helps to avoid the tendency to develop a "fortress journalism syndrome," that is, to think in terms of the media instead of the people. Second, we wish to avoid a pigeonhole approach whereby each media system is placed in one category only. Instead, we suggest that each national media system and medium—even each individual journalist—shares more than one intellectual tradition, and that typologies serve the purpose of analytical distinctions and not of totalizing labels.

Our attempt at a new beginning was easier said than done, as shown by the years that passed while we worked on it. These years have brought us new food for thought regarding both media and society, including the Internet, the digital divide, and new social movements. All this has fed the intellectual challenge of our task. We have felt that the state of the art not only invites but demands that we examine the foundations of normative theory of public communication as expressed in a range of models of democracy.

Accordingly, we wanted to write this book to provide a framework for dialogue between traditions having their roots in different civilizations and religio-philosophical systems. Our own perspective is naturally shaped by the traditions of the Western world, but we advocate an inclusive approach and an open mind. Hence we acknowledge that ours is not a universally applicable answer to the question of the media in society in general or journalism in a democratic society in particular. Even within the Western framework we do not claim to present a final answer but rather an intervention into ongoing scholarly work, hoping that our contribution will stimulate debate and encourage others to continue the work. At the same time, we wish this to be an educational book that explains and explores the field, addressed also to students with an instructional purpose, instead of merely a scholar-to-scholar book with a more select focus.

The book is composed of three parts, in addition to its introductory and closing chapters. The introduction reviews how the literature in journalism and mass communication articulates the tasks for media in society, and how our book attempts to enrich this scholarship. Part I reviews normative theory and the ways that thinking about social communication has changed over the past two millennia as crystallized in four traditions. Part II focuses on democracy and the role played by the journalistic media in it, both in theory and in practice. Part III presents four ideal types of media roles in democracy—not as new sacred models to be canonized but as yardsticks to sensitize the professionals of the field to being more responsible. The final chapter offers reflections and assessments, as well as opening prospects for the future.

This book is an outcome of collective work by the authors, with Christians acting as coordinator. Principal authorship of the chapters has been Nordenstreng: chapters 1 and 8; White: chapters 2 and 3; Glasser: chapters 4 and 9; McQuail: chapters 5, 6, and 10; Christians: chapter 7.

Clifford G. Christians, Urbana, Illinois
Theodore L. Glasser, Stanford, California
Denis McQuail, East Leigh, England
Kaarle Nordenstreng, Tampere, Finland
Robert A. White, Mwanza, Tanzania

Introduction

1

Beyond *Four Theories of the Press*

Since the 1960s a rich expansion of thought has taken place regarding normative theories of public communication, models of democracy, and the roles of journalism in democratic societies. The media world has become far more complicated, and the analysis is increasingly widespread. In this chapter we review American, European, and other perspectives as a basis for our own synthesis later in the chapter. The debate following the publication of *Four Theories of the Press* by the University of Illinois Press in 1956[1] provides a convenient starting point because that typology, so very controversial, stimulated a variety of contrasting models of media systems. Many important issues in journalism and democracy have been clarified over these five decades, and many original arguments have emerged.

The Debate Beginning in the 1950s

Four Theories of the Press, by Fred Siebert, Theodore Peterson, and Wilbur Schramm, was important above all for its typological thinking. As spelled out in the subtitle, it introduced "The Authoritarian, Libertarian, Social Responsibility and Soviet Communist Concepts of What the Press Should Be and Do." These four concepts were the authors' response to their basic question: Why do the mass media appear in widely different forms and serve different purposes in different countries? They argued that "the press always takes on the form and coloration of the social and political structures within which it operates. Especially, it reflects the system of social control whereby the relations of individuals and institutions are adjusted" (Siebert, Peterson, and Schramm 1956, 1–2).

Such a thesis makes sense, and in its time *Four Theories* provided a welcome stimulus to reflection about the media's role in society by suggesting that press systems are linked to different political systems and philosophies. While it was customary in the social sciences to take a value-free stance, leaving aside the question of social norms, these authors oriented the new field of mass communication toward an explicit analysis of how the press relates to society in terms of political values, professional ethics, and intellectual history. The method of contrasting different paradigms of press and society was not only useful theoretically but provided an important didactic tool for training journalists.

In fact, with the growth of the media since World War II there was inevitably a need to articulate the roles and tasks of the mass media in society, including the relationship between the media and politics. But in this respect, the emerging scholarship had little to offer, and therefore even a casual collection of essays found a niche and became in its way a classic. The book filled an obvious intellectual gap between the academic study of communication and the professional practice of journalism (see Nerone 2004). A bestseller, it was reprinted more times and translated into more languages than perhaps any other textbook in the field.

As suggested by the "beyond" in the title of this chapter, however, this classic has been challenged. Many have pointed out its oversimplified framing of history and its analytical inadequacy. Its political and cultural bias has been recognized since the 1960s, especially by critical approaches to communication research. *Four Theories* was a child of the Cold War era, when the world was deeply divided between the capitalist West, the socialist East, and the underdeveloped South. The fall of Soviet Communism, increasing independence in the global South, and new academic awareness among scholars have called into question the type of normative thinking that *Four Theories* reflected. Consequently, the question today is no longer whether or not the classic is passé but what is the best way to get beyond it. As Hallin and Mancini starkly put it, "It is time to give it a decent burial and move on to the development of more sophisticated models based on real comparative analysis" (2004, 10).

While the book's basic question and thesis were valuable, its four theories typology turned out to be a poor response to the authors' own challenge. A useful eye-opener in this respect was provided by a group of scholars from the University of Illinois at Urbana-Champaign, where the three authors of this book once worked. *Last Rights* (Nerone 1995), published by the University of Illinois Press in 1995, revisited *Four Theories* by critically assessing its relevance in a post–Cold War world. As the editor pointed out, "*Four Theories* does not offer four theories: it offers one theory with four examples" (1995, 18). "It defines the four theories from within one of the four theories—classical liberalism. . . . It is specifically in classical liberalism that the political world is divided into individual versus society or the state" (21). "*Four Theories* and classical liberalism assume that we have freedom of the press if we are free to discuss political matters in print without state suppression" (22).

In a wider perspective, *Last Rights* clarified the moment in intellectual history at which *Four Theories* was written: "By the mid–twentieth century, liberalism had reached a philosophical impasse. And, while political theory has moved beyond the impasse of liberalism, mainstream normative press theory in the United States has not" (Nerone 1995, 4). The stalemate was mainly caused by the fact that it was no longer feasible to view individuals as atoms, with natural rights, at a time when "politics became the stuff of institutions rather than of individuals" (5). Moreover, the press had become an institution, separate from the people, and "it became more intelligent to talk about the public's rights—the right to know, the right to free expression—rather than the press's rights. The press had responsibilities; the public had rights" (6).

One crucial chapter in intellectual history that gave rise to *Four Theories* was the Commission on Freedom of the Press in the mid-1940s.[2] Known as The Hutchins Commission, it elaborated on the media's idea of social responsibility later adopted by Siebert et al. as the third of their four theories. The Commission's report *A Free and Responsible Press* (1947) built a philosophical and moral foundation for the idea that the press owed a responsibility to society. It argued that democracy depended on a flow of trustworthy information and a diversity of relevant opinions. The report in fact elaborated on the idea of social responsibility that the media already subscribed to. The authors of *Four Theories* later adopted this idea as their third theory—that of the social responsibility of the press. One could argue that, if liberalism in general had reached a philosophical impasse by the mid–twentieth century, this theory was a last attempt to revive liberalism in the field of journalism and mass communication.

One of the lasting contributions of *Four Theories* has been the consolidation of thought regarding the media's responsibility to society. Several books have attempted to remedy *Four Theories'* defects by adding typological dimensions or presenting alternative typologies, but none of them managed to gain the acceptance of *Four Theories*. Nevertheless, each new formulation brought out important dimensions and provided valuable insights for a new synthesis.

Other Proposals

Last Rights helped deconstruct *Four Theories* as typology, scholarship, and ideology. Such a critical analysis was indeed a logical first step for anyone who wished to move beyond *Four Theories*. Yet there are a number of other typologies worth recalling, regardless of their relationship to the four theories. In fact, the European examples we list below have little or no kinship with the American four theories, and therefore it would be misleading to view the four theories as a universal baseline. On the other hand, several typologies have been proposed, especially in the United States, to complement and revise the original four theories, as follows.[3]

THE UNITED STATES

The first American among the revisionists was John Merrill, best known for his *Imperative of Freedom* (1974). He criticized particularly social responsibility theory and related notions of people's right to know, the right of access to the media, and the press as the fourth branch of government. For him these were "libertarian myths" that limited true freedom of media and journalists; his thinking boiled down to a dichotomy between authoritarianism/totalitarianism and liberalism/anarchy (1974, 42). This ultralibertarian position led Merrill to advocate nonutilitarian (Kantian) ethics and "existential journalism" (1977).

With his colleague Ralph Lowenstein, Merrill elaborated press philosophies into four types: authoritarian with negative government controls, social-centralist with positive government controls, libertarian without any government controls, and social-libertarian with minimal government controls (Merrill and Lowenstein 1979, 186). Lowenstein refined this classification in the second edition of their textbook, adding a fifth philosophy, social-authoritarian (Merrill and Lowenstein 1979, 164). Lowenstein and Merrill (1990) gave a final shape to Merrill's typology but did not manage to replace his original four theories as a canonic way of thinking about the media's role in society.

In 1981, William Hachten proposed a revision of the original four theories within the context of the global media debate of the 1970s. *The World News Prism* (1981) retained the authoritarian and Communist press concepts but combined the libertarian and social responsibility variants into an overall Western concept. In addition, he introduced two new categories: revolutionary and developmental. A revolutionary role was played by the early *Pravda* as well as various samizdat outlets—from mimeographed newsletters to audiocassettes and email—that challenged the prevailing political order. A developmental role was obvious to everyone who was aware of the Third World realities (Hachten had experienced this in Africa). Accordingly, his typology consisted of five dimensions; but his 1992 updated edition of *The World News Prism* accounted for the collapse of Soviet Communism, suggesting that we might be back to four types: authoritarian, Western, revolutionary, and developmental (this typology is retained in the latest edition, Hachten and Scotton 2007).

Later in the 1980s, Robert Picard added one more variant to earlier typologies: democratic socialist (1985). His source of inspiration was Western Europe and especially Scandinavia, where he observed that state intervention in media economics was exercised to ensure the survival of free media "as instruments of the people, public utilities through which the people's aspirations, ideas, praise, and criticism of the state and society may be disseminated" (70). Picard's democratic socialist theory along with the original libertarian and social responsibility theories are three forms of Western philosophy; whereas the rest of the world were covered by Hachten's developmental and revolutionary concepts as well as the original authoritarian and Communist theories (69).

Another notable American author is Herbert Altschull, whose *Agents of Power* (1984; 1995) presented not just a revision of the original four theories but an alternative paradigm based on the view that all systems of the news media are agents of those who exercise political and economic power (the first of his "seven laws of journalism"; 1984, 298; 1995, 440). He divided the world of media systems into three, following the traditional lines of First, Second, and Third World: market or Western nations, Marxist or communitarian nations, and advancing or developing nations. In these political regions, journalists tend to hold different views of press freedom and the purposes of journalism.

A similar tripartite division of the world was introduced by John Martin and Anju Chaudhary (1983) in their classification of mass media systems as Western, Communist, and Third World. While these were ideological systems with normative undertones, their concept of a media system was an analytical composite of functional elements such as the nature of news and the role of the media in education and entertainment. In fact, this work stands as an illuminating example of blending the two levels—normative and analytical—a blending that was present already in *Four Theories* and became typical in talking about media systems.

In short, American attempts to go beyond the original four theories make up a fairly rich reservoir of ideas and pedagogically useful typologies (for a summary of these revisions, see Lambeth 1995; Mundt 1991). These various proposals clearly suggest the limitations of *Four Theories*, but it has enjoyed considerable respect and has been widely used until the present day. For example, a standard undergraduate textbook of the 1990s, *Modern Mass Media* (Merrill, Lee, and Friedlander 1994), still listed the original four theories in a chapter on press and government. A fresh textbook, *Mass Communication: Living in a Media World*, sets out "to fully integrate twenty-first-century developments into the text in a way that older books cannot" (Hanson 2008, xxii). But it presents media ideals around the world according to *Four Theories*, while noting *Last Rights* and adding "development theory" as the fifth one (496–503).

EUROPE

The first notable European proposal for classifying contemporary media systems was offered in the early 1960s by Raymond Williams, a British cultural historian and classic source for critical media scholarship. His landmark *Com-*

munications (1962) suggested a typology of four systems within the context of the British controversy over culture and communication: authoritarian, paternal ("an authoritarian system with a conscience"), commercial, and democratic. It was an openly normative typology, highlighting the necessity and feasibility of democratic communication "not only as an individual right, but a social need, since democracy depends on the active participation of all its members" (Williams 1962, 93; see also Sparks 1993). Others followed, including Peter Golding and Philip Elliott (1979), as well as James Curran (1991a,b). Williams's useful classification did not achieve larger recognition among these, nor did they subsequently elaborate it.

The German social philosopher Jürgen Habermas provided another important dimension of normative theory in public communication with his proposal that the best foundation for the morality of public life in today's highly pluralistic societies is to be found in a theory of communicative action (1990). His concept of the public sphere became an increasingly influential theoretical framework, following the translation into English of his classic *The Structural Transformation of the Public Sphere* (1989). Briefly put, public sphere refers to the space of civil society between state institutions and citizens. In democratic societies, it should provide a more or less autonomous and open arena for public debate and the formation of public opinion along pluralistic lines. Access of all parties to the public sphere should be unhindered, and freedom of assembly, association, and expression are guaranteed. Habermas concluded that within the public sphere the means of public communication (initially by way of the political press) have played an essential part in maintaining diversity and association as well as in providing vital channels of communication and control between people and their rulers.

Habermas's position is open to criticism for idealizing the condition of free debate promoted by the press and for ignoring the political biases of the mass media. Despite this, the notion of the public sphere and the linked idea of civil society offers a framework for analyzing how the media gain centrality and influence in contemporary public debate (see, for instance, Dahlgren 1995; Keane 1995).

Much of the normative theorizing about the media did not attempt to link the question of systematic differences in the media to the types of social systems in which they operate, as *Four Theories* had done. *Four Theories* examined historically the progression from autocracy to democracy and took note of a world still much divided by state-sponsored ideologies of nationalism, Communism, colonialism, and even fascism in Spain and Portugal until the 1970s. European revisionists focused more on divisions internal to media systems within the boundaries of states, emphasizing differences between forms that were commercial or publicly owned, populist or elitist, and serving democratic or ruling-class purposes.

Scandinavian media analysts also produced different typologies based on the media systems in their countries. In Finland the broadcasting reform of the 1960s provided the basis for a classification of confessional, commercial, and informational media (Nordenstreng 1973; Pietila, Malmberg, and Nordenstreng 1990). In Sweden, Borden (1995) distinguished the types of media in terms of their functions in a democratic society: to inform, to critique, and to provide a forum for actors representing different views. This latter typology represents a long Scandinavian media policy tradition that not only defends the media's freedom but defines the parameters of this freedom in a democratic society. The policy also establishes criteria for the quality of journalism in terms of truthfulness, depth of information, and relevance for public decision making. A vital part of this normative tradition is promoting the diversity and pluralism of media content and avoiding the tendency toward concentration of media control. This typology of media functions has become a permanent part of media policy guidelines both in the Scandinavian countries and regionally within the European Union.

Normative struggles over the feared consequences of press concentration and over the place of public broadcasting in political, cultural, and social life have a long history in Europe and the United States. In 1947, the year the Hutchins Commission issued its report, the United Kingdom established a Royal Commission on the Press. The motivation was more directly political in this case, as press unions and the Labour Party sought an end to what they viewed as the right-wing dominance of the national press. The inquiry was thus an official one, appointed and paid for by government. Nevertheless, the Commission's powers were limited, and its recommendations required parliamentary approval. The principle of press freedom could not be challenged, but certain structural changes were sought to limit concentration and increase access for alternative voices.

In many respects, the conclusions of the Royal Commission echoed the earlier American report. The Commission concluded that "democratic society . . . needs a clear and truthful account of events, of their background and causes; a forum for discussion and informed criticism; and a means whereby individuals and groups can express a point of view or advocate a cause" (Royal Commission on the Press 1949, 100–101). The report had little direct consequence aside from its endorsement of the press's public responsibility and the need to restrict monopoly. However, it did eventually lead to the formation of a General Council of the Press, empowered to hear and adjudicate complaints from those affected by alleged press misconduct, although with no powers of compulsion or retribution.

Across Europe, especially where they had been controlled by fascism or liberated from occupation, press institutions were reestablished according to more open and democratic principles. Pressing social and political conditions legitimated intervention, especially in the form of subsidies for more vulnerable areas of the press and legislation to limit concentration. These interventions ranged from uncontroversial postal subsidies to disputed financial grants for some weaker press organs in order to support competition or innovation. Limitations on monopoly were also involved, and most of these interventions were justified according to principles of political diversity and editorial independence. Legislation supporting the press still exists in a number of European countries, especially in those that conform to the "democratic corporatist" model of Hallin and Mancini (2004). Nevertheless, the view that the press should be essentially a private and commercial undertaking has not been challenged. The formation and widening of the European Union has—if anything—consolidated this view, making it very difficult for national governments to make any intervention of economic significance.

In the postwar era, broadcasting gradually took over much of the task of providing the public with information. The idea of social responsibility was enshrined in various public broadcasting bodies. They were designed to be publicly financed and independently directed, subject to the goals and rules laid down, and reviewed by elected governments. To some extent, these developments reduced pressure on the press to meet the wishes of political parties and offered a new and more promising arena for the formulation and implementation of normative principles for the media. Although public broadcasting began as an administrative solution to the problems of regulating and controlling radio, it developed into a sector of the media that was regarded as more accountable to the public than the print media and as essential to achieving many of the requirements of democracy. Scholars concentrated on formulating roles and responsibilities for European public broadcasting (see, e.g., Atkinson and Raboy 1997; Blumler 1992; Hoffmann-Riem 1996). Although there was not a great deal of novelty in the roles they envisaged, these roles did represent a coherent formulation of the idea of public interest in media performance.

Given the general emphasis on objectivity in the sphere of news and information, and out of respect for a national consensus, the main obligations of public broadcasting were to reflect the pluralism of society and diversity of audience, to avoid offense to significant streams of opinion, and to promote cultural values. A balance had to be found between pleasing the audience and fulfilling cultural and informational tasks that were dear to political and cultural elites. Private alternative services were gradually introduced, in terms of terrestrial broadcasting, but were usually subject to many content restrictions and certain license obligations. For practical and principled reasons, these limits have been relaxed in the age of media abundance but have not entirely disappeared. Public broadcasting remains, but the wider media context has changed considerably in the last decade.

In continental Europe, early German sociology and political science offered important reflections on the media–society relationship (Hardt 2001). However, this tradition of theorizing was broken by the experiences of the Nazi era. After World War II, German communication research came to be closely associated with the empirical tradition, following the mainstream American pattern. Among theorists, a wave of New Left criticism of capitalist media emerged in the 1960s and 1970s. However, the incorporation of new principles regarding the role and independence of broadcasting within the German federal constitution was an important marker for media theorists as well as for lawmakers (Hoffmann-Riem 1996).

The first European-based revision of *Four Theories* was presented by Denis McQuail in 1983. He took the authoritarian, libertarian, social responsibility, and Soviet theories more or less for granted, especially since they were still in evidence at the time. But he added two more: development media theory and democratic-participant media theory (McQuail 1983, 84–98). However, in later editions of this textbook (1987; 1994; 2000; 2005) McQuail continued his reservations about the limitations of the press theory approach. For instance, with a focus on political news and information, there is "little of relevance in any of the variants of theory named which might realistically be applied to the cinema, to the music industry, to the video market or even to a good deal of sport, fiction and entertainment of television, thus to much of what the media are doing most of the time" (1994, 133). He also reminded his readers that *Four Theories* defined freedom of the press almost entirely according to interpretations of the First Amendment of the U.S. Constitution, which opened the way to associating freedom with property ownership and identifying government as the only enemy of freedom.

In a subsequent work concerned with issues of media accountability, McQuail concluded from a review of normative perspectives on the media that three main "traditions of press theorizing" could be identified as applying to Western media: market liberalism, professionalism, and democratic theory (2003, 63–64). The latest edition of *McQuail's Mass Communication Theory* elaborated this classification into four models of normative theory: a "liberal-pluralist or market model," a "social responsibility or public interest model," a "professional model," and an "alternative media model" (McQuail 2005, 185–86).

Another influential scholar from continental Europe is Karol Jakubowicz from Poland, who focused on media transformation in central and eastern Europe in the 1990s (see, e.g., Jakubowicz 1990; 1995). From the beginning, he was unimpressed by the prospects for true freedom and democracy, first following "glasnost," introduced by Mikhail Gorbachev in the mid-1980s, and then following the collapse of Communism around 1990. Jakubowicz (2007) provides an overview of the media change in these countries as a consequence of the processes of liberalization and democratization on the one hand and commercialization on the other. The media scene of these changes is full of contradictions and national particularities, but it does illustrate how the peoples of central and eastern Europe have traveled from the "imagined socialism" of official ideology to an "imagined capitalism" of their hopes and dreams. This "imagined capitalism," however, experienced a rude awakening to "real capitalism"—as people found themselves living a copy of the Western social order but without its prosperity and stability (Jakubowicz 2007).

There are also separate reviews from post-Soviet Russia, notably by Yassen Zassoursky (2001) and Ivan Zassoursky (2004). Both of these display Gorbachev's glasnost as a paradoxical arrangement in which media were turned by government into a collective mouthpiece for reforms and democratization. This was followed by a brief period of "the golden age of Russian journalism" in the early 1990s, when the media functioned according to the "fourth estate" model—perhaps more than anywhere else in the world. A new alliance of politics and private corporate interests took over the Russian media system by the mid-1990s, under such labels as "corporate authoritarian," "media political," "federal state," or "regional elites." Accordingly, the Russian landscape—like the rest of central and eastern Europe—provides many variations on the main theme of the role of media in society, but there is little that is qualitatively new. No "post-Communist theory of the press" has emerged, although De Smaele (1999) has suggested a "Eurasian model" of the Russian media system.

A major contribution to the task of replacing the paradigm of the *Four Theories* is a proposal by Daniel Hallin and Paolo Mancini (2004) to abandon normative theorizing as such and instead go back to the root idea of *Four Theories*: that media systems take on the form and coloration of the political and social system in which they operate. Hallin and Mancini search for empirical linkages between political systems and media systems. On the basis of a comparative analysis of a number of European and North American countries, they submit three basic models or ideal types of the media-politics relationship. The first is a liberal model, characterized by market mechanisms and dominant in Britain and North America. The second is a democratic corporatist model, in which commercial media coexist with media tied to social and political groups, with the state having a limited role, a model that prevails typically in northern continental Europe and Scandinavia. The third is a polarized pluralist model, in which media are integrated into party politics and the state has a strong role; it dominates the Mediterranean countries of southern Europe.

These models have subregional identities—a useful reminder of realities in the world of regional integration and globalization. While Hallin and Mancini's work is limited to the Western world, it has inspired Roger Blum (2005) of Switzerland to propose a more comprehensive typology of media systems with six models: an Atlantic-Pacific liberal model, a southern European clientelism model, a northern European public service model, an eastern European shock model, an Arab-Asian patriot model, and an Asian-Caribbean command model. This latest proposal shows how the question of classifying media systems, including their normative foundations, continues to stimulate scholars.

THE DEVELOPING WORLD

Despite their distinctive and rich cultural and philosophical traditions, Asia, Africa, and Latin America have not nurtured major innovations in normative media theories. Relevant contributions by scholars from the developing countries typically reflect *Four Theories* or its revisions—which could be another proof of the dependencies involved. Yet it is obvious that Islamic perspectives represent not only concepts of media ethics (Mowlana 1989) but also normative media theories of a different kind. Similarly, moral philosophies, such as the African *ubuntu* with its emphasis on community and collectivity, have stimulated the development of doctrines about the indigenous role of the media— and warnings about the misuse of such doctrines to limit media freedom and human rights (Christians 2004; Fourie 2008). Moreover, there is a significant movement in Asia and Latin America to resist Western models and explore alternative ethical and normative bases for public communication, even where systems, in a global media age, tend to look rather similar (see, e.g., Christians and Traber 1997; Servaes and Lie 1997; Weaver 1999).

An example is a conference on press systems in the countries of Southeast Asia that was held in Indonesia in the late 1980s and led to the assertion that "unlike the individualistic, democratic, egalitarian and liberal tradition of Western political theory, some societies value their consensual and communal traditions with their emphasis on duties and obligations to the collective and social harmony" (Mehra 1989, 3). There are, indeed, grounds to talk about "Asian values in journalism" (Masterton 1996; Xiaoge 2005).

Jiafei Yin (2008) clarifies the task ahead by explaining in detail how Asian media systems do not fit press theories developed in the West. She proposes a two-dimensional model with freedom and responsibility as coordinates (46–49). She integrates the key Asian cultural emphasis on responsibility into the Western preoccupation with freedom. With Western and Confucian philosophers dominating this model, it is considered a starting point for additional nuances and perspectives. However, it is disputable whether a distinct theory of society and media has been articulated at the conference, apart from political phrases about nation-building, freedom, and responsibility. Obviously, developing countries with a basically Western orientation are bound to some intellectual dependence on Western political philosophies and media theories. Therefore, the media reform movement toward a New World Information and Communication Order (Vincent, Nordenstreng, and Traber 1999) has provided a widely resonating window of opportunity for alternative, developing world perspectives.

Another perspective is opened up by Shelton Gunaratne's "humanocentric theory of the press" in his *Dao of the Press* (2005). He argues that *Four Theories* and the surrounding literature are too exclusively based on Eurocentric history, theory, and practice. In this view, Eurocentrism and universalism are presumed to be the same when the *Four Theories* framework is used to evaluate the press around the world. Gunaratne—from Sri Lanka and settled in the United States—interprets press theory in terms of Eastern philosophy, world systems analysis, and the theory of living systems. He integrates Western epistemology with Eastern mysticism into a "dynamic, humanocentric theory of communication outlets and free expression to replace the static, deontic normative theories of the press" (Gunaratne 2005, 56). He replaces the individualism and self-interest that dominates liberal democracy with interdependence and mutual causality.

Changing Climate for Media Theory and Policy

This review of the post–*Four Theories* landscape and the seeming inadequacy of the harvest after five decades of considerable growth of media scholarship must be seen in today's twenty-first-century context, in which the media scene is dominated by big media, and critical theory influences the academy. Much effort has been invested in demolishing the walls and foundations of the fortresses occupied by both the capitalist media industry and the quasi state bureaucracies that have controlled broadcasting and telecommunications in many countries.

In the academic world during the postwar period, critical theorists of the neo-Marxist and political economy traditions had little interest in explanations of the role of the media in relation to society, since the critical paradigm offered a clear message that the established, mainstream media were inevitably on the side of an unjust social order and a fundamentally flawed institution. Theorists and researchers worked at revealing the class bias and ideological character of media content and the general tendency toward hegemony. Those engaged in this task include many of the best known names in the field of communication, including Herbert Marcuse, Dallas Smythe, Herbert Schiller, Noam Chomsky, Raymond Williams, and Stuart Hall. The material for a fundamental critique of the media was found in structures of media ownership and in patterns of media content. These patterns included a persistent bias in domestic news toward the views of, or supporting, all forms of state authority wherever dissidence or unrest threatened; unquestioned support for capitalism; low-level racism and xenophobia plus high-level ethnocentrism; support for the overarching framework of the Cold War and reliance on the threat of nuclear war; and unbalanced international flow of communication between North and South, West and East. It is not surprising that interest in any other normative theory was at a low ebb.

The dominant hold of this version of critical thinking did not long survive the end of the Cold War at the start of the 1990s, not so much because it was discredited or disproved as a theory but more because the media and their context of operation started to experience quite fundamental changes. There were several components of change. One was technological, with the effective discovery in the 1980s of the potential of international cable and satellite transmission and the beginnings of rapid innovation in the use of computers for communication. The embryonic Internet was already challenging the dominance of old media, and numerous other innovations were working in the same direction.

Parallel to technological change, there was a political–ideological shift away from social responsibility in media governance and toward deregulation and entrepreneurial growth. In Europe this meant reduction in public monopolies' influence over broadcasting and over telecommunications. Deregulation and privatization became the driving forces of communications and media from the mid-1980s onward. In Europe, thoughts of revolution soon came to be seen as quixotic, and former critical theorists turned their attention to defending what was left of the old public sector and achieving by way of media policy some restraint on the new private electronic media sector. The demise of Communism in eastern and central Europe also furthered change, speeding up market liberalization and globalization.

The main point is that communication researchers and educators were confronted with a largely new set of questions and circumstances. For the most part the theoretical formulations of the post–World War II and Cold War eras were not very helpful in dealing with the new challenges. Entire new branches of communication law and governance were being established, and journalism itself became a target of reassessment (Deuze 2005; Hanitzsch 2007). A need for new thinking and new policies was not satisfied by drawing on the maxims and nostrums of normative and critical theory designed for older conditions (Van Cuilenburg and McQuail 2003). There was no way back, for instance, to a time of close regulation, restricted access to scarce channels, and national media sovereignty. Fundamental issues about communication and society were still at stake, including those relating to freedom, diversity, access, accountability, and quality (see McQuail 2003; Napoli 2001). But new forms and new arguments were needed to sustain the values these concepts implied (see Hamelink and

Nordenstreng 2007). One trend was de-Westernizing research paradigms in a new global context (Curran and Park 2000).

The foregoing panorama of proposals for normative theory and the changing landscape of communication policy illustrates that no grand theories have emerged out of various approaches. Proposed typologies seem to diverge rather than converge. Moreover, some scholarly voices suggest giving up the attempt to replace the original four with a new set of theories. However, this does not mean that a normative approach has come to a dead end and that there is a tide away from the prescriptive and toward description. On the contrary, a normative level of theorizing still occupies a central place in communication studies, with many issues of law, policy, and governance being highlighted by current changes in media technology and structure, as well as by the pressures on media freedom stemming from the so-called war on terror. The changes under way in a context of uncertainty and anxiety have undermined both the liberal consensus supporting complete media freedom and the more or less accepted rules of the game that help to reconcile freedom with accountability to society on essential matters.

A New Beginning

We think that despite its limitations, *Four Theories* had a great didactic advantage, as it introduced a typology of press systems, each type implying a different political system with its own political philosophy. The problem was that it collapsed into one level of consideration at least three levels of analysis: philosophical approaches, political systems, and press systems. Further, it identified each type with a very concrete historical case situated in specific countries.

Our methodological point of departure is to separate these three levels of analysis—philosophical traditions, political systems, and media systems—but also to show how they are intimately related. Each of these three levels has its own logic which does not translate to the others, but for an overview we list all three here:

> Philosophical—*normative traditions:* corporatist, libertarian, social responsibility, and citizen participation
> Political—*models of democracy:* administrative, pluralist, civic, and direct
> Media—*roles of media:* monitorial, facilitative, radical, and collaborative

There is no one-to-one correspondence between the types at the three different levels. None of the four historical traditions of normative theory corresponds exactly with a given model of democracy or with a given media role. To force such a correspondence would only repeat one of the errors of *Four Theories*. This typology of the three levels—philosophical, political, and media—should be seen separately in the context we will give them in the chapters to come. Moreover, it should be noted that our typology here does not introduce a comprehensive approach to philosophical traditions, political systems, and media systems. At each of the three levels we focus on a particular aspect—normative traditions of public communication, models of democracy, and media roles—that leaves considerable room for other possible approaches and typologies.

Acknowledging the didactic and heuristic advantage of typologies, we should also recall that a typology does not mean that each concrete case is placed in one and only one pigeonhole. For example, contemporary journalists may represent in their professional thinking several streams of the normative tradition simultaneously—not least the oldest, corporatist one. Media roles as held by media institutions or individual communicators are typically composites of different and sometimes contradictory traditions. Thus the different types should be seen as vehicles of analytical understanding rather than sets of fixed locations limiting actual phenomena.

Consequently, our new beginning recognizes the complexity of the question of normative theories of the media, the deep historical and cultural roots of the issues, and the multiplicity of levels at which normative issues have to be confronted. We cannot provide any single integrated framework that will encompass the variety of problems that arise. Instead, we have tried to simplify the task by distinguishing between different levels of generality. According to this approach, we propose three typologies that to us seem to cover the main range of variation at each level of analysis. By chance, or mischance, each typology contains four main entries. However, there is no intention to promote the legacy of the original *Four Theories*. As this book's title suggests, our overall reference point is democracy. We follow democratic political systems with the multifold philosophical conceptions of the human and the social that the history of discussion about democracy implies. One might argue, as we do in chapter 2, that discussions of what should be the ideal form of public communication can only occur when there is some degree of public participation in the collective decision making of the community, and this implies that participants are equal and free. The claims here are more modest: we refrain from discussing the normative conditions of autocratic or authoritarian communication as not relevant for this book.

We think that anchoring the normative in democratic culture and political systems avoids the problem of moral relativism, but we recognize that there have been and could be many combinations of democratic institutions in different historical and cultural contexts that provide guarantees of liberty and equality and the respect for human existence that this framework implies. We introduce a typology of democratic expressions but do not identify any type with any historical political system. Rather we see the types as tendencies or vectors on a quadrant that can combine into many institutional forms. The same logic of tendencies and combinations is applied to the portrayal of types of historical–philosophical traditions and media roles. For example, in a democracy, journalism could be called on for a more collaborative role in some circumstances, without violating principles of liberty and equality, but at other times the role of radical change agent would be more appropriate.

We have attempted to present systematically the repertoire of normative principles that are available in order to guide concrete action in the field of public communication today. We hope this will enable media professionals to see both their normative role in concrete circumstances and the underlying moral grounding that justifies them. At the same time, we view these normative principles as open and continually advancing in an era of globalization, localization, and interaction of moral traditions.

THE THREE LEVELS OF ANALYSIS

The first level of analysis is the most general and deals with the historical contexts and debates that have generated philosophical traditions to give guidance to public communication, including media and journalism. We term these traditions "philosophical" because they tend to link norms of good public communication with deeper explanatory justification in terms of conceptions of the human, of society, and of the good life. For this reason, we take the discussion back to the debate about the ethics of public communication in such classical authors as Plato, Aristotle, Cicero, and Augustine. It is also essential to discuss the many dimensions of normative theory associated with the concept of citizenship. This concept presumes freedom of expression, the right to participate in the public decision-making process, and a definition of public communication as essentially dialogical and discursive. A normative tradition is not just a limited number of theories but a complex set of values we think both professionals and the public should know.

The second level of analysis allows a more precise discussion of the media's contributions to the working of democracy. As noted, we recognize the existence of alternative forms of democratic institutions and procedures within an overall agreement on the notion of popular sovereignty. It is quite clear that different societies have developed their own practices of democracy, according to variations in historical circumstances and political cultures. For these reasons, we identify the main alternative political models of democracy, each of which makes somewhat different normative demands on the media of public communication.

At the third level of generality, we focus on the media themselves, especially their journalistic task. We see journalism, as James Carey noted, as a set of practices that "are justified in terms of the social consequences they engender, namely, the constitution of a democratic social order" (1996, 9). Some might think that in our era of infotainment and the wide political implications of entertainment media, it restricts the range of applications of normative theory to focus on the press and journalism. We prefer this focus, however, recognizing that journalism is more clearly and explicitly related to the defense of democracy. We choose not to deal with genres such as music videos or the monologues of talk show hosts (Entman 2005), even though these no doubt serve as sources of information and commentary. However, we have taken account of new developments with the Internet such as blogging and podcasting, although their implications for democratic institutions have not been sufficiently explored. There is great breadth in Michael Schudson's (2003) definition of journalism as that "set of institutions that publicizes periodically (usually daily) information and commentary on contemporary affairs, normally presented as true and sincere, to a dispersed and anonymous audience so as to publicly include the audience in a discourse taken to be publicly important" (11). Insofar as the media in general have this more explicit normative purpose of furthering democracy and democratic institutions, they should take on the guidelines developed in the context of discussing press roles in journalism.

The rest of this chapter summarizes our typologies on the three levels, as a preview of the chapters to follow. Taken together, they aim at a normative theory of public communication. *Normative* means that explanations are based on choices among cultural values and ultimately on some premises about the nature and purposes of human existence. *Theory* is here understood to be a reasoned explanation of why certain actions lead to certain outcomes. *Public communication* refers to those forms of human communication that maintain a broad public sphere and serve as an instrument of political governance from small communities to national and global societies. Mass media and journalism are central but by no means the only elements of public communication, which also includes much of culture, religion, and politics.

Normative Traditions of Public Communication

At the philosophical level, we distinguish four major stages that have evolved in two and a half millennia of debate over the way public communication should be carried on: corporatist, libertarian, social responsibility, and citizen participation. At each stage of development, we are interested in how communication values relate to the development of democratic systems of governance. For methodological reasons, we begin with the experience of direct democracy in the Mediterranean city-states. One might have traced the evolution of the philosophies of public communication in other civilizations. But many of the central concepts, such as "democracy," "ethics," and "rhetorical modes of communication," derive from Attic Greece. Many of the same issues of freedom and truthfulness were first introduced in the debates in classical Greece. Yet we prefer not to assume, as do *Four Theories* and other similar treatments, that the discussion of these questions began only in early modern Europe. Each historical stage of the debate usually takes up all three levels—the philosophical underpinnings, a system of just and responsible governance, and the concrete mode of carrying on "good" public communication. Each configuration of normative values, such as the insistence that all citizens have a right to participate in the democratic process, tends to be linked with the search for what good and just public communication consists of in a particular historical context.

The debate carried on by major thinkers of an era is based on philosophical values that have been so widely received and accepted that they have become part of the mainstream tradition of normative principles of public discourse. Thus we prefer to call them traditions instead of theories or paradigms, since each is too fragmentary to claim status as a theory as that term is understood today. Moreover, the term *paradigm* implies a degree of precision and explicit formulation that usually is not available. Yet we see these traditions as relatively stable historical entities—they are indeed paradigmatic traditions.

We offer a typology in terms of a set of received values and traditions that has a certain coherent internal logic linking together various principles. For example, in the libertarian tradition, citizens' freedom to express their views in the public forum goes together with the obligation to respect the freedom of expression of others and to keep the debate open to all positions even when these are widely thought to be erroneous. Each tradition expresses a set of values that are relatively consistent with each other and that emerged in a particular historical situation. As chapter 2 indicates, we see each of the traditions as part of a continuous conversation that gained its written expression in the works of classical Greek authors such as Plato and Aristotle but that certainly has even deeper roots in the interchange of living cultures with which the Greeks were in contact. Political philosophers and other writers of early modern Europe were very aware of the received tradition of classical Greece, which came to them through a medieval tradition itself very much influenced by the philosophers of Islamic civilization. Today, we can identify a distinct configuration of principles of public communication termed "citizen participation" that emphasizes the right of all citizens to directly participate and is far more open to women and many other groups than in the past. With globalization, the conversation is being much enlarged in many parts of the world.

Following the logic of our typologies, we see the four historical traditions not as fixed sets of ideas but as tendencies on a quadrant, as shown in figure 1. Fundamental issues in the history of debate on public communication are the degree of sociocultural consensus and pluralism. Consensus refers to a unified

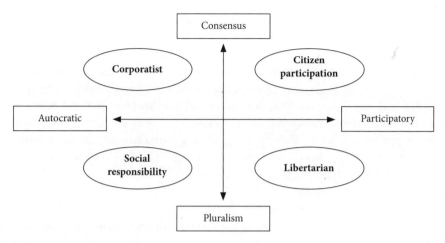

Figure 1. Four Normative Traditions

central state, a national religion, or a homogeneous culture, while pluralism stands for a condition of cultural and ethnic diversity, a dispersal of power, and greater freedom and diversity of expression and belief. The opposition between these tendencies sets out the vertical dimension in figure 1. The horizontal dimension is based on varying degrees of political mobilization, ranging from a condition of authoritarian governance to one of extensive participation in decision making.

As noted, we have identified four traditions in the history of debate on the norms of public communication: corporatist, libertarian, social responsibility, and citizen participation. The first and second of these traditions tend to be sharply contrasted historically, while the third and fourth are closer to each other and tend to take on many different forms. While the four traditions can be distinguished as relatively solid and paradigmatic, they are brought about by a historical evolution and should be seen as similar to schools of thought in political philosophy. We do not argue, however, that the more recent traditions have displaced the earlier ones or that the newer ones are to be regarded as superior for providing guidelines for public communication. Each tradition implies a set of institutions that time has tested and that continue to be an important source of norms for the roles of journalism in democracy.

THE CORPORATIST TRADITION

This tradition has its origins in the direct democracies of the relatively small Mediterranean city-states, especially in the political culture of Athens, some twenty-five hundred years ago. The tradition is termed corporatist because it rests on a cosmic worldview of organic harmony in the universe. A classic statement of corporatist public philosophy was perhaps best expressed by Aristotle in his treatises on ethics, rhetoric, and politics, but a stronger communitarian philosophy is found in contemporary political theorists. A corporatist philosophical worldview is still influential today as a foundation for public communication in many parts of the world, especially in Asian and Islamic cultures. This worldview differs from the "authoritarian" one that *Four Theories* attributes to autocratic monarchies and twentieth-century military dictatorships because it is open to democratic processes of public communication. In most cases, however, it is a tradition that expects the media to be cooperative in matters of national interest and in relation to other social institutions such as religion, education, and the family.

In a society with limited cultural pluralism, one finds virtual consensus on norms in various aspects of life, including those of good public communication. In these societies there may be little debate regarding the commonly held worldview and conception of the existential order. There is a tendency to identify a given cultural order with an underlying metaphysical order of being or divinely ordained set of norms.

The corporatist tradition could seek a high degree of centralized political control or, as in ancient Greek society, it could encourage a free and open debate among privileged male citizens. In contexts of a high degree of external threat and low internal social consensus, it is more likely that there will be a high degree of centralized control or even coercive mobilization. Ancient Greece had a fairly strong corporatist worldview and philosophical tradition. Plato, especially, appealed to the order of being as the foundation of truthful public communication. Aristotle, too, appealed to a knowledge of first principles as the basis of sound public discourse. But Athens was a small, socially and culturally compact society. It made sense to work toward consensus on decisions in order to gain the full cooperation of all in collective action. In fact, this principle was the basis of public decisions in many Mediterranean city-states throughout antiquity and the Middle Ages.

Many Southeast Asian democracies, with their underlying religious and cultural consensus, represent more consensual and less contestatory media policy. The relatively high degree of value consensus underlying a corporatist worldview often leads to media that are more respectful of authority. Democracies with a high degree of development mobilization may appeal to a corporatist worldview and a collaborative approach in politics. The media are expected to be cooperative on matters of national welfare and less critical of economic enterprise, religion, and education. Media elites are likely to be closely aligned to social, political, and cultural elites and dominated by a policy of national cultural unity.

THE LIBERTARIAN TRADITION

This tradition might also be called "liberal-individualist" since it elevates the principle of freedom of expression to the highest point in the values hierarchy that the media are expected to uphold. The libertarian ideal of public communication emerged in the late Middle Ages and the Renaissance in reaction to deeply entrenched monarchies and religious institutions of Europe, which combined to resist any challenge to their authority. Religious and political dissidents were generally repressed, but the very fact of dissidence—especially when based on principles of justice or true religion—planted the seeds for new claims to freedom of expression. There were secular philosophers, such as Thomas Hobbes, whose work *Leviathan* (1651) elevated the ultimate power of the state to being the indispensable source of order and civilization. Around the same time, the Puritan author John Milton published his eloquent plea for an end to censorship of the press in England in his *Areopagitica* (1644).

Many of the central libertarian values were also the values and thinking of the entrepreneurial class. An article of faith was that individuals could freely own, and owners could use, the media for whatever purpose they wished within the law. Accordingly, the interests of all participants would be best served by a free media market, and the benefits to the whole community would be maximized. There was no public right to publish nor any collective "right to know." The enemy of liberty was government and the state, and no good could come from public intervention to secure some supposed public objective.

In this tradition, the claim to liberty is paramount and absolute. This view suggests that there is no place for external accountability, even though failings can be expected. If there are limits to freedom in the way of intervention, they are only justified if they assist the better working of the market. The medieval norm of trying to protect the public against unscrupulous vendors in the marketplace is swept away. Let the buyer beware (caveat emptor). Given the suspicion toward all large institutions, especially the church and the state, organic unity is to be found not in the rationality of the corporate structure of society but through the inborn rational capacity and conscious choice of the individual. Social unity and coordination is to be found in some form of social contract.

The libertarian tradition came to full fruition in the nineteenth century, especially in the writings of John Stuart Mill. In Mill's *Essay on Liberty* (1859), freedom is the superior path toward uncovering truth and utilitarian benefits that accrue from the free flow of information and ideas. According to utilitarian philosophy as a whole, only liberty in the expression of ideas contributes to the greatest happiness of the greatest number.

THE SOCIAL RESPONSIBILITY TRADITION

This tradition retains freedom as the basic principle for organizing public communication, including the media, but views the public or community as also having some rights and legitimate expectations of adequate service. The term *social responsibility* itself was largely the product of the Hutchins Commission. Ultimately, freedom of the press has to be justified by its fruits. This may call for limits to media activities or interventions designed to supplement or control the media market. However, within this framework there is a wide spectrum of views about how far the state may legitimately go to achieve an acceptable level of public service. Different versions of social responsibility as it applies to the media have been espoused that have varying degrees of strength. A minimalist version expects the media themselves to develop self-regulatory mechanisms of accountability, based on voluntary promises in response to demands from the public or the government. The development of professionalism is thought to play a key part in this process. A more interventionist approach embraces press subsidies and laws to ensure diversity or innovation, as well as the founding of publicly owned media, especially public service broadcasting.

The emergence of the social responsibility tradition is illustrative of a kind of dialectical logic in the evolution of normative theories, the institutions of democracy, and our understanding of the role of media in a democracy. Once the libertarian solution became the formula for many nation-states, typically in the nineteenth century, and the negative results of unrestrained entrepreneurial freedom became evident, the need to balance freedom with responsibility also came to light.

During this transition, the information and entertainment needs of the mass public made it necessary for expert and responsible personnel to staff the media industries. The response was, in part, the professionalization of the employees of the media industries with the typical codes of ethics, expert training, and self-regulating bodies that are currently part of professional status. Also important was the development of an ethos of "service to the development of democracy" as a contribution to the advancement of industrial societies. In this new role of the media, the reference point for public communicators was less one's personal conscience and more the assumption of a personal responsibility to serve the needs of developing a democratic society with mass participation. However, it took more than a century to work out what we call the social responsibility formula.

In terms of the two underlying vectors discussed earlier and shown in figure 1, the social responsibility tradition lies close to the vector of pluralism but also close to that of autocratic control. The genius of the social responsibility tradition has been its ability to find a balance between freedom and control, self-regulation and public regulation, respect for both national culture and cultural diversity, personal needs and community needs, relatively high cultural quality and mass comprehension. Our new approach should be open to the immensely varied ways that different nations and cultures devise a normative tradition that is faithful to its culture but also faithful to both the demands of democratic institutions and the practical realities of media institutions.

THE CITIZEN PARTICIPATION TRADITION

This tradition, while more recent than the others named, already has a history of three or four decades. Its distant roots are found in the dissident religious and political movements of the sixteenth century and in the struggles for a right to freedom of the press in the eighteenth century. Precursors also include the radical press of the early labor movements in the nineteenth century. Even so, the modern notion of a citizen participatory press is more usefully dated from the alternative presses and then through the free radio of the 1960s and 1970s, and is inspired by a wide range of ideas and motivations. Not least important were grassroots activist media in many protorevolutionary situations spanning much of the twentieth century (see Downing 2001).

The basis of legitimacy for this tradition is the idea that the media belong to the people, with an emancipatory, expressive, and critical purpose. The media are typically engaged in some form of struggle for collective rights. Where political change is achieved, they may expire or become institutionalized as the true voice of citizens, without being beholden to the market or government authority. Citizen participatory media rightly are placed at the end of the vector that is opposed to the more centralized authoritarian control of the media.

This tradition has mainly emphasized the role of the local community, as well as small-scale and alternative media. In fact, there is an intrinsic difficulty in applying this tradition's thinking to extensive, mainstream national or international media like network television or the mass press. Nonetheless, this perspective furnishes a critique of such media and sets up certain criteria of desirable operation. Even large-scale media can have a concerned and responsive attitude to their audiences and encourage feedback and interactivity. They can employ participatory formats and engage in surveys and debates that are genuinely intended to involve citizens.[4]

Models of Democracy

Our second level of analysis begins with the simple view that democracy is governance by the people, for the people, and of the people (see, e.g., Gunther and Mughan 2000). However, democracy is not only a matter of accountability of rulers to the people but encompasses many other ways people act together to influence their rulers and their own lives, including the various forms of public communication now available. There is no one-to-one correspondence between the normative traditions we outline and a particular model of democracy. Indeed, there is no agreement on how to classify or arrange the various concepts and forms of democratic politics in the modern world. Still, there are good scholarly roadmaps for conceptualizing democracy (notably Held 2006), and on that basis we single out four models: liberal-pluralist, elitist-administrative, deliberative civic, and popular-direct.

As we will show in chapter 4, there is one dimension that cuts across most democratic theory and practice: the distinction between individual rights and liberty on the one hand and equality and the collective rights of the community on the other. Emphasis on the former is more typical of the Anglo-American condition, while the latter is typically a Continental model often associated with France and inspired especially by Rousseau. Habermas makes a similar distinction between a liberal or Lockean view of democratic politics and a republican view. In a liberal view, politics "has the function of bundling together and bringing to bear private social interests against a state apparatus that specializes in the administrative employment of practical power for collective goals," whereas in the republican view, "politics is conceived . . . as the reflective form of a substantial ethical life" involving an awareness of mutual dependence of citizens within communities (1998, 240). He writes: "besides administrative power and individual personal interests, *solidarity* and the orientation to the common good appear as a *third source* of social integration" (240). Chapter 4 also makes clear that theories of democracy inevitably carry a normative or prescriptive element as well as an empirical or descriptive one. Each of the alternative models outlined below and explained further in chapter 4 makes a claim to desirability based on argument and an appeal to basic values.

PLURALIST DEMOCRACY

This model is well represented in our time by many countries that give priority to individual freedom, look to the market as the main engine of welfare, and prefer to restrict the role of the state to what is necessary for the orderly running of a free market society. This model's connection with the libertarian tradition we outlined earlier is quite obvious and is well explicated by Hallin and Mancini's (2004) liberal pluralist model.

However, not all issues concerning the media are solved by the convenience of a compatible theory of democracy. For example, in practice the media market may not serve the needs of pluralism by failing to give access to competing voices. The media market is as much, if not more, subject to tendencies toward concentration as other industries. Unrestrained pursuit of profit has also periodically been blamed for a variety of harms to individuals and society, in a reaction especially against content representing crime, violence, sex, and other kinds of socially disapproved behavior and tendencies. Accordingly, democratic social order is not necessarily well served by libertarian media. Solutions may not be available in effective self-regulation, even if promoted in theory. At times of crisis, the state cannot depend only on the vagaries of supply and demand in media markets. Aside from problems of control or regulation that are inconsistent with a minimal state, there is some difficulty in consistently identifying a role for the free media in a free market society. The media can choose or avoid roles in society as they wish. And this difficulty is becoming more and more acute with the proliferation of the Internet.

ADMINISTRATIVE DEMOCRACY

This model emphasizes the need for institutions of professional administration and other expert bodies to look after the people's welfare. Neither politicians nor ordinary citizens have the knowledge to govern a highly complex modern society. In the past, there was a tendency to rely on public bureaucracies to run essential services, sometimes even major industries. More recently, the trend has been away from direct public control and toward private ownership, subject to review by regulatory bodies. The elites appointed to carry out essential government roles are accountable in various ways, including by way of public opinion, and if need be, by intervention in the market. Modern democracies seek to maintain reasonable standards of welfare for citizens and make collective provisions for social security and some basic services that are regarded as unsuitable for market provision. Yet, there are still considerable differences between Europe and the United States in what might be recognized as expressions of administrative democracy.

The relation between the administrative form of democracy and the media is typically ambiguous, even when there is a symbiosis between social responsibility theory and social-democratic politics in a number of societies, as exemplified in the democratic-corporatist model of media and politics proposed by Hallin and Mancini (2004) and still to be found in several northern and western European states. Within the terms of this model, the attitude of the state toward media is consistent with the principles of administrative democracy. The media are taken to task from time to time for their failures to support governmental and political institutions and not fully trusted to have complete independence. Attempts to increase accountability and retain public broadcasting against the tide of media deregulation reflect this lack of trust and desire to keep a degree of residual control. The clash between the British government and the BBC in 2003 over reporting the steps to war in Iraq is one clear example of the permanent tension in these relations.

CIVIC DEMOCRACY

This model takes a variety of forms. However, its general message is that any healthy democracy should be characterized by the active involvement of citizens in formulating opinions and representing certain shared interests, especially at the local level. As a form of democracy, this model is not very compatible with government by elites and experts and is clearly differentiated from the democracy of society-wide aggregates of individual voters. Admittedly, the model of civic democracy is somewhat problematic as a guide to norms for the media, but it appears to call for more use of all forms of participatory media such as the Internet, as well as reinforcing the need for diversity and localism. In fact, it is difficult to see how this could do more than serve the participating minority.

A challenge is thus posed to many political uses of established large-scale media. Solutions typically call for the media to provide increasingly relevant and higher quality information and news, to open their channels to more voices, to listen to the concerns of citizens and reflect them, and to play an activating role on citizenship issues. The media are also asked to avoid the denigration of politics and politicians that promotes cynicism and detachment from government. However, many such proposals risk coming into conflict with the economic interests of the news media under highly competitive situations. Therefore, they are unlikely to amount to much unless backed by the professional commitment of journalists and significant consumer demand.

DIRECT DEMOCRACY

We can interpret direct democracy even more diversely than the civic type. The classical form of direct self-government by an assembly of people is not possible in extensive contemporary societies. The modern equivalent is government by referenda and plebiscites, with majority decision making the rule. Political systems differ in the degree to which they offer such possibilities. But governments have various devices for listening to the populace, by way of surveys and focus groups, for instance, even if the people have no power over decisions. Electronic government has been canvassed as a practical possibility, yet has not been widely applied in practice. Populism as a form of politics is usually reserved at present for grassroots movements that seek immediate radical solutions for problems that are perceived by the public at large to be serious and ignored by elected governments. This often applies to issues such as crime and punishment, immigration, taxation and regulation, and sometimes foreign policy, with variations from country to country.

Leaving these issues aside, the requirements of direct democracy for the media are primarily that there should be media channels available that allow all significant voices and claims to be heard, especially where they may otherwise be ignored by established elites. Opinionated bloggers and uninhibited critics of those in power, in whatever media channel they appear, can make a contribution. Direct democracy is likely to be promoted by large numbers of small-scale and grassroots media voices or by recognition in the marketplace of the unmet demand for content that will please some majority or significant minority that is otherwise being ignored.

The Roles of Journalism

These reflections on the relation between normative theories and democracy have focused on the media's role in society. The media sometimes refer to their own role in the sense of their purposes or the services they provide. Public debate about the media makes similar references, although more likely in a prescriptive way about what the press ought to be doing. The concept of media role fits quite easily in such different discourses.

In sociology, the role idea is typically found in functionalist or social systems theory, where it usually refers to activities that have to be performed by some person or unit in order to ensure the proper working of the system as a whole. In the case of the mass media, early theorists (e.g., Lasswell 1948; Merton 1949) pointed to three main social functions of communication that were readily expressed in terms of roles: surveillance (providing information on the world), correlation (promoting social cohesion), and continuity (transmitting values and culture across generations). These ideas were elaborated by others to give expression to more specific expectations about the role of the news media in a democratic society. They were supported by general notions of the press's role as a fourth estate (B. Cohen 1963) and by arguments in support of greater social responsibility of the press (Commission on Freedom of the Press 1947). A typical way of expressing the tasks and role of the media in society is the formulation used by most public service broadcasters (following the BBC): to inform, to educate, and to entertain.

The rationale for news media roles is examined in greater detail in chapter 5. It should be kept in mind that just as theories of democracy have an empirical and a normative dimension, so, too, the media's various roles have both elements. The role of media, or of journalists working within media, has a component that describes journalistic tasks or practices and another dimension that refers to their larger purposes and obligations. Because a free press in a democratic society cannot be compelled to follow any particular purpose, the normative element in media roles is normally a matter of choice, often reinforced by custom and the force of social ties. In any case, we are concerned with purposes that are considered desirable according to the kind of values advocated in normative theory or in models of democracy as outlined.

The main components in the range of ideas about media roles in society, and democratic politics in particular, can be summarized in terms of the following practical tasks:

- Provision of *information* about events and their context
- Provision of *comments,* including guidance and advice, in relation to events
- Provision of a *forum* for diverse views and for political advocacy
- Provision of a two-way *channel* between citizens and government
- Acting as *critic* or watchdog in order to hold the government to account

Such a list of possible roles reminds us that the media can serve the interests of the sources of information and ideas, whether political or otherwise, as well as the interests of the public as receivers. Another dimension through which media roles are typically differentiated contrasts the media as observers of events with the media as participants, corresponding to the media as a mirror of reality and as an instrument of social action. Common metaphors to characterize media roles are different kinds of dog: a watchdog controlling the power holders, a lapdog serving the master, and a guard dog looking after vested interests.

The formulation of roles in conventional ways is mainly based on the news media of the traditional kind—still often typically referred to as "the press"—and posits a certain institutional relationship between media and politics. The nature of the media is changing in ways that affect the delineation of social roles. The Internet, in particular, opens up possibilities for a new or different formulation of roles, with particular reference to its massive capacity to carry information, its open access to senders and receivers, and its interactive potential.

Despite the difficulties, we have opted to discuss the news media's social roles. In so doing, we have chosen four general formulations that do not correspond exactly with the foregoing headings and are not limited to any one normative tradition or type of democratic system. They are not intended to be exhaustive of the full range of possible media activities, but they do deal with what we believe are the central issues today. These relate to the transparency of society and flow of information within it; the facilitating of social and political processes, especially the democratic system; the critical role for communications media that has to be fulfilled independently of vested interests and established institutions; and the collaboration, or not, of media with authority.

THE MONITORIAL ROLE

The natural first role is that of vigilant informer, which applies mainly to collecting and publishing information of interest to audiences, as well as distributing information on behalf of sources and clients that include governments, commercial advertisers, and private individuals. The aims of both sources and media are very diverse, including such goals as profit, social missions, and propaganda. The term "monitorial" includes the notion of providing advance intelligence, advice, warning, and everything of general utility for information seekers. For example, information about celebrities, sports, fashion, entertainment, and consumption cannot easily be distinguished in format from political and economic information. Essentially it applies to the work of journalists, but covers a wide terrain.

THE FACILITATIVE ROLE

As the main channel of public information, the news media are inevitably caught up in a wide range of political and social processes. They are relied on by other institutions for certain services in many areas, including politics, commerce, health, education, and welfare. The media provide access for legitimate claimants to public attention and for paying clients. But they also make a virtue of the facilitative relationship, provided that it is voluntary and does not compromise their integrity, credibility, or independence. Consistent with the normative character of journalism's roles, the news media do not merely report on civil society's associations and activities but support and strengthen them.

THE RADICAL ROLE

This role is at some distance from being facilitative and is a clear departure from collaboration with authority. The media enact this role when they provide a platform for views and voices that are critical of authority and the established order. They give support for drastic change and reform. The media may also be a voice of criticism in their own right. This role is the focus of attempts to suppress or limit media freedom and also provides the main justification for freedom of publication. Without the radical role, participatory democracy would not be possible.

THE COLLABORATIVE ROLE

Collaboration refers specifically to the relationship between the media and sources of political and economic power, primarily the state and its agencies. Historically, this was the natural first role for the press when employed by various institutions, including the emerging political parties as vehicles of democracy. Even today, under certain circumstances, the news media are called on to support civil or military authorities in defence of the social order against threats of crime, war, terrorism, and insurgency, as well as natural emergencies and disasters. The claim to media cooperation can be more general and involve demands that journalism support the national interest or be patriotic and respect authority. In developing societies, journalism may be directed to serve particular development goals. This role is not just imposed on the news media from outside but is often consistent with their everyday activities or performed by choice under special circumstances of societal necessity.

In practice, there is a good deal of overlap between the different roles. The provision of information in particular is essential to all of the other three roles, and in that sense it is the most basic one. The typology is less a classification of media tasks than of primary purposes and of the mode and spirit in which a given medium chooses to operate. From this perspective, there are certain oppositions and potential conflicts of role. Most distant from each other are the collaborative and the radical roles. Even if criticism is sometimes constructive, the radical role usually involves a position of opposition to established authority. This is a reminder that the media do not operate in a societal vacuum but are continually engaged with other social actors as well as with their audiences. As noted, the media can be differentiated in terms both of their relations with power in society (dependent or oppositional) and of their degree of participation as actors in political and social events.

While this typology of roles offers food for thought, we do not present it as our alternative to *Four Theories*. We rather open several perspectives for a critical look at the way people—particularly professional communicators—speak and think about journalism in society. It is our intention, as expounded in the second half of the book, to explore the territory once occupied by the four theories in terms of some essential roles of the news media in relation to society.

Conclusion

Our three levels of analysis—normative traditions, models of democracy, and media roles—provide alternative routes into the complex problem of the relation between media and society, although the three levels are not fully independent of each other. There is bound to be a certain correspondence between the values underlying any one normative tradition of the media and the prominence of a given model of democracy. A similar link can logically be made between a specific value orientation and the priority given to one or another of the four roles. Nevertheless, there is much free play between the three levels, and they offer different perspectives on the issues that arise. The level of normative traditions is most appropriate for describing and evaluating a complete media system at a given historical period, while the starting point for models of democracy involves a choice of political theory and usually a given set of political institutions. The third level of media roles applies to the work of journalism in virtually all democratic societies, of whatever type and in whatever epoch.

We begin the discussion of the interrelation of the three levels in chapter 2 with a concrete analysis of the historical development of normative theories.

We wish to see how a political community in a specific sociohistorical context links its philosophical worldview with a particular form of democracy. Chapter 3 demonstrates that what links together the three levels—philosophical explanation, the form of democracy, and the press' role—is a normative theory. We attempt to explain how the community works out, through public deliberation, a set of guidelines for good public communication, within the development of a democratic system of governance. Again, we recognize that to keep this book to a manageable size, chapter 2 examines only one civilization. However, we suggest a methodology that could be applied to other value systems, for example the important Confucian and Muslim traditions.

Notes

1. Wilbur Schramm's *Responsibility in Mass Communication* (1957) was supported by a grant from the Department of Church and Economic Life of the National Council of Churches (U.S.A.). The finances not needed for completing that project were used to support the preparation of the four essays in this book, with permission granted by the NCC.

2. The Commission was an independent inquiry under the chairmanship of Robert Hutchins, president of the private University of Chicago. It was convened and paid for by the publisher of Time, Inc., Henry Luce, in response to the criticisms that had long been leveled against the mass circulation press. The popular press had developed in the United States throughout the twentieth century and was widely seen as indulging in sensationalism and scandal-mongering, as well as being criticized from the left for its monopolistic tendencies and the abuse of power by press magnates. As such the Commission was initially welcomed by the press itself, although its final report was not, because of its alleged hints at the need for limitations on freedom (Blanchard 1977). In fact, there was no call for more government regulation. Instead, a strong claim was made for the acceptance of a public responsibility to provide full and truthful news accounts, alternative views of matters of dispute, a representative view of different groups in society, and to present and clarify the "goals and values of society."

3. The following overview is based on Nordenstreng (1997), which included also our first outline for this present book, with five paradigms built on models of democracy rather than models of communication: liberal-individualist, social responsibility, critical, administrative, and cultural negotiation. These paradigms have since been abandoned in favor of the three separate typologies we introduce in this present book.

4. The decision to select an emerging dimension of the normative tradition illustrates how important it is to be aware of the contemporary situation, but also how difficult it is to define current trends accurately. The choices are important; if there is a significant and profound shift in the values and expectations of the public regarding the media, this has implications for our conception of democracy and of the roles of the media in contemporary society. Choosing is difficult, however, because we cannot always detect whether currently discussed communication values are passing fads or represent a new development in a tradition that has been evolving for more than 2,500 years. To

designate this as a tradition is based on a methodology, which sees a convergence of radical changes in philosophies, in conceptions of ethics, in communication cultures, and virtually all other aspects of public communication. It is motivated not by any one evolving phenomenon, but by the convergence of the cumulative evidence from different sides.

PART ONE

Theory

2

Evolution of Normative Traditions

Where does a history of normative theory of public communication begin? Some historically based typologies of normative thinking about the media such as *Four Theories* are widely recognized as flawed in part because these typologies locate the beginning of contemporary normative theory in the rise of the libertarian ideal and ignore or judge negatively the historical origins of Western normative theory in classical thinkers such as Plato and Aristotle (Nerone 1995, 21–28). The founders of the libertarian and social responsibility traditions themselves recognized their indebtedness to a long history of normative reflections on public communication. John Milton, for instance, took the title of his libertarian declaration in 1644 from the name of the Athenian public judicial forum, the Areopagus. Words such as "democracy," "ethics," and "public" originated as ideas in the Greco-Roman world. The Athenian writings about rhetoric, public debate, and politics in the work of Plato, Aristotle, and others were a point of reference for a thousand years in that world. The Islamic and European medieval revivals of institutions of public discourse were based on the thought of classical Greece.

The thesis of this chapter is that contemporary norms of public communication are the result of a continuing conversation that has been evolving for more than twenty-five hundred years. Each major historical era has been based on earlier phases of the debate, and each has contributed something to the current normative traditions. This chapter organizes the relevant history in terms of four historical periods, each with its dominant concern and tradition:

1. The classical period, from 500 BC to 1500 AD, in which the major concern of theorists was the truthfulness of public discourse within a *corporatist* order
2. The early modern period, from roughly 1500 to 1800, in which the major concern was the freedom of participants in the public sphere within a *libertarian* order

3. The period of modern populist democracies, from 1800 to 1970, in which the major concern has been the *social responsibility* of participants

4. The contemporary "postmodern" period, since the 1970s, in which a major concern is *citizen participation* in the public sphere

Pooling the normative elements of public communication into such historically wide—even huge—aggregates might seem to experts on each period a conflation of major differences. While recognizing this difficulty, we want to highlight what can be seen as core elements in the worldview of each period.

Several factors influence the emergence of a new phase or tradition of normative theory. One is the tendency to appeal to a fundamentally different philosophical worldview in order to define a particular form of public discourse as good or true. In the classical period something was considered true, good, or just if it corresponded with the organic unity of existence, a unity generally seen as resting on the mind of a creator. This dominant worldview of organic unity can best be summarized as a corporatist view of existence and society. After 1500, this supposed unity of the universe seemed less tenable, and social philosophers such as Locke, Rousseau, and Kant argued that sociopolitical harmony and well-being should be constructed not by philosopher-kings but by ordinary citizens acting on inborn reason and the desire for the good. In the nineteenth century, however, the individualism of the libertarian tradition seemed less a universally acceptable foundation of what is true or good, and the ethical commitments of social responsibility in the organic interdependence of society as summed up by Marx or Durkheim seemed to be a more solid foundation. Today the grounds of the normative appear to lie in intersubjective dialogue between persons and cultures, as explained by Jürgen Habermas, Seyla Benhabib, Charles Taylor, or Emmanuel Levinas. The emergence of a new tradition is complex, but usually involves a combination of this worldview factor and many others as described below.

Corporatist Tradition: 500 BC–1500 AD

One of the premises of the present book is that normative theory of public discourse is about communication in a democratic society, and chapter 4 attempts to establish at least the basic parameters of democracy. It is important to recognize that this democratic orientation is in part a coincidence of the historical, cultural context in which the evolution of normative theory began; in other words, the beginnings influenced the subsequent evolution. Four sets of cultural values regarding public discourse emerged in the period termed "corporatist" that played an important role in pointing the evolution of normative theory toward the democratic framework we find today: (1) that collective decisions are best arrived at by participatory debate among all in the community; (2) that deliberation should be oriented toward the common good; (3) that deliberation should be based on a rational, reality-based criterion of truthfulness; and (4) that cultural practices should be rooted in a literate, reflexive culture of theoretical justification.

PARTICIPATORY DEBATE

For participatory democracy to work, a criterion for the right to participate had to be found; that criterion was citizenship. Riesenberg notes, "it is clear why the Greek city-state world created the peculiar Western institution of citizenship" (1992, 3). Most of these city-states had rejected monarchical forms of government, and public communication concerned the common welfare of the people (though limited to male citizens), not the welfare of a royal house. It was the genius of leaders such as Solon and Cleisthenes to see that granting the right to participate, and guaranteeing personal rights, not only motivated people to contribute to the wars and works of the community, but passed a sense of responsibility to those who argued for the decision (Ober 1989, 60–73). Athens, with 125,000–150,000 inhabitants, found the services of different classes and subcultures sufficiently important for economic survival or armed protection of the state to guarantee participation of free men in all decision making in an open assembly (Cartledge 2000, 17; Riesenberg 1992, 3–6). The simple criterion of permanent residence had a democratizing influence because it removed the exclusionary standards of divine choice, noble breeding, education, and achieved wealth. Once the institution of citizenship was introduced into a city, as in Rome or later in the Middle Ages, there were continual pressures to expand citizen rights (Sherwin-White 1996). Plato, Aristotle, and other authors of ideal republics in antiquity were quick to theorize citizenship, and this made it an integral part of the tradition of normative theory of public discourse (Nichols 1992, 53–56).

Few city-states in antiquity had the freedom of expression and citizen-based participation of Athens, but this ideal was followed in various degrees in many Greek colonies around the Mediterranean (Ober 1989, 127–55). Romans maintained the tradition that major public decisions were made by the debates of the patrician-based senate and the public voting assemblies of the people (Senatus Populusque Romanus—SPQR) (Wood 1988, 22–37). The Hellenistic and Roman empires absorbed the city-states but incorporated many of the principles of citizenship, leaving the cities much cultural and deliberative autonomy (Fowler 1893, 317–20). When commerce and education reawakened in the Middle Ages, it was usually in terms of small city-states that obtained charters of independence, especially in the Mediterranean basin (Jones 1997).

A further foundation of decisions by participatory debate was to reinforce political equality with communicative equality. In Athens and other Mediterranean city-states, the recognition of the right of ordinary citizens to voice opinions in a public assembly introduced an important institution. The assembly in Athens met forty times a year with an average of some six thousand persons present (Ober 1989, 132–33). The assembly's agenda was prepared by the Council of Five Hundred, in which all citizens could participate at least once in a lifetime. The members of the council who determined the agenda were selected annually by lot, implying that any person at random was considered politically competent. Major offices were also filled by lot. Athenians did not believe in the election of officials or in delegating deliberation to elected officials. The state paid citizens a normal day's salary when they participated in the deliberations of governmental bodies (Ober 1989, 127–55).

However, the right to voice proposals in public assembly would not, in itself, have meant communicative equality if the institution of education for public participation had not become widely available. The systematic teaching of public speaking in the courts and in public assemblies is said to have originated in Sicily and to have been brought to Athens about 450 BC. Throughout the Mediterranean, the Sophists taught not only rhetorical speaking itself but the knowledge of science, culture, and philosophy that enabled these men to impress crowds with their capacity for systematic, rational argument (Kennedy 1994, 7–8, 17–21; Schiappa 1991, 54–58). The sophistic teachers of civic participation were a major factor in bringing political equality to the level of communicative equality (Swartz 1998, 65–70). They fashioned rules of persuasive rhetoric based on the ability to aggregate interests into proposals for decision making that all could agree with or at least tolerate (Schiappa 1991, 157–73). Not the least of the sophistic rhetorical skills was pleasing and cleverly holding the attention of an audience; as Ober notes, the moment a crowd of six thousand became the least bit bored, they began to shout down the speaker (1989, 138).

Aristotle in his *Rhetoric* argues that personal character is one of the major qualifications for being a good participant in public debate (Garver 1994, 172–96) and being a person of balanced virtue is essential for influence in the political regime. Rhetoric, along with dialectic, became the foundation of educational systems in the Hellenistic and Roman cultures and in medieval Europe.

A third important foundation of the use of participatory debate for making public decisions was the commitment to resolving conflict not by force but by persuasive rhetoric based on good reasons. Athens in the fifth and fourth centuries BC was a society of great cultural diversity (Reed 2003), continual litigation in the courts, political debates, and love of philosophical discussion (Schiappa 1991, 145). The Mediterranean city-states were proud of their enormously diverse skills, trades, and professions, and they carefully protected the agonistic, competitive pluralism of their societies (Ober 1996, 172). What emerged is what Ober calls the "regime of truth" rather than a regime of economic power, bullying, vendetta, and other forms of violence (106). Underlying this regime was the citizen's right to take action in the face of injustice and the acceptance of the political equality of all citizens even in the face of economic inequality (Ober 1989, 293). Ober (304–11) argues that the great achievement of the Athenian constitution was that it balanced the economic power (and indirectly military power) of elites with the political power of the poor in the assembly.

Cicero, who dedicated a lifetime to studying rhetoric, argued desperately against the passing of the Roman republic and the onset of imperial government by military commanders, even if no viable democratic form of administering an empire presented itself. His ideal statesman was one who resisted the lust for domination, respected the deliberation of the people, found peaceful solutions, and was himself a persuasive speaker (Wood 1988, 176–205). This deep distrust of the "lust for domination" is found in Augustine's *City of God* argument that the downfall of the Roman Empire came from forgetting its respect for liberty, and from its admiration of brute power (von Heyking 2001, 22–23). Augustine, himself a teacher of rhetoric, thought that great world empires were built on the exercise of domination and preferred a political order of small nations linked in relations of continual accord (108–9).

With the rebirth of public deliberation through the formation of parliaments in the 1200s, education in rhetoric became important again (Graves 2001). Around 1200, trials of the accused by ordeal and by bloody battle were replaced with deliberative juries, and the practice of persuasion before judges and lawyers was revived. As a result, some training in rhetoric became part of the education of lawyers in the late Middle Ages (Levy 1999). The logic of using persuasive discourse instead of military or economic power to create a narrative of future action that had truth value for decision makers continued to be an ideal of public discourse.

Still another dimension of decisions by participatory debate that entered into the normative tradition was the trust in the participation of even the unlettered. When participation of all citizens was introduced, the question quickly emerged whether the unlettered masses could produce good public decisions or not. Aristocrats, including Plato and especially Cicero, had grave doubts; nonetheless, Cicero's and other model republics featured a "mixed constitution" providing for some combination of monarchy, aristocracy, and popular participation, on the premise that this provided a protection against the tyranny of any one group. Aristotle in his *Politics* expressed the view that the common sense of the majority of ordinary citizens was less likely to misrepresent the common good than a few well-educated experts (Ober 1989, 163–66). Underlying the acceptance of mass participation was the tradition that the masses had a better grasp of the people's values than did the elites.

EVERYONE MUST CONTRIBUTE TO THE COMMON GOOD

Aristotle rested his theory of ethics and politics on the widely accepted assumption that the person is, by nature, political. The people of the small city-state, who shared a common history, culture, language, and religious ritual, simply took it for granted that a person could not exist outside the community's history. Early modern Europe, faced with the challenge of building large nations out of city communities, emphasized the free contractual nature of national solidarity. But in a context of small city-states it seemed obvious that persons were by nature social, that persons became human in a sociopolitical context, and that human welfare depended on how strongly one's social interdependence was articulated.

In the corporatist worldview, especially under the influence of the Stoics, the social harmony and prosperity of the political community was seen to faithfully reproduce the rational, teleological order of the universe in the social order of human life. Cicero is a point of reference because he provided the first major formulation of this concept of law (Wood 1988, 70). People have the rational capacity to understand the harmony of the universe, as this is built into the nature of everything. By understanding this law-like structure of existence, it is possible to have good laws in the human community. Initially, this community might be thought of as a city-state, but under Stoic and later Christian influence, the community came to be understood as a universalistic, cosmic one. Knowledge of the logic of the universe (wisdom) could be gained by human study, but Platonism, Stoicism, and Christianity believed that ultimately only divine wisdom understood the rationality of the universe. True wisdom could be gained by philosophers who had mystical insight into the mind of divine reason.

From the Stoics came the sense of duty, especially as that was refracted through Roman leaders such as Cicero. Cicero linked to governance roles the Stoic emphasis on duty for duty's sake, forsaking the quest for personal wealth and committing oneself to principle even to the point of sacrificing one's life. The concept of duty as outlined by Cicero emphasized loyal service to the community and nation, absolute honesty in all dealings, and subordination to the deliberations of the Roman senate. Cicero battled corruption among officials of the empire, fought the development of imperial government based on the brutal military dictatorships of the Caesars, and paid for this campaign with his life.

This understanding of public discourse sustained the corpus of Roman law. One of the major legacies of the Greco-Roman culture to Western civilization is a legal tradition. Greek public culture stressed that good laws had to be based on public debate, weighing verifiable evidence for and against alternatives. In Aristotle's summary, the person is a reasoning animal (Johnstone 2002, 22–23).

Cicero incorporated ideas of Aristotle in his work *On the Orator,* and Cicero's ideal of education for public discourse was fundamental for Quintilian and for the Western tradition of public communication (Kennedy 1999, 113–18). Christianity, which did not have an elaborate theory of public life in the New Testament, took over much of this view. For example, *De Officiis,* the treatise of Ambrose, bishop of Milan, on the duties of the clergy, written in the late 380s, explicitly followed Cicero's template and became one of the major influences on professionalism among the clergy. It was cited by virtually all writers from Isidore of Seville in the early 600s to Thomas Aquinas, with repeated editions and printings up to the nineteenth century (Davidson 2001, 1–112). One can argue that the institution of such professions as the clergy, law, and medicine, centered in the medieval universities, goes back to the definition of professional duty in antiquity.

Although the political philosophers of antiquity proposed the relative merit of different constitutional organizations of government, they put far more faith in educating citizens and rulers as the basis of good public discourse and good government than in, for example, careful organization of the balance of powers (Kennedy 1994, 115–18). Greco-Roman society did not have an elaborate system of public security or social services such as one finds today. There was little to stop unbridled greed or power. The well-being of the community depended much more on the internal, disciplined goodness and magnanimity of citizens. In a culture with a harmonious corporatist worldview, having a balanced, temperate character was viewed as the source of other virtues such as courage, justice, wisdom, and above all, practical wisdom or prudence. A person with these virtues was much more likely to orient public discussion toward reasonable debate, emphasis on the common good, and the reconciliation of conflicts (see Tessitore 1996, 28–37). Good governance depended on the goodness of whomever was governing.

Gradually the various training programs for civic leadership became the universal system of education in the Roman Empire, which continued through the Middle Ages into early modern Europe. Virtually every significant contributor to the Western tradition of public communication—from Cicero to Augustine, Machiavelli, John Locke, and down to John Dewey—wrote treatises on how education for participating in the public sphere should be carried out. In China, India, and all other civilizations, there is also the general belief that the best guarantee of good governance is the character formation of future governors.

CRITERION OF TRUTHFULNESS

From the beginning of citizen participation in decision making in Athens, many questioned whether this babel of partisan, self-interested voices could produce wise, prudent public decisions. This doubt came to a head in the lifetime of Plato.

In 450 BC, Athens was at the height of its sociopolitical and cultural influence, but the humiliating loss of the Peloponnesian War (431–404) with Sparta and internal civil war set in motion soul-searching as to what had gone wrong. Among those accused of causing the problem were the sophistic teachers. Plato, Isocrates, and many others felt that the Sophists, often foreign newcomers to Athens, had turned deliberative assemblies and juries into a show of empty words full of demagogic half-truths. They appeared to be more interested in swaying the crowd, enriching themselves, and defending ideologies than devising good solutions to public problems (Poulakas 1995, 113–49).

A major effort in this period was to find some universally verifiable conceptions of justice, virtue, good, and evil. Athens was a meeting place in the Mediterranean of many different tribal, ethnic cultures, each with its own gods and history, each tradition claiming to be the unique truth. Trying to find a common basis for public agreement was a challenge. In response, Socrates and his followers, including Plato, introduced a method of education based on dialectic question and answer that led young people to think critically about issues (Poulakas 1995, 99–101). Above all, Plato's dialectical method attempted to get speakers to base their statements not just on opinion or emotion but on commonly accepted evidence from the world of experience. Truth could be arrived at by exchanging honestly perceived evidence in a cooperating community of truth seekers. The ideal was a form of public deliberation in which the relevant ideas and moral claims of every party would be listened to, debated, and brought together to form a consensus about the best course of action. The goal was to establish universally applicable principles of justice and truth similar to our contemporary universal declaration of human rights. Plato hoped to save Attic civilization by educating statesmen who would form a univocal, universal, consistent concept of justice and with this concept identify clearly the just actions that needed to be supported and unjust situations that needed to be rectified (Gadamer 1980, 93–123).

As Aristotle noted, Plato turned philosophy away from issues of nature to social, political, ethical, and communication issues instead (Irwin 1992, 58). Plato's controversial *Republic*, attempting to fashion a model of education, communication, and governance in the good society, remained a continual stimulus to new formulations of normative theory of public discourse. Following Plato, a central issue in scientific thought in the classical period was the question of how truth can be reached in public discourse. Underlying this process of truth seeking was the assumption that there is a rational, harmonious order in the universe and that true wisdom is the ability to perceive how all reality fits together so that people can live in accord with that order. Plato's concept of truth corresponded with this rationality but also grasped the rational coherence of all existence (Jenks 2001).

Aristotle emphasized dialectic, but as a community process—becoming social, political persons. He believed that the first step toward living in harmony with the universe was to develop a rational, balanced integration of the emotions and intellectual powers in one's own personality. In order for citizens to be able to promote harmonious decisions in the city-state, they had to have balanced integration in their own personalities.

As the Platonic tradition was picked up centuries later by Christian philosophers, they placed the rational coherence of the universe in God's mind and in the creative plan for the world. The Christian ethic—summarized well in Augustine's *City of God*—was to know the will of God through personal and group discernment of the action of God's creative spirit of love in one's consciousness, in communal consciousness, and in the surrounding world (von Heyking 2001). Dialectic—posing questions in terms of debate about alternative truth claims— was the framework of the theological and philosophical reflections of Aquinas and other major thinkers of the Middle Ages. Dialectic eventually became the central aspect of education for participating in public life across the Greco-Roman, medieval, and early modern eras. Throughout the Hellenistic, Roman, and late antiquity periods the bearded, ascetic philosopher, dedicated to seeking wisdom, was an important institution. Most Roman political leaders kept such philosophers as members of their households to help them discern how to make public speeches (Sandbach 1989). As Christianity became more common, the philosopher was replaced by the ascetic monk seeking to know and live in union with the will of God (Brown 1992, 71–117). In later medieval times, the monastic bishops of the Church became the guide for temporal rulers regarding the will of God in temporal matters. Knowledge of the unity and rationality of the universe became the basis of the truth of all public discourse.

THEORETICAL EXPLANATION

In the technically developed societies of the Mediterranean, virtually every social role, from medicine to ship building, required theory— that is, an explanation of why a certain technique obtained given results and why it was necessary to apply the knowledge of technique in a precise way. For example, the art of persuasive public speaking developed as a science, with quite complex theories and systems of explanation.

Plato, Isocrates, and many other teachers in Athens developed explanatory theories of effective public speaking and the relation of public communication to good governance. Aristotle, however, took the ideas of the Sophists and other teachers and created a comprehensive system of metaphysics, theory of knowledge, philosophy of the person, ethics, and politics. By systematizing rhetoric and ethics into a method, Aristotle made insights regarding public dialectic into a teachable subject matter.

Plato's explanation of knowledge, the quest for truth, public communication, and the emphasis on good governance were an attempt to base public discourse and governance on solid, unchanging universal values; but it was utopian and difficult to apply in a real world.

The more practical Aristotle thought that a knowledge of both universal, unchanging principles and of local interests and opinions was necessary for the artful application of principles (Bodeus 1993, 65). Thus, Aristotle introduced the basic logic of the syllogism, which started with the unchanging principles (the major) and then inserted the cultural situation (the minor) in order to arrive at the recommended course of action. Of course, the context of this deductive logic was immensely complex, and Aristotle outlined many different ways of using it. In the end, Aristotle was convinced that only with a highly developed habitual capacity to grasp the proper course of action was it possible to lead the community in forming laws that respected both the rationality of the universe and shifting historical circumstances (66–67).

At the center of Aristotle's explanation of public communication and political leadership was his theory of *phronesis,* a term generally translated "practical prudence." This much-debated concept can best be understood as the capacity to relate the fundamental, widely agreed on, perennial values of a civilization to the practical contexts of political decision making (Bodeus 1993, 36–37). The young learned *phronesis* through great literature, history, drama, and above all the experience of participating in the ongoing public debates about politics. Aristotle's theory was based on a commitment to universal values and a general formation in virtue, but it could only be developed through the practical experience of trying to solve real political problems that respected values but got the job done. An essential aspect of *phronesis* was empathic insight into the diverse cultures and life contexts of people in a community and the ability to bring the community to some degree of consensus that respected all positions.

Aristotle came at the very end of the Athenian city-state democracy, and he lived to see it absorbed into the Hellenic empire, which later became part of the Roman Empire. In many ways, Aristotle continued the process of taking the search for public truth to the transcultural level by making it a systematic exploratory science abstracted from any given cultural context (Poulakas 1995, 150–86). Aristotle took dialectic out of Athens and made it a potential practice in medieval and early modern Europe. Cicero spent a period of his life studying in Athens in contact with the tradition of Plato, Aristotle, and Stoic thought and was able to apply it to the practical issues of public speaking, governance, and administration (Wood 1988, 70–78).

Remarkably, these competing theories of good public communication developed in literate societies became the foundation of a continuous 2,500-year tradition of normative theory until today.

The Libertarian Tradition: 1500–1800

During the Middle Ages in the West, the ideal of citizens seeking wisdom to-gether through dialectic debate was sustained in some protected spaces such as the Italian city-states, the universities, the monastic communities, the emerging commercial cities, and to some extent the nascent parliaments (Jones 1997; Luscombe and Evans 1988, 308–15; Marongiu 1968). The emerging European nations, however, developed a concept and practice of public discourse that was closer to the Platonic model of the philosopher king as envisaged in the medieval theory of the monarchy. This was based on an alliance of the monarchies and the nobility with the Church (Canning 1988). The Church legitimated the belief in the monarchs' right to preserve the harmony of the corporate society in which all social actors had their divinely ordained positions. The knowledge of the proper order did not rule out philosophical dialectic, especially in the context of the medieval universities, but it had to take place within the givens of divine revelation defined authoritatively by the Church. The ritual of anointing gave the monarch God's authority in temporal matters, and the members of the kingdom looked on the monarch, however weak, as the sacred cornerstone of the nation's solidarity. The state, in turn, with its monopoly of coercive power, supported the religious belief system. Theoretically, the norm of truthfulness was whatever the Church considered to be in conformity to its theological interpretation of scripture, traditional Church teaching, and great philosophical writings such as Aristotle. These were judged to be good indicators of the harmonious order of the nature of God's creation. In practice, the ruling classes managed to gain from their ecclesial advisors the legitimation of the legislation and form of governing that they wanted. The Protestant Reformation movement contested the authority of the Church of Rome, but practically it allowed monarchs to choose whatever ecclesial order was most willing to give sacred legitimation to their rule. Given the corporatist worldview, it seemed logical that the Church and civil rulers, as guardians of the truth, should control all publishing so that no error would disturb the harmonious vision of reality. Truth is one.

In the fifteenth century, this sacred worldview began to lose its credibility. The corruption and unfaithfulness of the Church to scripture undermined belief in its ecclesial authority. Increasing conflict began between the church and commercial, political, and technical interests over issues such as interest on loans. Concentration of power in the monarchies led to increasing abuses. New scientific discoveries regarding such things as the planetary system brought into question the harmonious order of the world. Increasingly, the defense of traditional wisdom appeared to be a false ideology protecting the power of a hierarchical order and suppressing the evident truth through coercion.

Technical and economic progress gradually came to be central values, but there were competing views of how national progress might be achieved. One model of development upheld an orderly process, centrally controlled and planned by monarchs and their advisors. Another model argued in favor of a multitude of individual initiatives building a national unity through voluntary personal and group exchange agreements. The feudalistic ideology was gradually dismantled in favor of a new philosophical worldview that affirmed the equality and freedom of all persons. Over a period of nearly three centuries from 1500 to 1800, the corporatist normative theory of public communication was modified to guarantee the individual freedom to transmit and obtain whatever information might be considered of personal benefit (Siebert 1965). This new paradigm transformed and expanded normative theory of public discourse to include a series of new institutional conceptions.

POWER IN EVERY PERSON

The libertarian tradition of normative theory highlights the fact that all persons have the capacity to reason and to transform the world around them creatively. This is based, in part, on a profound belief in the freedom and dignity of the person. For John Locke, all persons are born rational, free, equal, and capable of governing (Locke 1960). From this flows the guarantee of the right to affirm one's own equality and universal human equality. Locke's thinking opened a public forum to challenge the institution of slavery, the subjugation of women, and all other major exclusions that had characterized corporatist thinking throughout its history.

In the libertarian tradition, positions of governance are delegated by citizens and are accountable to the people. This gives the public the right and responsibility to denounce in the public sphere abuses of power by delegated officials and to insist on change. Instead of depending on privileged access to knowledge of elites, all persons are supposed to be encouraged to take the initiative to think for themselves and develop their own belief systems. There is an assumption that no one person or institution has all the truth, and that individuals should be encouraged to create their own belief systems, which are potentially significant contributions. All institutions are susceptible to influence by distorting ideologies. The guarantee of freedom encourages every person to continually question the cultural context in terms of his or her own sense of right and wrong, justice and injustice. The principle of a pluralist society and maintaining diversity in the media can be traced back to this value of the right to one's own convictions (McQuail 1992, 141).

The encouragement to think for oneself is guaranteed in most civil constitutions and in lists of basic human rights such as the United Nations Universal Declaration of Human Rights. The right to one's beliefs includes the right not to be forced to disclose them or be punished for them (Emerson 1970, 30–41). Most educational systems and conceptions of socialization are designed to develop the capacity to be aware of and consciously defend one's own convictions. Many religious organizations also today affirm respect for the freedom and integrity of the belief systems of others.

EXPRESSING PERSONAL CONVICTIONS

Not only is freedom of belief defended but also the right to persuasively project one's beliefs into the sphere of public debate. This guarantee rules out all external, public criteria of truthfulness as long as the expression is not a threat to the rights of others—the famous "freedom to be mistaken" that Milton included in his *Areopagitica*. Freedom of expression is buttressed by the defense of private ownership for the media and by guarantees of immunity from all censorship or reprisals before, during, and after publication. The right to free expression places a high value on all citizens' duty to make their views present in public debate and on the value of being a fully informed citizen. People are expected to reject all forms of economic, political, or religious influences on their public expression. Public policy encourages speaking out in the public sphere with a multiplication of media for ease of access and by removing economic barriers to access. Maximum free expression is seen as one way to ensure that citizens have access to the alternative sources of information about a public problem, and to ensure that the public has full, fair, and objective information (McQuail 1992, 101). When there is a conflict between the free publication of information and privacy or personal reputation, courts tend to favor freedom of expression as the more important value (Bollinger 1991, 1–23).

The best way to guarantee truth in the public sphere is free, open, and unchecked debate in which both error and truth have equal access. Rather than setting up some organizations to judge the truthfulness of public statements, the "invisible hand" of the market place of ideas is the best guarantee that some approximation of the truth will be reached. The premise "that truth naturally overcomes falsehood when they are allowed to compete" was continually proposed in the eighteenth century (Smith 1988, 31). The classic marketplace-of-ideas theory was based on the assumptions that the truth is discoverable, that people are capable of distinguishing truth or reality from nonreality, and that people can agree on evidence. It assumes that people are able and willing to put aside their social biases and sift through data to get to the core issues in a discussion (Baker 1989, 6–7). Although some of these premises may be questionable, it is generally thought better to err on the side of free expression.

To promote open debate, it is important to encourage the organization of interest groups with articulate cultural values and a readiness to express positions on any given collective-decision-making issue (Friedland, Sotirovic, and Daily 1998, 191–220). Thus, freedom of expression is defended by a series of other rights including assembly, religious organization, access to education, and geographical mobility. In effect, the normative theory of the marketplace of ideas is based on a broader theory of civil society's role in democracies.

Freedom of expression has meant, concretely, freedom of the publishing enterprise and is interpreted as the protection of media owners from intervention by the state or other major social institutions (McQuail 1992, 102–5). The reduction of ideas and information to an impersonal monetary value introduced a public sphere of universal access unrestricted by particularistic criteria of social privilege, religion, ethnicity, profession, or other artificial barriers.

TOLERATING DIVERSE BELIEFS

The tolerance of diverse, contrary, and mutually hostile beliefs is expected as a characteristic of public discourse. Most of the major libertarian theorists, such as John Locke and John Stuart Mill, wrote essays on tolerance, exploring ways to avoid the violent suppression of minority views. Tolerance is the practical acceptance that points of view one thinks erroneous or even dangerous not only have a right to existence but may be, in the long run, beneficial—presuming that those holding these views are tolerant (Nederman and Laursen, 1996). John Stuart Mill in his treatise *On Liberty* argued that minority positions and new ideas should be encouraged as a way to counteract the "tyranny of the majority" (1859; 1951).

Tolerance defends the right of every group to maintain its own culture and to project into the public sphere what it considers to be its reasons for existing in society. It also encourages an attempt to know and judge fairly the positions of other groups and promotes the understanding of how each group is contributing to the well-being of the whole society. Tolerance means that there is a continual dialogue between cultures in the public sphere and that society's members are attempting to discover what common values are shared by all groups.

MECHANISMS FOR CONTROLLING POWER

To protect freedom, it is important to introduce institutional checks and balances of power and mechanisms for the continual redistribution of power. Locke, in his influential *Second Treatise on Government,* written in approximately 1680, located the power of government in individual members of society and in the capacity of every person to reason. "Men being . . . by Nature, all free, equal and independent, no one can be put out of this Estate and subjected to the Political Power of another, without his own Consent" (1960, ch. 8). Locke proposed a division of the powers of government into legislative, executive, and judiciary, but the supreme power lies in the legislative one, which is directly responsible to the people who have elected its members.

The power of the people over legislative action, in this view, depends very much on the press's continual reporting of legislative activities and the debate, from different perspectives, of these legislating activities. In eighteenth century-Europe, especially in English-speaking countries, it was increasingly accepted that the press had the function of checking the misuse of authority and revealing the oppression and abuses of oligarchies (Smith 1988, 19–26). With the growing consensus that governments exist by the people's consent, the view that the people can dissolve the government if it is not responding to the rightful interests of the citizenry became increasingly strong. The press was continually gauging the legitimacy of degrees of forceful action against abuse of rights (26–30).

The libertarian tradition placed great faith in personal property as a kind of defensive wall to protect individual freedom of expression. Property is the fruit of personal endeavor, of applying one's talents to the development of nature's resources (Simmons 1992, 222–77). The right to own and operate a press came to be considered a sacred bulwark against the abuses of tyranny.

The libertarian tradition also preferred to base society's moral order on the freedom of individuals to seek their personal goals rather than on communitarian norms and on contractual relationships of quid pro quo mutual advantage. In this perspective, the essential idea of justice is the fulfillment of contracts. Freedom of expression will be respected if everyone sees that the respect for laws protecting freedom is eventually to the benefit of all.

An important dimension of the libertarian tradition is the continual critique of the concentration of power in the media and a continual unmasking of ideologies that defend interests in the media (Hocking 1947, 135–60). The freedom of public discourse requires that there be diversity of ownership and diversity of views so that the press itself can be the object of continual critical evaluation.

ENLIGHTENMENT AND EDUCATION

Throughout the eighteenth century, publishers emphasized that the public debate in the press is a major source of education and moral uplift (Smith 1988, 42–53). Benjamin Franklin, for example, in his newspapers continually directed readers to look at the concrete evidence for any belief—not to accept anything on the basis of superstition, magic, or blind acceptance of authority. A systematic skepticism encouraged the analysis of the causes of all phenomena, and especially looking for the most efficient means of improving one's life. Readers were to be encouraged to think for themselves, to be just in their dealings, and to demand justice from others.

An underlying theme in the thinking of the Enlightenment from Descartes down to Locke and Rousseau is that there is a natural goodness in the internal reasoning powers of persons. Corruption is more likely to come from dependence on the external structures of society. The inherent reasonableness of the person is, in Locke's view, the foundation of the person's capacity to govern and is the basis not only for self-realization but for real social progress (Schouls 1992, 168–72). Kant likewise rooted his ethics of duty in the evidence of reason, the perception of the contradiction of wanting good treatment for myself but not also wanting to do the same for others. Debates in the press sharpened one's freedom to respond to an internal sense of reason and duty (Merrill 1974, 195–99).

THE MEDIA AS COMMON CARRIER

The freedom of the press implies that it serves as a common carrier of opinions and news from all sources. Although printers and publishers defended the right to publish what they liked on the basis of the press being their property, in practice the printers of newspapers tended to argue that a press is free if it offers to everyone the same liberty. Especially printers in smaller communities, where there were not large partisan groups, were inclined to be neutral and open to printing all opinions. In part this was pragmatism elevated to the level of moral norm by grounding it in a broader sociopolitical philosophy. One of the best known statements in favor of an impartial press was Franklin's *Apology for Printers*. When he was attacked for publishing it because it gave offense to the local clergy, he responded "that when Men differ in Opinion, both Sides ought to have the Advantage of being heard by the Publick" (Botein 1981, 20). As Botein comments, "Here was a principle consistent with advanced eighteenth-century doctrines of the public good, defined in terms of free competition by individuals or interests"(20).

The Social Responsibility Tradition: 1800–1970

With the Industrial Revolution at the end of the eighteenth century, the formation of great cities began, and a social stratification system structured around industrial production and the service industries coalesced. Newspaper entrepreneurs quickly saw a market for cheap, mass-produced newspapers for the less-educated classes who were looking for information about the cities to which they were immigrating. The popular press appealed to the less educated, with information about robberies, murders, and other dangers in their neighborhoods, and in the people's colorful, sensationalist language.

With the gradual extension of voting rights to nonpropertied classes, these newspapers also became a major source of political information and a strong influence on the popular vote. The democracies that evolved in the nineteenth century presumed that members of legislatures and governments were representatives who were to do the voters' will. Thus voters had to be continually informed of elected officials' performance in order to monitor and evaluate their service to the public. This information became particularly important as education, health, transport, and other services were assumed by local city, regional, and national governments. The eighteenth-century press had already assumed a major political role in forming democratic governments in Europe and America and now was anxious to consolidate its role as the "foundation of democracy." Elite readers got their information about their city, nation, and empire from firsthand oral sources, and they were more interested in quality newspapers for their reporting of trends in political opinion. The less-educated classes did not have this privileged, firsthand access to information in private clubs and homes and depended on news the press gathered. Journalists became the trustees of the public, giving eyewitness accounts of situations the voting public had to make decisions about. Thus the penny newspapers gradually introduced news reporters, rapid telegraphic news delivery, vivid descriptions, and photography. The press also assumed the role of protagonists of nationalistic progress, and nothing was more lucrative than selling newspapers that recounted a nation's wars of expansion.

Critics of the popular press in the late nineteenth century, especially in the United States, accused the so-called yellow press of being a serious threat to democratic values and family morals. Many called for government control of these excesses. The evidence against the press showed criminal negligence in handling news, suppression of important news because of vested interests, false advertising and conspiracy with advertisers, and promotion of antisocial prejudices. In 1912 Congress passed legislation regulating newspapers, and in 1913 some 20 states were considering some form of regulation (Marzolf 1991, 64).

Nothing aroused the press's antagonism more than the threat of government intervention. The moral high ground of the press was that the freedom from government control or any form of censorship was essential for democracy. The more pragmatic concern was that the kind of regulations envisaged often interfered with the press's lucrative sources of income. In response to the swelling tide of public criticism, the press promised to carry on its own in-house reforms under the principle of "social responsibility," a term widely used by press critics. How to resolve the conflicting moral claims of media autonomy, with accountability to the public's information needs, remains one of the thorniest issues of normative theory of public communication (Glasser 1989; McQuail 2003). And it is complicated by the fact that the moral foundations for this conflict were often taken from the Progressive movement, which was itself the source of much press criticism (Botein 1981, 40–57).

PROFESSIONALIZATION

In the new industrial democracies and in the industrial cities of older nations, the traditional occupations of noble distinction based on a feudal past were absent. The most prestigious occupations instead were the classical professions— clergy, law, and medicine. These professionals' claim to distinction in a community was their university education and their corporate professional identity. The medical profession stood out because there was rapid scientific progress in medicine. As the other theoretical and applied sciences progressed rapidly at the beginning of the nineteenth century, people with this technical knowledge also sought professional status. New professional careers were rapidly added to universities, especially in newer secular universities in new nations such as the United States. By the middle of the nineteenth century, the process of what Bledstein (1976) calls "universal professionalization" was well under way in America.

The most frequent proposal for improving the responsibility of the press by leaders in the movement, including Joseph Pulitzer, was to make journalism a profession (Marzolf 1991, 50–61). Journalists had already taken the first step toward forming a profession by establishing associations and founding professional journals such as *Editor and Publisher* in the United States. What Pulitzer and other leaders in the newspaper world wanted, however, were university degree programs. The first degree program was established by Walter Williams at the University of Missouri in 1906. Pulitzer's own program at Columbia University followed a few years later, and by the 1920s dozens of journalism degree programs had been established.

Professionalization brought to journalism, first, the assurance that through systematic, accredited training, proved by examinations and witnessed by the diploma, the professional had duly mastered the science and could be trusted by the public. In the case of journalism, the tradition of a science and its grounding in research had to be invented. Second, a profession has a code of ethics that is freely assumed in conscience by an oath (in the case of medicine) or quasi oath in many professions. This is generally a public promise to provide a service to clients (in this case the media-using public), loyalty to one's colleagues, and high levels of competence. While supervisors control wage workers, the truthfulness and accuracy of what journalists report depend entirely on their personal consciences. This creates a serious ambivalence in the commitment of media professionals: on the one hand there is a commitment to one's conscience and to the public and on the other hand there are the pressures of a profit-oriented or government-controlled organization.

Third, and most important, a professional becomes part of a corporate association that provides a personal sense of identity and a social identity of prestige in the association and in the community. The prestige one enjoys in the institutional association depends on the degree to which individuals fulfill the norms of professional competence. Prestige in the community depends on how much importance the community assigns to the services of the profession. The main motivation that drove journalists to become professionals was precisely to raise their prestige in the local and national community. The community, however, is ready to attribute prestige only if the typical professional lives up to the community's expectations. The uncertainty and contradictory expectations of the public regarding the media create still another set of ambivalences for the profession.

The other aspects of professionalism, such as regular updating of one's scientific competence by attending special courses and conferences and through journals, are also encouraged in the media profession. Professionalism in media occupations is increasingly defined by having a university degree based on training in a systematic science of communication, and knowledge of continued research on communication problems is a significant reference point for evaluating the media world normatively.

DEFENDING POPULAR DEMOCRACY

In the libertarian tradition, the media tend to ground their moral obligations in the principles of freedom of expression and loyalty to one's conscience. The social reform movements of the nineteenth and early twentieth centuries gradually established a consensus regarding the moral obligation that comes with ownership of a media business, especially the press, to respect its social responsibilities (Hocking 1947). The media have responded, in the social responsibility tradition, by seeking moral grounding in terms of their importance as defenders of democracy. In fact, democratic political cultures do attribute this purpose to the media. The press played an important role in the eighteenth century as the forum in which people circulated and developed proposals for how a representative government should be formed. The press had increased its privileged access to and comment on political leaders to the point where it came to be considered a part of the mechanisms for balancing power, the so-called fourth estate (McQuail 2003, 51–52). Maintaining its identity as a defender of democracy has become central in the press's normative tradition, and the institution of the media, especially its academic wing, began a process of constantly evaluating the media's moral performance in terms of how they are or should be defending and promoting democracy (Gans 2003; McChesney 1999; Schudson 2003).

INFORMATION TRUSTEE

The media quite eagerly assumed its role as an information trustee, delegated by the public, because this legitimated privileged access to information and the credibility of the public. Having gained a moral claim to autonomy and noninterference by government, the media became ambivalent about accepting the citizenry's insistence on being accurately informed about public affairs. In response, the civil society has established a series of institutions to continually scrutinize media performance. Periodic major evaluations such as the Hutchins Commission report are part of this. Press councils, complaints commissions, and ombudsmen are also intended to defend the public's rights (Bertrand 2003). While recognitions of good media performance such as the Pulitzer Prizes contribute to better standards, also important are the numerous public condemnations of the major lapses of newspapers and the broadcast media.

The advent of trustee journalism changed the obligation of the publisher from expressing the publisher's ideas and values to responding to the public's information needs. New newspaper formats of large headlines, inverted pyramid organization, and division of news according to the great variety of social-status tastes all made newspapers easy to use even for semiliterate people. Newspapers defended their new more popular and sensationalist style by emphasizing their educative, informative, and moral uplift functions (Dicken-Garcia 1989, 158–61). Serial novels, so popular in the nineteenth century, presented solutions to problems in the narrative language readers were accustomed to in their oral culture. Advertising not only lowered newspapers' prices, but told urban immigrants what kind of mass-produced products were available, where prices were lower and, for upwardly mobile people, what styles were currently acceptable.

As Hallin and Mancini point out (2004), the forms of new journalism vary greatly with political institutions and political culture. In general, however, the codes of ethics of the new professional journalism revolve around providing a complete and realistic representation of events that enables readers to make personal judgments about the events' implications. The primary obligation of the reporter is accuracy, a well-rounded narrative account, and a nonpartisan presentation. This ethic generated technologies such as telegraphy and vivid photography, word-for-word quotations through interviewing methods, and journalistic ethnography that enabled readers to be present from a distance (Dicken-Garcia 1989, 163). New technologies are often even better ways to make the user present in the situation and help him or her experience the event as if directly.

INVESTIGATING ABUSE

A further ethical dimension of the social responsibility ethic was a journalism that catered to populist political interests: supporting popular political movements and candidates, exposing graft and dishonesty in political machines, promoting nationalism and community boosterism, attacking concentrations of power, and revealing the desperate plight of poor minorities (Dicken-Garcia 1989, 107–8). The media, however, developed a moral foundation for this rather pragmatic activity, namely, that the media are important for promoting social justice, redistributing social power, revealing abuses in public services, and debunking the mythologies of privilege and social caste (Gleason 1990).

The development of journalism as a systematic critique of abuses of power has generated another dimension of the social responsibility tradition: forms of investigative journalism (Ettema and Glasser 1998; Protess et al. 1991). In this case, the purpose is not simply to report events that are public and have public importance but to systematically discover social problems or abuses of power and to use rhetorical resources to move the public to act on these problems. These are recognized as the highest and purest forms of social responsibility.

PUBLIC REGULATION OF THE MEDIA

Although government legal regulation was anathema to the press's tradition of autonomy, insistence that the enterprise had social responsibilities and fear of economic monopoly prepared the way for a new perspective. Regulation implies that the media have obligations to the public and that government has the right to represent public interests. The introduction of radio opened the door for government regulation, at least in the area of the electronic media (Bensman 2000). The media, in turn, have acquiesced because the government provides an impersonal coordination of media industry services. One of the central aspects of regulation is to ensure a diversity of services responding to all sectors and tastes (Einstein 2004). The government has also provided a forum in which all major social actors having to do with the media can meet to negotiate acceptable norms. The landmark 1933 legislation in the United States and the organization of public broadcasting services in Europe were moments when governments were able to convene the media to agree on norms to guide the industry.

In the context of the progressive, social responsibility movements of the early twentieth century, there was recognition of the enormous plurality of social interests and the tendency of certain hegemonic alliances to distort cultural reality with a biased ideology. In the face of a constant tendency toward concentrations of social power and the exclusion of some interests in democratic decisions, it is important to maintain an enforced diversity of voices so that all interests can be taken into consideration in public collective decisions and tendencies toward totalitarianism can be avoided (McQuail 1992, 141–81). Diversity of media content is also considered important in order to serve the great variety of cultural interests, information needs, and tastes in a pluralistic society (Hoffmann-Riem 1996). A system of diverse media ownership, of diverse styles and content, is also important for questioning the concentration of power.

PUBLIC SERVICE

In many countries, especially in Europe, the corporatist tradition of sacred institutions with the remnants of monarchy, an established church, the chartered universities, and other major cultural institutions is stronger than in the United States. In these societies the media have taken on the character of a sacred institution essential for the solidarity of the culture and society. Most countries now have a mixed system of commercial, public service, institutional, and community media. All of them are expected to have public service as their primary goal. However, media supported by public funding are supposed to serve as a standard of service and quality for the culture industry as a whole. The public service sector has an obligation to provide services such as education, which the commercial media feels it cannot support. Those media specifically referred to as "public" are expected to be the norm and the paradigm of social responsibility.

The Citizen Participation Tradition: 1970–

It is always difficult to characterize the present historical moment because we are still in the process of defining what the current age is trying to create. Critiques by leading theorists regarding the social responsibility and public service tradition are some of the clearest signs that a new set of norms for public discourse are beginning to be affirmed. Typical is James Carey's (1999) observation that trustee journalism of the social responsibility tradition has generally played into the hands of hegemonic interests and has failed to bring into public debate the most pressing social issues. Davis Merritt's characterization of the journalism profession as elitist, a "high priesthood" that excludes the people from the public agenda, finds many supporters (Rosen 1999, 41). There is widespread criticism of public service media as being elitist because it takes as its norm of quality the culture of the privileged classes. A new set of values points out a glaring deficiency in the normative tradition: the exclusion of women, non-European racial groups, the handicapped, and the poor.

A central critique is that the media do not expose the concentrations of social power that are a major threat to democracy. Contemporary societies are characterized by an increasing gap between the rich and the poor, great social insecurity, and a social rigidity that makes upward social mobility far more difficult (Gans 2003, 1–20). Glass ceilings continue to block access to opportunities for those of a certain gender, ethnicity, and race. Worse, gaps between high and low status, and growing cultural confrontations are simply accepted as part of the system.

This analysis points out several dangerous tendencies. Increasingly, the media are part of a financial conglomerate, in which decisions are made not by editors concerned about public issues but by financial officers interested solely in shareholders' profit. News staff is being reduced, and the media are depending more on public relations handouts or uncritical reports of executive spokespersons. The mass media, in the view of many, are generally about actors at the top of the political-economic pyramid, and they present concentrations and consolidations of power to the passive spectator public as simply routine (McChesney 1999, 1–11). The occasional critical, evaluative reporting of public actors and investigative journalism's occasional revelation of remarkable corruption, only correct the worst abuses and give a false impression that power is being challenged. The media do not stimulate the discussions of perspectives across cultural barriers but turn the public into passive, even cynical spectators (Cappella and Jamieson 1997). Although media institutions introduced by the social responsibility tradition are important in confronting concentrations of social power, the changed situation of postmodern cultures calls for new approaches.

Proposals regarding the role of media and communication institutions in bringing about redemocratization and redistribution of social power assume that movements toward change will originate with the poor, the marginal, and the disempowered or groups in alliance with these movements. One response to this problem is to support and improve the local, small, alternative media that assist the spontaneous movements described by Clemencia Rodriguez (2001) and John Downing (2000). The alternative media articulate the complaints of the public ignored by the mainstream media, and help both the public in general and the movements to formulate proposals for major reforms in health, education, and other public services. Another line of proposals attempts to get existing media institutions to provide more support for grassroots citizens' movements (Gans 2003, 113–25). Other proposals aim at governments' media policy toward opening alternative media in public broadcasting, strengthening nonprofit and noncommercial media, encouraging the opening of the mainstream media to alternative voices through regulatory agencies, and working through consumer movements (McChesney 1999, 300–319).

At a still broader national and international level are movements attempting to influence public communication policy, legislation, definition of juridical claims, and international treaties to take into consideration citizens' communication rights. One of the strongest approaches is the emphasis on human rights and people's communication rights (Hamelink 1994; 2000). This has helped legitimate normative conceptions underlying efforts toward community media, public access media, and communication policies favoring alternative forms of citizen participation in the public media, such as press councils and media complaints commissions.

ETHICS OF DIALOGUE

In the background is a deeper critique of modernity, emerging from the postmodern emphasis on the importance of the multiplicity of cultural identities. Contemporary societies have an enormous variety of specialized knowledge and occupational subcultures. Globalization puts once separate cultural identities in direct interaction. Every subculture has its own electronic channels. Newspaper editors complain that the traditional newspaper cannot respond to the immense variety of interests (Kovach and Rosenstiel 2001). Nation-building and populist social reforms—part of the vision of progressive, unilinear social evolution promoted so strongly by the social responsibility ethic—are now experienced as an overarching ideological conception of history that stifles personal identities.

For further evidence that a new tradition is emerging, observe the shift away from the individualistic Kantian ethic of solitary, interior convictions and toward an intersubjective discourse ethics as a foundation for public communication. Greater awareness of the diversity of moral claims of individuals with different cultural backgrounds calls into question the Enlightenment universalist premises that assume that moral reasoning transcends cultural differences. Feminist and minority reflections on the roots of ethical sensibilities suggest that the systems of public ethics are based too exclusively on male, professional, political economic experiences. There is increasing support for discourse ethics based in Habermas (1990) and developed especially by Seyla Benhabib (1992; 2002). These argue that moral reasoning must involve a listening, negotiating dialogue between the variety of cultural and personal identities.

Dialogue has emerged as a centerpiece of contemporary communication theory, and with it the dialogic ethics of authors from Buber through Levinas. Conceptions of moral practice have been based too exclusively on models of instrumental reason, commerce, negotiations of political power, and professional service (Elliott 2002). The ethics of dialogue needs to be broadened to an ethics of community spaces where the concerns of family; religion; and leisure, geographical, and interest communities can be expressed. Instead of reducing morality to the neutrality of the pattern variables, the ethics of community provides a space where people of different identities, cultural backgrounds, social classes, and ethnicities can meet precisely at the level of differences and confront various perspectives (Bracci 2002; Nussbaum 2001). This is an ethic for reestablishing the public sphere as a space for the hybridization of cultures.

PARTICIPATORY MEDIA AND MOVEMENTS

The cultural tendency to affirm one's unique personal and subcultural identity has led to the primacy of an "ethics of authenticity" (Taylor 1992b). The new tradition values types of communication in which identities are expressed and enhanced: the multiplication of channels, the proliferation of fanzines and zine culture (Atton 2002, 54–79), and the increased importance of audience ethnography and reception analysis. This paradigm calls for a new regulatory perspective that values opening up greater dialogue between cultural groups in communities (Horwitz 1989).

To be encouraged are the community radio, indigenous newspaper, television, and multimedia movements now proliferating all over the world (at least where the national states will permit them). Community media insist that programming be produced by nonprofessionals, that all people and groups of the community have direct access, and that the content be decided by citizens' groups in the community (Jankowski and Prehn 2002). These media are owned by cooperative-like councils, and policy is set by the members of the community who care to participate. There is a commitment to the talent of amateurs in the community and confidence that people are entertained by their neighbors and friends, at least as an alternative to the slick performances of commercial entertainers. Community media are a celebration of local cultural identities and an affirmation of personal rather than universal criteria. Often local community media generate new styles and genres of media that can have great mass attractiveness, but the decision to remain small and local is firm, in large part as a resistance to mass culture.

Through participatory media a space of participation is opened for a community's marginal and less powerful members, such as women, youth, ethnic groups, and immigrants (McChesney and Nichols 2002). The prototype is the animator of a group discussion of people who have long remained silent and fatalistic about their dependency and oppression in the community. In local radio, video, or television, the animator becomes an anchor team that gives the first voice to oppression in a community institution. The animator brings out more clearly the faint protest, invites others to comment through letters or interviews, opens up studio debates, and fosters a general discussion of the issue in the community or region. Several normative issues are present in this scenario: the animator team is not primarily interested in objective reporting but in getting oppressed groups to speak out and take action. The norm is not common carrier distance but revealing injustices and bringing the public to consensus about social change. Public discourse is defined not by the leadership and power holders but by *all* people in the debating community, especially minorities, the poor, and the marginalized who are less articulate.

Another variant of participatory media is what Clemencia Rodriguez calls "citizens media" (2001). The protagonists are not animators who stand somewhat apart from the process of change in power relations but rather spontaneous local movements of marginal, less powerful people who challenge, without too much organization, exploitations that are a part of their everyday life. Because these groups are closer to the suffering of the poor, they create a discourse that delegitimates the ideologies and hegemonic discourses. Without much theory involved, these movements redefine communication as dialogical, participatory, continually shifting in its languages, and nonprofessional. These small movements come and go quickly—Rodriguez uses the image of swamp bubbles—but they gradually bring respect for their identities and demands. Change happens in terms not of great movements of "them" and "us" that "take power" and "control the media" but of a proliferation of small movements that gradually undermine existing power structures until simply no one believes in them any more.

In contrast to these small, seemingly ephemeral movements are much more visible movements that confront the existing organization of public discourse much more directly. The public journalism movement began in the United States largely among local and regional newspapers that interpreted their falling circulation and the disaffection of their journalists as due to losing contact with the real issues of the communities they serve (Rosen 1991b). Editors became aware that they were manipulated by leaders of election campaigns and public relations offices that invented nonissues to avoid taking unpopular stands on real issues. This parallels a general concern over the apathy of voters and the decline of civic life because people feel that their participation makes little difference. Newspapers have experimented with surveys and public meetings to discover what issues concern people in everyday life, especially education, health, public security, local cultural life, and so on. The news media also reorganized news-gathering methods, changing from the beat system, which is dependent on the handouts of power holders, to use of specialized staff who do economic or education reporting around specific aspects of central issues in communities.

News presentation attempts to follow the natural history of an issue so that the public gains a much more coherent understanding of the causes and consequences of an acutely felt problem. The norms of good journalism have shifted from focus on professional procedures to meaning creation in the community and the quality of civil society organization in the community (Lambeth, Meyer, and Thorson 1998). This seeming involvement in community social power changes—a key characteristic of all of these citizens' participatory media approaches—has set off a major normative debate between the advocates of public journalism and those who defend a more traditional neutral, trustee type of journalism (Glasser 1999a).

COMMUNITY BUILDING

Finally, at the level of normative theory itself, the movement toward communitarian philosophies of the public sphere has, in the area of public discourse, directly challenged the liberal, social contract, and progressive social responsibility theories of communication (Christians 2004; Christians, Ferré, and Fackler 1993). There have been various approaches, but they share the view that attempts to ground the public discourse on the projection of individual interests, to help each actor achieve individual goals, does not provide a basis for the common good of the society. The libertarian marketplace logic, in itself, can lead toward great concentration of social power and social exclusion. This has been moderated by the fragile consensus around the values of functionalist economic progress and instrumental rationalism undergirding much social responsibility as normative theory, but even so there has been relatively little value consensus in industrial societies. Public deliberation has led toward a certain negotiation of moral claims among major actors, but little real dialogue and moral consensus to sustain a given moral order has been achieved. What appears to be moral consensus based on dialogue among various cultural groups is really the use of power and resources to subsume these different voices under one or another hegemonic voice, such as WASP + Male + Professional. In the end, this leads toward collective decisions always in favor of the cultural capital of major power holders.

Communitarian normative theory argues in favor of a cultural dialogue form of public deliberation. It seeks a foundation in philosophies of communication such as those of Buber and Levinas, Daryl Koehn, Paulo Freire, and Charles Taylor, which ground communication in the communicative relation as such. For Habermas, moral consciousness must be nurtured under conditions of instrumental technocracy and institutional power that stifle autonomous action in the public arena. Thus Habermas's (1990) discourse ethics is relevant also, especially the versions that are constructed through the challenges of Nancy Fraser (1992; 1997) and Seyla Benhabib (1992). Daryl Koehn moves beyond a feminist ethics of care, nurturance, and empathy to a dialogic version that is public and wide-ranging in application (1998, ch. 3). The dialogic lineage of Buber, Freire, and Levinas make their normative commitments unequivocal, and they insist on transformative action. In Freire's language, only through dialogic communication can we gain a critical consciousness and become fully human (1970; 1973). For Buber (1958), restoring the capacity for dialogue ought to be our primary aim as humankind (209–64). He asserts prophetically that only as I-Thouness prospers will the I-It modality recede (1958). Levinas's (1981) interaction between the self and the Other makes peace normative; nonviolence is not only a political strategy but a public philosophy. Edith Wyschogrod represents a dialogic ethics of the self and Other rooted in Levinas, but her emphasis on compassion makes it distinctively her own (1974; 1990).

Conclusion

It is evident that the formula of normative communication theory emerging as reasonably satisfactory to the major communication actors in a given historical period depends very much on the culture of the time and national adaptations of a cultural era. The ethos is very much related to the major power holders' worldview and efforts to work out a satisfactory normative basis for some degree of collective action.

It is also evident that no era has been satisfied with the formula of normative theory that eventually found some degree of acceptance. This historical review leads us to central questions that are the basis of the following chapter: what are the characteristics of a more satisfactory state of normative theory, and what are the social conditions or strategies that lead toward an adequate normative theory?

Current efforts to define a new dimension of normative theory have been summarized well by another history of the twenty-five-hundred-year conversation about good communication, John Durham Peters's *Speaking into the Air* (1999). Peters concludes from his historical review that "communication . . . is more basically a political and ethical problem than a semantic or psychological one. As thinkers such as Hegel and Marx, Dewey and Mead, Adorno and Habermas (1999) all argue, *just* (emphasis added) communication is an index of the good society" (269). Communication is not simply a matter of greater technological power, as is so commonly promoted by those who say that communication problems will be solved by new technologies. Rather, good communication is a matter of mutual understanding. The major current developments in normative theory of public communication stress that a criterion of the media's effectiveness is the extent of the role they play in human and community development.

3

Characteristics of Normative Theory

The historical review of the previous chapter shows that the clarification of normative theory is not a deterministic process of historical progression, but a continuous conversation among major social actors seeking to understand how public discourse *should* be carried on in a given sociopolitical context. The past formulas are drawn upon, but the normative is best described as seeking consensus on how to carry out communication for public decisions in the present circumstances. At times there is a high degree of satisfaction with the new formulas of public communication, but these conceptions are always being challenged by new actors and new media technologies. This search continually generates new ways to guarantee respect for the moral claims of various actors, and it takes on new meaning as the conversation becomes increasingly global.

Accordingly, we define normative theory of public communication as the reasoned explanation of how public discourse should be carried on in order for a community or nation to work out solutions to its problems. It is a theory in that it attempts to *explain* how certain forms of public discourse lead to good collective decisions. As noted in chapter 2, libertarian formulas were widely accepted in early modern Europe because they fit well with the spirit of free enterprise and the desire to challenge the remnants of a stagnant feudalistic power structure. Milton's *Areopagitica* and later Mill's *On Liberty* summed up well the libertarian consensus of the time. These formulas seemed to explain simply and clearly how many of the major problems of carrying on public discourse should be solved: how and why to guarantee freedom of expression, how everybody can quickly get the information they seek, how consensus can be reached without coercion, and how to sort out so-called erroneous proposals.

By the twentieth century, however, there was a new sociopolitical context with new social actors and different communication needs. The libertarian formula, which made media the private mouthpiece of the proprietor was no longer working to the satisfaction of all. A new formula that said that proprietors also had social responsibilities had to be worked out to explain how issues of truth, freedom, and participation could be achieved in new circumstances, where the media became large corporate enterprises. Formulas such as the one offered by the Hutchins Commission report, and its popular adaptations in books such as *Four Theories,* explained to generations of young media professionals how the social responsibility system worked and why it was more satisfactory than earlier frameworks.

We also explore in this chapter *why* the theoretical grounding is so important for gaining a more satisfactory organization of public communication. What is the significance of having a commonly agreed-on theory or explanatory formula of norms? Why does a society that works out a commonly held theory have more effective public communication? Does a tradition of public discourse clearly and directly grounded in normative theory orient the media much more strongly toward the support of a democracy? Finally, we ask *how* a community or nation arrives at a more satisfactory normative formula, so that we can work out an effective normative underpinning for press roles in a democratic society.

Single or Competing Theories?

Four Theories and subsequent discussions of normative theory have tended to emphasize competitive models. Analysis of the historical evolution suggests, however, that we are speaking not about competing normative theories but a relatively unified body of explanatory resources that can justify specific public policies or help judge the validity of certain actors' moral claims. There are obviously diverse and competing orientations within the tradition of normative theory. For example, there has been a long debate between advocates of the individualistic, libertarian conception of how to realize truth or freedom in public discourse and advocates of the conception of communitarian, socially oriented approaches to normative theory. Here we shall refer to these competing orientations as paradigmatic traditions. A paradigm is a model or basic logic that colors all aspects of a field of meaning. For example, if the libertarian orientation is the dominant paradigmatic tradition of normative theory, this will influence all aspects of the normative in public discourse—personal ideals of good communication, codes of ethics, preferable communication policies, and the performance of the press that the public demands. Every tradition provides a different resource for explaining why a particular normative approach is preferable. The particular normative system supporting the policy tradition of a given society usually combines elements of the four paradigmatic traditions described in chapter 2. In Great Britain, for example, with its strong public service institutions, one can find elements of the corporatist, libertarian, social responsibility, and citizens' participation traditions.

Normative theory is perhaps best understood as a repertoire of explanatory resources, a continuing conversation that can be called into play when a given context lacks clarity about democratic procedures of public discourse. When new nations in the developing world build their systems of press and broadcasting to fit their cultures and their political systems, they tend to be eclectic, adapting ideas from many parts of the world. When the Japanese initiated their new democratic public communication system after World War II, Japanese representatives traveled the world to examine U.S. commercial systems, the British tradition of public service broadcasting, and other national media systems. What emerged in Japan was closer to the European public service tradition, but with many influences from the United States.

In each major debate that brings to bear aspects of the normative theory tradition, the explanations become clearer and more explicit. The formulas evolved by classical Greek authors assumed freedom of expression in the public sphere, but a much fuller understanding of freedom emerged in early modern Europe. Over centuries of conversation and debate, the contemporary conceptions of normative theory of public discourse have become much richer, and different dimensions have become much more explicit. If the problem in a given context is freedom of expression, we find that the available explanatory resources have a much more varied and deeper concept of freedom than was once the case.

Today, normative theory is becoming a global dialogue. The normative theories of the West are entering into conversations in other parts of the world. Participants from a great variety of cultural traditions in Asia, India, Africa, the Islamic world, and Latin America are joining the discussion. Doors are opening that permit these participants to utilize a great variety of normative resources in their cultural traditions.

Democracy and Media Roles

In this book, normative theory of public communication is understood to be the conceptual foundation, the explanatory rationale of a particular institutional organization of communication in a democracy, and the rationale of media roles in democracy. We may consider a democracy to be essentially a form of communication in which citizens communicate the decisions of governance and monitor the governing activity of those delegated. The normative theory explains and justifies the institutions of democratic communication at any particular point of history and sociocultural development.

It is obvious that media roles in Western democracy have changed considerably since John Stuart Mill and even since the Hutchins Commission a half century ago. Citizens expect far more direct participatory communication, and attempts to justify and provide normative theoretical foundations for citizens' participation in public discourse are much more central today in most societies of the world. This chapter argues that a foundation of normative theory is extremely important for the vitality of democratic communication institutions and for media that support and implement democratic communication.

To help locate normative theory on a map of elements that constitute such normative domains as communication ethics, communication policy, and professional leadership, figure 2 organizes normative issues as a hierarchy. At the top are analytical foundations—the communication values of a culture (a "public philosophy") and the organization of these values in normative theory. At the bottom are the specifics—the day-to-day practices of media production groups and the personal normative criteria guiding media professionals in their ordinary choices and decisions. Figure 2 indicates schematically the typical major actors in a normative system and is open to other dimensions. One can start from the communication values of a culture and argue that professionals must

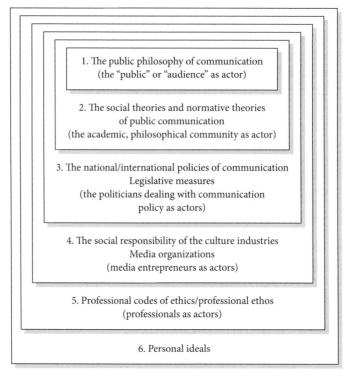

1. The public philosophy of communication
(the "public" or "audience" as actor)

2. The social theories and normative theories
of public communication
(the academic, philosophical community as actor)

3. The national/international policies of communication
Legislative measures
(the politicians dealing with communication
policy as actors)

4. The social responsibility of the culture industries
Media organizations
(media entrepreneurs as actors)

5. Professional codes of ethics/professional ethos
(professionals as actors)

6. Personal ideals

Figure 2. Major Social Actors

work in accordance with these. Or one can start with the values of individual media professionals and argue that they influence in some way the communication values of the culture. Undoubtedly, there is a dialectical relationship between all of the various actors in the system.

At the base are the personal ideals and values of professionals in the field of public communication. All normative elements finally depend on persons acting according to their conscience about what kind of public communication represents truth, justice, and respect for human dignity. The personal ideals of professionals establish the tone for the corporate culture—the *ethos*—of newsrooms, the codes of ethics of professional associations, the principles of teachers of communication and for media institutions generally. The most important influence in the ethical formation of professional communicators is socialization into the accepted culture of the profession. If a culture is ethically demanding, then norms will be important. Codes of ethics are merely the formalization in public, written, and consensual form of the most important general principles of the professional ethos. These codes are formulated, adopted, maintained, and enforced by professional associations, and they generally mean only what the associations want them to mean.

The normative policies of media organizations are often the operating and enforced norms. Newspaper codes of ethics are notorious for not always being enforced and continuing to be loose guidelines for professionals. Communication today is the collective action of media organizations. Usually, when there is some violation of rights or when some issue of media morality is put before complaint commissions, media organizations are held responsible, not just individual journalists (Mnookin 2004).

Close to the normative policies of media organizations is the collective social responsibility of the culture industries. Abuses tend to be industry-wide, and when the public, directly or through elected members of government, begins to attack specific reporters and publications, then the relevant newspaper, broadcasting industry, or other media industries thereby come under attack. There is always a threat of economic or political action if remedial actions are not taken. The sense of social responsibility comes to expression in personal ideals and corporate ethos, but usually there is agreement in the industry when there are major abuses of power and position. When the Watergate issue opened up and when the origins of the Vietnam War were exposed by the publication of the Pentagon Papers, virtually all culture industries were involved and maintained solidarity.

Legislated norms move communication ethics across the boundary of voluntary action into the area of state action and the state's monopoly on coercive measures. The press and most other media have always tried to maintain their independence from the controlling powers of the state precisely to protect their freedom and their function as guardians of public social responsibility. The state is legitimated only because governments are democratically elected, and legislated norms represent some kind of negotiated standards desired by the general public. Usually media industries agree that some version of public regulation is in the interest of all. They generally accept the government's coordination as the most effective and fair way of setting common norms for the industry.

Virtually all nations or regional organizations of nations such as the European Union have landmark legislation that establishes the national or international policies of communication. Often a policy is introduced when there are significant changes in public communication, such as the development of a major new technology and the founding of a new communication industry, or after important changes in government regimes. In Germany and Japan after World War II and in eastern European countries following the political changes of 1989, their culture, basic sociopolitical organization, and particular development challenges were called on to formulate a normative theoretical foundation and a set of media institutions.

Finally, we arrive at the level of normative theory and, closely linked to it, theories of the way societies develop. Normative theory, we argue, addresses public policy most directly but provides the reasoned foundation for all of the elements. Sophisticated formulations of normative theory are often the actions of the academic, philosophical community, but those involved in public policy may also contribute. Some idealistic members of the industry may participate, as in the recent debate over public journalism. Typically, in the background there is a growing public criticism of abuses and an emerging consensus among professionals that a new systematic policy statement is needed. At a certain point, a representative group such as the Hutchins Commission or the MacBride Commission at UNESCO is authorized to formulate a state-of-the-art summary of recommended norms. Often there is significant philosophical and theoretical-critical scholarship that these commissions can utilize. The published statements draw on principles of moral philosophy and almost always seem idealistic, ahead of their time, even utopian. Almost invariably the formulations are controversial in the industry, partly because the statements criticize abuses and partly because the ideals they articulate place great demands on the industry's resources.

It is obvious that certain stages in the development of normative theory closely parallel and are influenced by a general theory of social development. The libertarian dimensions of normative theory emerged as part of a general liberal policy in early modern Europe. Social responsibility norms evolved along with nation-building popular democracies in the late nineteenth century.

Media diversity is an example of one element of the social responsibility dimension of contemporary normative theory. The ideal of diversity illustrates the sociocultural benefits of a public policy that prevents concentration of media ownership in the industry, while providing conditions that promote the diversity of media services. The theory of media diversity also legitimates a great variety of media skills and offers a basis for extending normative criteria to new media and new communication situations. The principles of media diversity may also validate emerging norms in newsrooms and at the level of personal ideals. Normative theory becomes much more robust when it is closely based on moral philosophy and broader philosophical premises. Certainly normative theories in the classical and early modern periods couched their arguments in a metaphysical discourse that assumed they were talking about the givens of nature and not about arbitrary cultural conventions. Public discourse is a cultural action that depends on human inventiveness, but this creativity must take into consideration the constraints of existence. Virtually all normative formulas of public discourse make some assumptions about the nature of human and social existence.

A final normative element in communication ethics is what can be called the public philosophy of communications. By this is meant the communication values and commitments that are generally diffused in a society's culture. As Weaver (1986) has shown in his study of the sources of professionalism, many of the values of journalists or other media professionals come from their family and community backgrounds. Professionals and the industry know that they constantly face the public's moral claims and expectations. The political will to defend freedom and social responsibility is only as strong as the people's values. Moral philosophers and academics are voices crying in the desert if the community does not respond to what they are saying. In many ways, normative theory articulates a reasoned argument that expresses the moral demands that are in the minds of the people.

Fundamental Issues for Normative Theory

It is clear that there are different traditions of normative theory in different sociocultural contexts, just as there tend to be different traditions of democracy in different cultures. Accordingly, regions in Asia and Africa may develop their own normative traditions of democratic public communication in forms different from those of the Western tradition. There seem to be, however, common issues or problems of democratic public communication that all normative theory must find a way of solving. Usually the role of normative theory is to explain and give a deeper philosophical grounding for given practices of public communication. This may also imply rejecting a practice as incompatible with indigenous values and philosophical traditions. At other times, normative theory may become the conscience of the people and promote more democratic public communication.

A first important issue normative theory must deal with is free and equal access to open public debate. Traditionally, normative statements defend some form of freedom to express an opinion in the public forum without reprisal, to defend a position in public debate, and to make public the arguments regarding issues facing the community. At the same time, open public debate must lead to truthful, wise decisions. In the Western tradition, one of the major lines of discussion about truthfulness began in the context of democracy in the Mediterranean city-states, especially Athens, after the Sophists began defending persuasive speech in a context of freedom for all citizens. If Plato criticized the mode of discourse the Sophistic teachers promoted, he was not questioning the process of public discourse as such. Indeed, the teaching methods of his Academy were based on the Socratic method of open debate. The writings of Cicero presumed the freedom of senatorial debate, the freedom to initiate forensic trials, and the freedom of publication. Later, Milton and other dissenters protested the anomaly of denying a free press precisely because England had a long tradition of open parliamentary debate and public trial by jury.

A second central issue for normative theory is finding ways to resolve conflicts through deliberation. Virtually all of the great declarations about the proper mode of public discourse were made at times when a crisis in society's institutions threatened free and open debate. The statements of the Academy in Athens came at the end of Athenian city-state democracy. Cicero emerged as a normative theorist because he feared that the autocratic government of military administrators of the empire spelled the end of the Roman republic. Augustine saw barbarity smothering Roman civil life. The dissenters of early modern Europe were fighting off an encroaching system of absolutist monarchy in league with an absolutist Church that seemed to have rejected its own conciliar tradition. Today, Habermas critiques a society ruled by rationalist bureaucracies because they are dehumanizing, no matter how efficiently they seem to resolve the problems of industrial society. Habermas argues in favor of a discursive ethics based on deliberative reason, the recognition of the interests and rights of others, and the search for a solution that is acceptable to all parties. A major issue in many nations of Africa today is how to protect Africa's communitarian tradition of life and communication—where the good of the community is the prime value—and not fall into a rigid authoritarian type of public communication.

A third issue is how to balance the art of persuasive, elegant, popularly understandable public discourse that is also truthful. The issue of what defines public truthfulness is a central problem because cultural reality is constructed and truth is always to some extent a construction. Most significant normative statements on public discourse are produced in cultural contexts that have great esteem for an artistic style of communication. Classical public discourse was not simply a matter of pragmatic problem solving, but a delightful, inspired human experience that was somehow godlike in itself. Attic Greece cultivated and enjoyed celebratory oratory, poetry, drama, beautiful architecture, and various forms of artistic expression. Good public discourse brought into play every aspect of human emotion, intellect, memory, and reason. Most critics at the time, including Plato, Isocrates, and Aristotle, questioned the methods of the Sophist speech teachers because these methods often seemed to lead to untruthful, unjust, and unwise public decisions.

Milton was both a great poet and a believer in rhetoric. He defended his formula for freedom of expression, including speech and writing that many thought erroneous, because he felt that continued open debate would lead to the wisest, most truthful decisions. Robert Hutchins was a great humanist and admirer of philosophy, literature, and poetry. Out of that background, he led a commission that faulted the media of the day for failing to offer the public an accurate, unbiased, and balanced view of current issues in their social context. The media must not only be profitable but must also serve the public responsibly.

A fourth issue in developing an adequate normative theory is the relation of the academy and the arena of public discourse. Formal statements of normative theory tend to be the academy's work. One of the sins of the academy in the area of public communication might be called its theoretical perfectionism. Plato's passion for truthful justice and distrust of the messiness of public communication led him toward his theory of public deliberation, dominated by a philosopher-king, that tended to justify authoritarian public decisions. Virtually all authors of great normative statements were also teachers of public discourse. The men of the Athens academy, those who have framed the vision of social responsibility in our own era, and the current movement toward communitarian communication have all been dedicated to cultivating a love of dialectic in others and in the cultural environment. All have had a passion to promote the transmission of culture from one generation to another in a way that encourages each generation to rediscover the values of culture freely and to re-create it in innovative ways. But will this lead toward a truly open forum where others are encouraged to think freely and arrive at their own conclusions? Libertarians today, for example, are suspicious of the contemporary communitarian emphasis because they feel it endangers freedom of expression.

Normative Theory's Legitimating Function

Normative theory legitimates a particular model of public discourse in a specific historical period by rooting it in an acceptable foundation of moral givens. The moral givens are established by existential realities. Today, protecting the air, water, and environment for the future existence of the human race and other living beings is generally accepted as an unquestioned moral obligation. *Legitimating* means finding a formula for respecting the validity of the moral claims of all major actors in a particular public communication context and finding ways to respect the moral obligations of all. For example, at present many movements argue that a direct voice in the public communication process is crucial and that their right to participate is a moral claim. But media industries that feel they have moral obligations to investors and practitioners insist that they have professional ideals to meet. Parents feel that they have moral obligations to their children that the media should respect. The development demands of some countries establish still other moral claims. Finding an acceptable formula to respect the moral claims of all major actors is difficult and rarely accomplished to perfection. Nevertheless, one finds far more general satisfaction with the public communication system in some nations than in others.

The historical review in the previous chapter makes clear that a dominant normative paradigm of public discourse may maintain its validity for long periods but then change radically in a very short time. For example, a corporatist paradigm was dominant for almost two thousand years but shifted to an individualistic ethos in early modern Europe in less than a century. The new world of modernity reorganized the meanings of the world so that the meaning of every institution fit together into a logical whole. The marketplace metaphor spread from its initial emphasis on individual entrepreneurial initiative to the marketplace of ideas, the marketplace of pooled scientific information, even the marketplace of religions.

As a fundamentally different organization of history and time came into being around linear progress, the forms of public discourse in which meanings were harmonized changed, too. To make sense of this new world, thinkers from Locke to Rousseau explored different integrations of meaning until a normative formula for freedom of expression emerged that seemed to respond to all moral claims. In the end, even the established churches and the monarchies that had once defended a corporatist order with more centralized public deliberation came to see that freedom of expression was in their best interest. The new formula, which we refer to as libertarian, did not entirely replace the former corporatist formula but reorganized it to integrate the new meanings. The language of an order of nature persisted in speaking about the integrity of personal conscience, but with a quite new meaning.

Sometimes a single declaration of a single author gains great cogency for a whole era because it seems to explain so much of reality. It is said that Plato's *Republic* was the single most influential book in the Western tradition until early modernity. The fact that modernity finds it so difficult to make sense of the worldview proposed in the *Republic* only emphasizes how much it was linked to the worldview and ethos of that time. It would be wrong, however, to say that the *Republic* summed up the normative theory of public discourse until early modernity, for it was only one important resource. A normative theory is never limited to any one statement but exists in the ongoing debates about justifying a given mode of public discourse. Formulas such as Milton's *Areopagitica* or the Hutchins Commission report might be seized on as one good statement that comes close to what many people were thinking at that time. But usually no single document sums up all the normative theory of a given era. Often many documents come out, cross-referencing their mutual agreements, adding to or emphasizing one central element. The cross-referencing indicates that this is an ongoing debate in which every voice in the conversation has something important to say.

The state of normative theory at a given moment, as hard as it might be to pin down, legitimates the mode of public discourse by linking it to a broader structure of meanings. Plato's *Republic* attempts to link the model of deliberative public discourse with the ideal role of the statesman, the system of education, epistemology, and metaphysics. Most important, it fit the Stoic ethos that was widely agreed on in the era. Later, with small adjustments, it was easy for Christians to locate the Stoic perception of the rationality of the universe in the mind of God, the creator. At that time the purpose of public discourse, as Augustine pointed out, was to lead all to live in harmony with the creative plan. Through the influence of Aristotle, the dialectical method also became the method of Aquinas, which was to move from opposite to opposite by the argument of analogy until one arrived as close to the mind of God as possible. As noted, the Christian ethic dealt largely with interpersonal communication, but, linked with normative theories of public communication, such as that of Aristotle, also became a foundation for institutions of public communication.

Foundational Explanation

A normative theory provides a systematic connection between communication activities and moral claims, with an underlying moral philosophy that satisfies people's questions. It outlines a set of guidelines for acceptable actions in all areas of life dealing with public communication that are consonant with a widely held philosophical worldview. In antiquity, for example, Plato and Aristotle's explanatory system provided a reasoned explanation, in terms of the corporatist conception of existence, of how public communication should best be carried out in the context of relatively small city-states with essentially agrarian economies. Aristotle was useful because he wrote systematic explanations of ethics and politics, art and drama, and many other areas, linking these with each other and with a general concept of the person and the universe. Cicero, the Stoics, and literally hundreds of other lesser thinkers adapted the general explanatory systems of Plato, Aristotle, and Zeno in the attempt to provide something approaching normative guidelines for different areas of life, especially public communication. In the context of early modern Europe, Locke, Rousseau, Kant, and others worked out explanations rooted in the philosophical worldview of the Enlightenment that provide the normative guidelines for most of the current dimensions of public communication. Today, systematic thinkers such as Habermas are reworking explanations of the Enlightenment to take into account the contemporary intercultural contexts that require a constant process of communicative adjustment for understanding the enormous flows of information.

Habermas has written that after listening to broadcasts of the Nuremberg war trials as a young boy, he began wondering how such atrocities could happen in his country. That experience, he explains, inspired much of his work (Allen 2002, 97). Virtually all major philosophers today are trying to figure out what is going wrong with our systems of public communication that has permitted the mass atrocities of World War II, the genocides of Rwanda and Darfur, the frightening injustices of our advanced economies, and the many other irrationalities of our supposedly highly rational cultures. Normative theory attempts to link our everyday communication activities in the public sphere to a broader system of values that will help eliminate some of the contradictions in our actions. Considering thinkers as different as Herbert Gans in New York, Clemencia Rodriguez in Colombia, and Francis Nyamnjoh in Cameroon (2005), one asks what perceptions of reality inspire the normative guidelines they propose.

As noted, normative theory legitimates the system of public communication; it also legitimates the individual role of every major actor. *Actor in public communication* refers to groups of individuals who see their political, economic, or cultural interests to be affected by a particular way of organizing the services of public communication. These individuals have discovered a sufficient community of interest to organize an intercommunication network seeking change in the decision process regarding public communication and a change in the values legitimating these processes. For example, in many nations today, parents and others concerned about the negative influence of broadcasting on the young have formed associations to challenge broadcasters to respect the moral implications of this socialization.

Normative theory legitimates the right of groups to exist as public actors. In the example of those responsible for socialization, the public service tradition places a strong emphasis on education as one of the functions of broadcasting and thus gives far more legitimacy to this group of actors. Some would argue that the strong libertarian tradition in the United States, with its emphasis on commercial viability, gives great legitimacy to entrepreneurial initiatives but does not recognize sufficiently the rights of parents and consumers as significant actors. In this context, the operative normative theory does not sufficiently legitimate a very important set of social actors.

All social actors tend to approach public discourse in terms of the moral obligations shared by members of their group. Professional journalists think of themselves as having a moral duty to inform the public about major issues. When a democracy appears to be threatened, journalists see more readily the relationship between broad democratic values and their own work. The normative tradition of social responsibility has provided an explanation of why good journalism is important not only for the functioning of democracy but for the very existence of a free and just society, and ultimately for the freedom and dignity of the human person. When Plato attacked the Sophists and argued that intervention in public life should be based on a metaphysical dialectic, he represented the view of many that the moral well-being of Greek society depended on it. Normative theory, above all, gives moral legitimacy to the identity and action of various communities of interest.

Beyond the morality of personal identity, that is, being true to oneself, the proposals espoused represent a community of values, experience, and expertise that is of crucial importance in helping communication institutions fulfil their mission in society. For example, media consumer associations believe that they are an important source of normative reference regarding cultural values, order, and solidarity. Journalists feel that they are of crucial importance in maintaining the freedom and open debate of the system. Media owners consider themselves important in opening up new media services and greater media diversity. The challenge for normative theory is to provide a justification for each set of moral claims in a way that also brings the groups to recognize and respect the moral claims of others.

Social actors tend to define their relation to other actors in terms of their own particular role and sphere of interest. Creative producers typically define their claims in relation to others who have some role in media production. Figure 2 charts the major actors in contemporary public communication in a kind of hierarchy of responsibility for the quality of public communication. Most of these actors define their moral obligations in terms of codes of ethics or sets of informal moral principles. A code of professional ethics is a group's attempt to set norms for its own members, but also to tell other actors that the group's practices are not just personal interests but follow moral principles. What is often unsaid is that a code of ethics is derived from an underlying normative theory and has legitimacy only in terms of a much broader social morality.

As we noted about the legitimacy of the public communication system, a mature normative theory in a given historical period harmonizes the moral claims of all major actors in the arena of public communication. In a period of major sociocultural transition, when there is little consensus among major actors regarding the mode of public discourse, one set of actors often bitterly attacks the other as immoral. An example is the centuries-long dispute in early modern Europe between two models of modernization. The groups associated with monarchies felt that only highly centralized and highly planned bureaucracies legitimated by the sacred authority of the kingdom could properly push through industrialization and rationalized modernization. The entrepreneurial sector felt that only individual creativity and initiatives, united in a market of goods, inventions, ideas, religions, and philosophies, could act with the flexibility and speed that national competitiveness required. One might argue that the social responsibility formula brought a measure of balance to these two traditions.

The Importance of Quality Dialogue

It is evident from historical analysis that not all societies and not all historical periods are able to develop a normative theory that legitimates truthful, free, socially responsible, participatory, and communitarian communication. Not all societies at all times are able to generate a moral consensus about what kind of system of public communication they want and need. Not all forms of public communication that claim to be democratic are truly so. Great injustices remain in the modes of public discourse, and large sectors of the population remain without the information they need. In some cases, many are excluded from the opportunity to voice their claims for justice, or a significant subculture may be denied the freedom to express its values. At times the inadequate organization of public communication blocks effective decision making and problem solving. A central question is how a society achieves an optimum level of democratic public discourse.

We argue here that a key condition for establishing a satisfactory normative formula that harmonizes the moral claims of all social actors is the quality of dialogue between social actors (Habermas 1990; Pasquali 1997). If dialogue evokes a sense of respect for the moral claims of all actors and sustains the collective search that does not cease until all moral claims are dealt with, then it is fulfilling its central role. Quality dialogue brings about a deeper awareness among all groups in a society of their organic interdependence and the conviction that if the moral claims of one party are ignored then all parties will suffer. The following criteria, very similar to the principles of discourse ethics outlined by Habermas (1990; 1994), Apel (2001), Benhabib (1992), and Arens (1997), are at least suggestive of the dimensions that should be present.

1. The process should encourage all potential actors to have an internal process of decision making regarding their community of interests and their moral claims. Often, giving a constituency a "seat on a board" or an "office in the building" provides a stimulus toward defining its role.

As noted, "moral claims" means that continued human existence demands a particular action (Christians 1997, 6–8). For example, the mother of a starving child senses a personal obligation to find food and feels that she has a moral claim to demand food from those around her. Peasant farmers in developing countries feel that they have a moral claim on the media to provide information that would enable them to increase their agricultural productivity to the level of day-to-day survival. The process of dialogue could help the actors responsible for rural development provide the information not only for productivity but also for good health and for a richer cultural existence. Needless to say, in most developing countries this kind of dialogue does not exist. Peasant farmers and their communities have little voice in the public communication process. The People's Communication Charter was an attempt to bring the moral claims of the marginalized public into the public consensus and implement the current emphasis in normative theory on citizens' participation.

2. All affected parties should be encouraged to be present in the negotiation process. If some parties are not present, then a proposed formula will lack support from this group in the eventual political process, and the group may even block it as illegitimate. For example, during the late 1960s and 1970s, a number of Latin American countries had movements to introduce stronger public service and social responsibility dimensions into communication policy. On the basis of ideological criteria, a number of major social actors were excluded from the process. As a result, the excluded parties managed to sabotage the movements, and the process never brought the proposals to the policymaking stage (Fox 1988).

In general, the poor and marginal are never adequately involved, and public discourse often excludes the resources of large sectors such as women, residents of rural areas, youth, and various minorities. This situation calls for an official convening body that is recognized as impartial and represents society's moral foundations. Whether this is a public legislative body or a group of citizen trustees depends on how the society has typically adjudicated moral authority.

3. The claims of all parties need to be taken not simply as pragmatic interests but as moral claims. All participants should be encouraged to define their concerns in moral terms, that is, in relation to the society's constitutive common good and for the defense of fundamental human rights and human dignity. At times what actors initially put forward as a very pragmatic demand gradually becomes defined as a moral claim because the discourse has been framed in moral terms. An example of this is the moral discourse introduced by Lord Reith in defining the BBC constitution in Britain. Initially, advertising was rejected as a source of funding for the BBC on very pragmatic terms as a concession to the newspapers, which feared that broadcasting would draw away their advertising revenues. Later, the elimination of advertising was widely accepted

as a moral issue: that some areas of the public media need to be free from the influences of advertising for the common good of the national culture (Paulu 1981, 13–14, 54–60).

4. Dialogue enables participants to take the perspective of others, that is, to see and feel deeply the moral claims of other parties as if these were their own moral obligations. In Habermas's view, following Robert Selman, the most developed level of moral consciousness is the ability to "see the need to coordinate reciprocal perspectives, and believe that social satisfaction, understanding, or resolution must be mutual and coordinated to be genuine and effective" (1990, 144).

5. Negotiation procedures will have greater success in reaching agreement when the discussion is located in overarching values that are "above" the interests of any one group but, at the same time, guarantee the interests of all groups. Formulas of overarching values would show how service to people and recognizing the right to good service would respect all interests. A normative theory that appeals to common values such as the progress of the whole community helps to bring agreement. A normative statement gains wider acceptance through appeals to the national and international values that have been accepted in the past as the ultimate justification of common action. An appeal to whatever new and emerging common values seem to be of interest to all the parties involved also brings all actors into the dialogue.

Moral discourse rooted in some version of a categorical obligation beyond the arbitrary construction of culture is the foundation of all appeals to respect the moral claims of others (Christians 1997). The ability to call into play a moral discourse depends on the integrity of the leadership of the process. If parties involved perceive the leadership as representing its own pragmatic interests rather than universal moral values, then the appeal will have less power to bring the parties to negotiation.

6. It is particularly important that the formula for negotiation does not require any party to give up part of its reasonable cultural values and fundamental moral claims. The formula of overarching values should be sufficiently polysemic so that all can recognize something of their moral claims in it.

7. The greater the organic social interdependence in a culture, the more likely its members will be to see that serving the interests of others will eventually return to serve themselves and their immediate reference group. Corruption, which is widely considered one of the major obstacles of socioeconomic development in many countries, is a form of stealing from the community to serve one's own family, regional, or party interests. What those involved do not acknowledge is that it eventually may come back to destroy the welfare of the corrupt themselves.

Social theorists such as Emile Durkheim argued that it was crucial for modern societies to develop this sense of moral interdependence. For Durkheim, the contractualism of Spencer, which made the economic marketplace the prototype of social relationships and turned others into economic objects, was destructive (1960). Durkheim would also have disagreed with Weber, who saw the instrumental rationality typical of complex formal organizations as the prototype of modern social relationships. Instead, in his *Professional Ethics and Civic Morals* (1957–92), Durkheim saw service and mutual concern as the prototype of social relationships. He felt that the ethics of professionalism was a way to harness the power of scientific knowledge in personal dedication to clients, the well-being of colleagues, and rational service to social progress. Professional associations, in his view, were to be the social intermediary between isolated individuals and powerful states, enabling a scenario approaching what today we would call the civil society (Turner 1992).

Underlying the desire for negotiating is the realization that a breakdown in elaborating a new normative formula will be detrimental to all involved. Especially important is a commonly accepted moral foundation, that is, a willingness to carry out an action simply because it is the good thing to do, even if it has no immediate pragmatic benefit personally (Kohlberg 1981). The alternative is a regime in which brute power, the law of vendetta, or the law of personalistic agreements among friends and family holds sway. Once the values of sectarian leadership dominate, then leaders compete to show they can reward their own constituencies better than other patrons. Likewise, sectarian leaders try to outdo each other in destroying any kind of consensus because consensus would undermine their form of leadership. As Benhabib and others have argued, the discursive process must go beyond the rationalistic sense of justice that Habermas introduces to a multiperspectival relationship that emphasizes caring for the other. Freire proposes a prototype of dialogue that leads to relations of mutual respect (Christians 1997, 9).

If the quality of the dialogue among major actors is important for arriving at a satisfactory normative consensus, no less important are the rules for elaborating a consensus that respects all moral claims. Indeed, the history of philosophical and scientific reflection on communication, from the earliest treatises of Plato and Aristotle on rhetoric, has consisted of attempts to define a formula for good public communication (Poulakas 1995). Different paradigmatic traditions have highlighted the importance of different aspects of public communication. For example, Plato stressed the importance of objective philosophical truth in public discourse. The movements for press freedom in early modern Europe tended, naturally, to emphasize the expression of authentic personal conscience. Other paradigmatic traditions have emphasized the social responsibility of all actors or the radical democratization of the system. Whatever the focus of the particular normative tradition, it must be able to explain to the major actors why they have a moral obligation to act in a way that respects the moral claims of other major actors.

A new normative formulation becomes important when consensus among the major actors breaks down and public communication becomes a chaotic situation in which might makes right. In this new situation, major public actors do not seem to be bound by any moral order and do not feel that older formulations apply. The process of arriving at a satisfactory normative theory often falters or fails in some major way. One condition is the quality of dialogue. Another condition is the quality of the normative theory that is engaged through the dialogue. Quality in this case means the degree to which all major actors agree to abide by established moral norms of good public communication such as freedom, diversity of content, credibility, and order (McQuail 1992). A normative theory of public communication emerges in the context of a particular sociopolitical movement that seeks a reorganization of society and a public communication system that will be part of this new society (White 1989).

A Moral Foundation for Media Activities

A given tradition of normative theory fulfils multiple functions to resolve the dissatisfactions and conflicts that may exist in the sphere of public communication at any given moment. One of the major criticisms of contemporary texts on media ethics is that they are basically a list of dos and don'ts with no systematic linkage to moral foundations. Christians, for example, has pointed out that without a unifying moral paradigm there is a hodgepodge of ad hoc codes, conflicting pressure group action, and supervisory commissions uncertain of their own principles (1977, 19–29).

A normative tradition underlying the specific codes and formulas usually emerges out of the worldview and social challenges of a particular historical era. Social theorists point out, however, that what gives a historical era moral coherence and creative dynamism is a fresh systematic moral vision that channels motivations into new roles and institutions. The libertarian tradition of early modern Europe, focusing on human freedom and equality, helped to shape the roles of the newspaper press and defined the norms guiding newspaper proprietors.

Robert Wuthnow (1989) has analyzed three great discursive movements that articulated the meaning of new social contexts—Luther in the Protestant Reformation, Voltaire and others defining the vision of the Enlightenment, and Marx summing up early nineteenth-century desires for social utopianism. Wuthnow thinks that what is causing contemporary cultural confusion, cultural wars, and major cultural contradictions is the lack of consensus on a basic moral vision. "What makes the study of public discourse of particularly vital importance in today's world is a widely shared perception that we are increasingly talking past one another, letting bureaucratic and technical concerns predominate, rather than finding effective ways of reaching consensus on matters of the common good" (1992, 8).

A central role of a particular paradigmatic tradition of normative theory is to relate practices and activities to the more fundamental values of a particular era. The printers of early modern Europe may have been unhappy with the royal and ecclesial monopolies because they deprived them of needed income, but they struggled for press freedom on much broader moral grounds. Likewise, many minority movements today may hope that community media will increase their influence on the services of local government, but they appeal to the right to communicate and the right to participate. A moral paradigm can have the following functions.

- It relates actions to an overarching moral purpose so that pragmatic activities are transformed into moral activities. Media activities are now based in moral obligation. For example, it provides a *moral* argument as a basis for codes of ethics rather than constructing them on a positivistic functional framework. All of the major values associated with good media—truthfulness, freedom, objectivity, diversity, and contributing to social solidarity— are infused with a moral sense.

- It provides a succinct formula that shows how a given media activity can respond to the moral claims of all major actors while satisfying and enhancing the pragmatic and moral claims of the party in question. The formula thus harmonizes conflicting moral claims.

- It transforms media use into a form of public philosophy with transcendent values. Using the media is now considered essential for society's moral foundations. One of the reasons that a new paradigm brings consensus is that it links new technology and new roles with the ideals of democracy and with long-standing social values.

- It provides a set of ideals for individual media professionals and a basis for socializing media personnel into these values. Wuthnow shows how the summary language of Luther and Voltaire redefined, in one stroke, a wide range of social roles (1989, 14–15).

- It provides guidelines for media policy and media legislation. The work of politicians is transformed into serving society, not just gaining favors for one's party and constituency.

Each of these functions of normative paradigms can be illustrated by the "social responsibility–public service" model, which is now sufficiently a matter of history to confirm the validity of the argument. The moral formula of social responsibility theory is that the media are the foundations of both modern liberal democracy and the rights of citizens to information and communication services.

Linking the media to the normative in general and specifically to the public philosophy of citizens lends legitimacy to many media uses. The media pragmatically increase usage when it is perceived that one cannot be a good citizen without using them. As contexts for advertising, the media pass on their prestige to advertisers. That is, of course, a double-edged sword. As the media enter many areas of social life, such as advertising, the morality of this relationship comes into question, forcing the media to rethink their moral foundations.

The classical professions gained their prestige by proclaiming that their scientific expertise was dedicated to the good of society and the good of their clients. In the same way, the formula that links media to democracy—the economic progress of the nation and the dignity of the individual—now differentiates all of the major media roles: journalists, editors, proprietors, correspondents, film directors. It gives them a quasi-sacred meaning as artistic creators. These roles are no longer simply part of an economic enterprise, like semiskilled factory workers, but involve responding to one's independent artistic genius to create the "sacred community" of the nation. This enhances the moral significance of media work so that, ideally, all are satisfied. Newspaper proprietors and editors must now respect the independence of reporters as professionals, just as all medical doctors must respect other medical doctors.

The normative paradigm transforms the use of media as entertainment into a democratic duty for citizens. Being vigilant to make sure that the values of democracy are found in the local newspaper and becoming a critical media user are now one's sacred duties. The moral claims of politicians are satisfied because they become the formulators of policy to ensure that the media serve democracy. The moral claims of media scholars are satisfied because there is now moral purpose in evaluating the media's role in democracy.

Public Cultural Truth

One of the fundamental concerns of public communication is the truthfulness of what is presented in the public sphere. If the statements of individual actors are not true, then the outcome of public debate may be fundamentally vitiated. The debating community loses contact with the reality in which it lives. The problem lies in determining what is truth in public communication.

One set of criteria argues that objectivity, accuracy, and fairness to sources are the bases of truth. But these criteria, as important as they might be, do not guarantee the truthfulness of public discourse. Often, the news may be accurate and fair, but may not reflect society's real issues. In some societies slavery has been justified and explained as a reasonable way to treat certain groups of human beings. In those societies at least, slavery or apartheid has not been publicly questioned. The "truth" of their justifications for denying human dignity, freedom, and equality seemed to be taken for granted. The same might be said for many other exclusionary criteria used to treat categories of human existence as inferior in some way, such as gender, sexual orientation, and race. What may be said to be "true" at any given time may be an arbitrary cultural construction and an ideology, a systematic distortion of reality to protect the interests of the powerful.

A more adequate norm for the media's truthfulness is what may be called "public cultural truth." The criterion of truthfulness is not just correspondence to reality in an epistemological sense but also serves social justice. A fundamental criterion for morality is respect for human dignity and the dignity of all other forms of existence. Public communication is debate about the community's best decisions, and the best decisions are those based on justice and compassion for human suffering. The most important criterion of the truthfulness of some event is whether or not social justice is being respected. Movements that question the truthfulness of a statement arise out of the sense that one's human existence is being denied and destroyed in some way. Thus, public cultural truth is the systematic representation of the injustices and human suffering that the society must collectively acknowledge and resolve if that society is to exist as a cultural unity. Democratic public discourse can exist only if all citizens are free to speak out according to their consciences. Since the definition of what is a problem depends on particular cultural movements and the cultural values in play at a given moment, public cultural truth is a continually shifting construction of meaning.

Some might feel that the emphasis on cultural truth is too relativistic and does not give sufficient emphasis to transcendental truth. In this view the context for conceptions of transcendental truth is philosophy and theology. The issues of public discourse, however, are more properly in the cultural sciences. Thus, to speak of public cultural truth based on the criteria of human dignity and the dignity of all existence is an attempt to build a link with the premises of transcendental truth but still remain within the cultural sciences.

The media must assess their own capacity to question the current construction of public cultural truth in terms of justice and human dignity. One of the crucial tasks in the search for a more adequate normative paradigm at any given historical moment is to continually redirect the media toward this self-assessment. If the media consistently ignore major social injustices or simply take them for granted as intractable, there is something fundamentally wrong with the media system. There is a constant tendency for public communication to be absorbed into pragmatic, self-serving activities and to forget its moral purpose. The media are then held hostage by an ideology and are no longer capable of being truthful.

But what is truthful? What Clemencia Rodriguez says about contemporary citizens' media gets to the heart of the truthfulness of communication:

> Citizens' media, where symbolic production is constantly happening, can be thought of then, as important sites where symbolic resistance and contestation can potentially take place. That is, as people experiment with words, images, sounds, and special effects—as they delve into the universe of signs and codes—selecting, rejecting, reaccommodating, and reappropriating the symbolic in order

to create their own grid, they may be relabeling the world, reorganizing reality, and reconstituting a new order where preestablished social and cultural codifications of power cease to make sense. (2001, 151)

Rodriguez stresses that labeling makes sense, is "truthful," when it changes power relations so that a person who has never been a producer becomes one. In other words, the person's creativity, dignity, and worth should be allowed to come forth. Rodriguez questions whether citizens' media should succumb to the temptation to try reaching larger audiences and get so big that they routinize themselves into a set method. In her view, remaining local, everyday, and ephemeral enables citizens' media to be more authentic.

It may be that a particular paradigmatic tradition of communication is best expressed not as an essentialist definition but rather as a formula that allows ordinary people in everyday contexts to remove power restrictions and to create labels that express their creativity. The corporatist tradition may have been at its best when it encouraged endless Socratic sophistic debates about the meaning of everyday lives. The libertarian paradigmatic tradition was a useful formula to allow anyone to have a press and let the world know one's thoughts. The social responsibility, professional tradition allowed every journalist to make a personal contribution.

Conclusion

This chapter has sketched out an explanation of how normative theory develops and the role it plays in public discourse. In many ways, this is a general theory of communication ethics.

The prolific outpouring of books on the content and practice of communication ethics over the last twenty years has provided a rich source for building such a theory. Typically, these texts present an outline of the duties of journalists or other media professionals. But what is the basis for saying that journalists have a duty to carry out this or any other set of activities? What is the criterion for including some activities as duties rather than others? What is the relation of codes of ethics to the broader normative issues such as media policy, normative theory, and moral theory? This chapter has sketched a theoretical map to guide us toward the deeper foundational questions of communication ethics. This map provides a vision of a way forward for creating dialogue among the major actors in the area of public discourse and a more satisfactory normative theory for developing moral consensus.

A fundamental premise of this analysis of the characteristics and functions of normative theory is that it emerges in the context of democratic public discourse. The most basic characteristic of normative theory is that it attempts to provide a reasoned explanation of the relationship between the conception of democracy in a particular society and the concrete roles of actors in public discourse. The following chapter provides an open, flexible conception of the basic dimensions of democratic culture and politics. Subsequent chapters attempt to delineate the major roles of the media in relation to this conception of democracy.

PART TWO

Democracy

4

The Principles and Practice
of Democracy

Democracy means popular sovereignty. In whatever particular form
it might take, a democratic community represents the triumph of the rule of
the many over rule by the few. Unlike monarchies, where individuals or an
individual family rules, or oligarchies, where a small group of individuals rule,
democracies promise rule by the people.[1]

While different theories of democracy define popular sovereignty in different
ways, they almost always agree on its two basic constituents: equality and liberty.
Equality implies identical or substantively similar opportunities to participate
in the decision-making processes through which the people rule themselves—
everyone gets to vote, for example, and one vote is worth no more than another.
Liberty denotes the right of mutual influence—freedom of communication, for
example, affords everyone, speakers and listeners alike, the benefits of uncoerced
debate and discussion. Taken together, these basic ideals—popular control based
on a commitment to political equality and individual liberty—amount to what
Thomas Christiano terms a "minimal conception of democracy in modern societies" (1996, 4). They provide a foundation on which to build a more detailed
account of what democracy means.

Detailed accounts of democracy vary considerably, of course, particularly
with regard to, as David Held puts it, the "prerequisites of *successful* 'rule by
the people'" (2006, 2). For some, democracy succeeds only when citizens rule
themselves by participating directly in the community's day-to-day affairs. For
others, democracy works best when citizens defer to elected officials whose
experience and expertise qualify them to deal with the difficult and time-con-
suming demands of self-governance. But whatever the choice or compromise,
there exists today a more or less united commitment to the general idea of democracy. As Held reminds us, this stands in stark contrast to the vast expanse

of human history, roughly between the time of the city-states of ancient Athens in the fifth century BC and the eighteenth-century revolutions in France and the United States, when the "great majority of political thinkers" were "highly critical of the theory and practice of democracy" (1987, 1).

If hardly anyone today disputes democracy as a worthy goal, not everyone expects it to apply to their own decisions and activities. Newspaper editors, to take an example close to home, often champion democratic values on their editorial pages but seldom apply those values in their own newsrooms. And editors usually see no irony in the gap between what they preach and what they practice, because for them democracy denotes a form of government and not a set of requirements aimed at private persons and their private enterprises. Others, however, view democracy more expansively. They regard it as a social, organizational, and institutional ideal that extends far beyond the realm of government in precisely the way George Seldes had in mind more than sixty years ago when he argued that freedom of the press means "letting the editorial staff run the newspaper" (1938, 382).[2]

What democracy means, then, depends on answers to questions about its proper domain: Where and when do we expect to find democratic arrangements? And answers to questions about democracy's domain rest ultimately on responses to two larger and related inquires about the prospects for democracy. The first concerns the principles of democracy: What, precisely, are democratic ideals and the grounds for them? The second concerns the practice of democracy: How should these ideals apply?

There are, obviously, important differences between the abstract and philosophical inquiries into the principles of democracy and the applied and concrete inquiries into the practice of democracy. But there are important connections as well. Just as an articulation of the principles of democracy needs to anticipate the forms of practice it implies, a description of the practice of democracy needs to reference the principles that inform it. It makes little sense to put forth a set of ideals so lofty and so unrealistic that no form of practice could ever approximate it. Paolo Mancini calls this "exacerbated normativism" (1996), and it happens whenever ideals or norms—about democracy, the press, or any human endeavor—bear little or no relation to cultural, sociological, historical, and other basically empirical accounts of the conditions and circumstances of everyday life. Whatever the purity of the principles that guide it, no form of democracy, to misappropriate one of Bertrand Russell's choice phrases, "can escape from the dreary exile of the actual world" (quoted in Barber 1996, 349).

But it also makes little sense to posit a set of ideals so closely aligned with current arrangements that it does little more than describe them. It defeats the purpose of any normative theory when no meaningful distinction exists between "what is" and "what ought to be." Properly conceived, a normative theory of democracy, like a normative theory of the media, explains and inspires. It amounts to the kind of "embedded utopianism," as Held describes his brand of political theory, that includes an examination of "where we are" as well as an analysis of "what might be" (1995, 286). It takes the "actual world" into account, of course, but it also offers an assessment of what it would take to make that world a little better, a little less dreary.

Thus our approach to democracy straddles the line between normative and empirical questions. We offer an account of democracy that focuses on a handful of principles that at a certain level of abstraction highlight the distinctive charter of any democratic community, but an account that indicates how in practice the same principles can become the basis for distinguishing between one democratic community and another. We begin with a quick sketch of the two principal traditions in modern democratic thought, which in turn provides a general framework for reviewing four broadly distinguishable models or theories of democracy. We then look at a handful of topics that vivify the complexity of the relationship between media and democracy: (1) the balance between liberty and equality, (2) the connection between community and communication, and (3) the nature of public opinion and popular consent. We conclude with a discussion of where divergent principles of democracy have converged in recent years and what this convergence might mean for new forms of democratic practice and new opportunities for public communication.

Two Traditions of Modern Democratic Thought

Just as democracy enjoys many sources of inspiration, it manifests itself in a variety of ways, as Held (2006) illustrates with his several models of democracy. But today's variants, rooted in the political turmoil of the French and American revolutions, are best understood with reference to two broadly distinguishable traditions in modern democratic thought, what Habermas (1996b) describes as the "two received views of democratic politics": civic republicanism and procedural liberalism. Although both traditions deal comprehensively with basic questions of rights and liberties, popular consent, and political authority, they differ in their approach to these questions and in their final assessment of what rule by the people means. They differ, that is, not in identifying the fundamental requirements of self-governance but in their definitions of these requirements and in the priority they assign them.

Civic republicanism, a Continental brand of democracy rooted in the French Revolution and the works of Jean-Jacques Rousseau, James Harrington, and others, emphasizes the importance of common goals and shared values. It expects the state to play a key role in securing and sustaining what is shared and valued, namely, the "commonwealth." Procedural liberalism, of Anglo-American origins and indebted to the ideas of John Locke, Thomas Hobbes, and others, accentuates the interests of free and autonomous individuals. It looks to the state to protect the means, usually defined in marketplace terms, by which individuals can pursue their own ends. Liberalism offers a democracy of means, a deontological view of community that focuses on individual ends that are known prior to, and independent of, any associations between and among individuals. Republicanism presents a democracy of ends, a teleological view of community that regards a life in common as the best way to discover a good together that we could not know alone.

Republicanism and liberalism differ not simply with regard to the role of the state but more basically on the very nature of the political process. A republican conception of politics takes seriously each citizen's commitment to a *civic* culture that transcends individual preferences and private interests. Through what Habermas calls "civic self-determination," individuals become "politically autonomous authors of a community of free and equal persons" (1996b, 22). A liberal conception of politics, however, rests on an essentially procedural mechanism designed to facilitate the expression of individual preferences. Habermas describes the procedure that characterizes politics in the liberal tradition as a "market-structured network of interactions among private persons" (21). Political autonomy serves to separate citizens in order to protect "their opportunity to assert their private interests," which "are finally aggregated into a political will" (22).

Indeed, the importance of understanding the essence of democracy in the liberal tradition "as a process of aggregating the preferences of citizens in choosing public officials and policies" prompts Iris Young (2000, 19) to describe liberalism as the "aggregative model" of democracy, which she distinguishes from the "deliberative model" of democracy that characterizes politics and political participation in the republican tradition. The goal of "democratic decision making" in the aggregative model, Young explains, is "to decide what leaders, rules, and policies will best correspond to the most widely and strongly held preferences." Democracy amounts to a "competitive process" through which individuals, acting alone or in concert with others, build support for what they want. The deliberative model of democracy rests on an entirely different premise. Rather than assuming that "ends and values are subjective . . . and exogenous to the political process" (22), as Young describes the basic assumption of the aggregative model, the republican tradition treats ends and values as products of public discussions. The deliberative model thus posits a mechanism for identifying and achieving common goals and shared values, such that, to return to Habermas's (1996b) conception of civic republicanism, political participation "obeys not the structure of market processes but the obstinate structures of public communication oriented to mutual understanding" (23).

Because the aggregative and deliberative models of democracy embrace different forms of political participation, they rely on different conceptions of freedom. And these different conceptions of freedom, along with the correspondingly different demands they make on the state, underscore "contrasting images of the citizen," which Habermas summarizes this way:

> According to the liberal view, the citizen's status is determined primarily according to negative rights they have vis-a-vis the state and other citizens. As bearers of these rights they enjoy the protection of the government, as long as they pursue their private interests within the boundaries drawn by legal statutes—and this includes protection against government interventions. Political rights, such as voting rights and free speech, have not only the same structure but also a similar meaning as civil rights that provide a space within which legal subjects are released from external compulsion. . . .
>
> According to the republican view, the status of citizens is not determined by the model of negative liberties to which these citizens can lay claim as private persons. Rather, political rights—preeminently rights of political participation and communication—are positive liberties. They guarantee not freedom from external compulsion but the possibility of participation in a common praxis, through the exercise of which citizens can first make themselves into what they want to be—politically autonomous authors of a community of free and equal persons (1996b, 22).

No "actually existing" democracy, however, falls neatly within one tradition or the other. Democracies exist as an amalgamation of principles, a creative and even contradictory mix of ideas that defies the orthodoxies of any particular school of thought or body of literature. Even in societies with rich democratic traditions, the practice of democracy can vary considerably from one place to another, from one generation to the next. Crises of almost any kind, such as terrorism, war, popular unrest, corruption, financial instability, and natural disaster, can quickly alter the state's role and thereby redefine what it means to live in a democratic society. Liberalism and republicanism, therefore, represent "ideal types." They do not describe democracy as much as they provide an intellectual resource with which to examine and understand the logic and application of democratic principles. As counterpoised perspectives, understood normatively and not empirically, the ideals of liberalism and republicanism set forth a certain tension that might usefully inform the development of additional democratic models.

Four Models of Democracy

To expand and refine the aggregative and deliberative traditions of democracy, and to bring them closer to current arrangements in democratic societies, we revise and reconfigure them into four discrete models: pluralist democracy, administrative democracy, civic democracy, and direct democracy. Although these four models, outlined in figure 1 and summarized below, hardly exhaust the range of democratic societies in the modern world, they provide a broad and accessible framework for examining the relationship between media and democracy. Still, models have their limits. Democracy will always be more complex, and more fluid, than the models used to depict it. Here and elsewhere, models of democracy need to be understood as heuristic devices; they invite thinking about the relationship(s) between different aspects of democracy. The models we settle on work in much the same way as Young says hers do (though without the depth and detail Young provides): "Each picks out features of existing democratic practices and systematizes them into a general account of an ideal democratic process" (18).

THE PLURALIST MODEL OF DEMOCRACY

Pluralist democracy, sometimes called "liberal-pluralism" or "interest-group" democracy, derives its legitimacy from the proposition that individuals can most effectively assert their interests and preferences by coming together in the form of groups, small and large, that compete with other groups in an effort to find or forge mutually satisfying policies and programs. These private groups, protected by the state and at the same time insulated from its coercive powers, compete in the marketplace in the same way other private enterprises compete—they seek popular support for their interests and for the resources needed to promote and secure those interests. Without discounting the danger of factions and the divisiveness associated with them, pluralists believe that a dispersion of power of this kind represents the best and most appropriate response to the conflicts that inevitably surface in any but the most homogenous of societies.

Because power in the pluralist tradition is dispersed and thus decentralized, rule by the people takes the form of a system of checks and balances. In other words, although pluralism, like other forms of democracy, recognizes the legitimate sovereignty of the people, it logically insists on limits to that sovereignty. To be sure, limited or shared sovereignty stands out as the "fundamental axiom" of the pluralist perspective, what Robert Dahl (1967), one of pluralism's most prominent theoreticians, regards as the very check on power that protects minorities from majorities: "Instead of a single center of sovereign power there must be multiple centers of power, none of which is or can be wholly sovereign. Although the only legitimate sovereign is the people . . . even the people ought never to be an absolute sovereign" (24).

Understood as a process, pluralism celebrates the freedom of choice individuals enjoy as they decide how and when to come together to pursue their shared interests and goals. Just as the marketplace emphasizes open competi-

Table 1. Models of Democracy

	Liberalism		Republicanism	
	Pluralist	Administrative	Civic	Direct
Sovereignty	Shared among competing interest groups; "multiple centers of power, none of which is . . . wholly sovereign" (Dahl 1967, 24)	Limited to substituting one government for another; "government *for* the people" but not "*by* the people" (Schumpeter 1942, 412)	Exercised collectively through appeals to common interests; "free and public reasoning among equals" (Cohen 1997b, 256)	Requires unmediated participation in public affairs "all of the people govern . . . at least some of the time" (Barber 1984, xiv)
Civil Society	Privatized, entrepreneurial; modeled on the marketplace	Highly circumscribed; limited to electing, replacing, or removing officials	Open and robust; public debate on the overall aims of society	Invites direct involvement in government; modeled on the New England town meeting
Liberty	Defined negatively; ascribed rather than achieved	Defined negatively; ascribed rather than achieved	Defined positively; affirmed by the state through its policies	Defined positively; affirmed by the state through its policies
Equality	Of opportunity; basically a private matter	In voting, guaranteed by the state	Of conditions, a public question of resource distribution	Of conditions, a public question of resource distribution
Public Opinion	Aggregation of individual and group opinions; based on a composite of private interests	Aggregation of individual and group opinions; based on a composite of private interests	Of public deliberation; outcome based on appeals to common goals and shared interests	Of public deliberation; outcome based on appeals to common goals and shared interests
Community	Instrumental or sentimental	Instrumental or sentimental	Constitutive	Constitutive
Journalism	Is partisan and segmented; mobilizes members of groups, advocates their interests	Covers crises and campaigns; acts as a check on power by alerting citizens to problems	Facilitates deliberation; accommodates and amplifies debate and discussion	Promotes dialogue; serves as a forum for debate and discussion

tion, with the expectation that what is good will prevail "over a long period of time" (Nozick 1974, 332), pluralism emphasizes "constant negotiation," with the expectation that the "consent of all will be won in the long run" (Dahl 1967, 24). Through the coalitions they form and the compromises they reach, groups of any size should be able to participate meaningfully in the give-and-take of pluralist politics. However unappealing a particular outcome might be, all groups in a pluralist democracy "have extensive opportunities for presenting their case and for negotiations that may produce a more acceptable alternative" (23). Accordingly, the pattern of power that characterizes the pluralist tradition, Dahl explains, "makes for a politics that depends more upon bargaining than hierarchy; that resolves conflicts more by negotiation and compromise than by unilateral decision; that brings about reform more through mutual adjustment and gradual accumulation of incremental changes than through sweeping programs of comprehensive and coordinated reconstruction" (190).

The process of pluralism depends in part on a system of segmented media, such that each group and its interests has, as Baker describes the role of journalism in a pluralist democracy, "its own media for internal mobilization, external advocacy, and recruitment" (2002, 177). Pluralism neither requires nor precludes deliberation (Young 2000, 19). It instead depends on the media to sustain the "constructive conflict" that fuels the process of competition, which in turn provides citizens with the palette of choices they need for deciding how to best satisfy their needs and interests. This calls for a decidedly partisan press, a range of committed and even strident voices commensurate with the range of values and beliefs in the larger community. Particularly under conditions of "polarized pluralism," the term Hallin and Mancini (2004) use to characterize the "sharply polarized and conflictual politics" of Italy, Spain, Portugal, and Greece, media content tends to be more politically charged than dispassionate. Through their coverage of policies and politicians, issues and ideas, news media serve as "instruments of struggle" in the conflicts that animate pluralist politics. The "notion of a politically neutral journalism," Hallin and Mancini observe, "is less plausible where a wide range of competing world views contend" (2004, 61).

More focused on mobilization than information, journalism in a pluralist democracy promotes negotiation and facilitates the process of bargaining by amplifying agendas and by providing platforms for specialized analyses and commentaries (Hallin and Mancini 2004). Even when moderate forms of pluralism prevail, political communication resonates with interested insiders whose knowledge and political disposition qualify them for special attention—or devolves into content that treats politics as a conflict or game that may appeal to, but seldom mobilizes, most members of the community. Insofar as pluralism neither expects nor encourages widespread citizen participation, news media either tailor their news content to meet the needs of politically active readers, listeners, and viewers or they depoliticize the day's news in ways that make it appealing to a politically inactive but considerably larger audience.

While pluralists may or may not call on the state to formally support a particular plurality of media through subsidies or other forms of subvention, they invariably look to the state to safeguard the conditions for media competition. The pluralist tradition stands opposed to local, regional, and national media monopolies on the grounds that competing interests need competing media. It is less clear, however, what the pluralist position would be on the escalating concentration of media ownership. If media firms find it in their self-interest to provide a diversity of media properties, does it matter who owns any particular property? Is there any necessary relationship between plurality of ownership and plurality of content? Baker puts it succinctly when he acknowledges that a lack of media "segmentation and diversity ... could suppress constructive conflict and undermine pluralist politics" but wonders why "national or global ownership concentration fails to provide pluralistic diversity" (2002, 178). Given the logic of market economics, a "single conglomerate often supports separate media entities or titles espousing radically different views and serving different groups. This diversity expands the corporation's overall market coverage without forcing it to compete against itself" (177–78).

THE ADMINISTRATIVE MODEL OF DEMOCRACY

This model of democracy rests on the premise that ordinary citizens lack the interest and expertise to effectively govern themselves.[3] In any but perhaps the smallest of communities, democracy demands more knowledge than most citizens possess and more of a commitment to politics than most citizens find reasonable. What most democratic communities need, then, is an elite corps of popularly elected leaders whose dedication to public service ensures that matters of legislation and administration receive the serious and sustained attention they deserve.

Usually associated with the writings of Max Weber (1978) and Joseph Schumpeter (1942), the idea of an administrative democracy represents the triumph of leadership over citizenship. Held (2006) describes the circumscribed conception of citizenship and political participation that characterizes an administrative approach to democratic politics as a "highly restricted model of democracy" (159). In this model, citizens involve themselves in little more than the election and occasionally the ejection of political leaders. Popular sovereignty means, basically, "the ability of citizens to replace one government by another" (142). In an account of democracy that exhibits a "low estimation of the political and intellectual capacity of the average citizen" (Held 2006, 143), Schumpeter (1942, 256) calls for "government for the people" but decidedly not "government by the people." Democracy, he writes, "does not mean and cannot mean that the people actually rule in any obvious sense of the terms 'people' and 'rule.' Democracy means only that the people have the opportunity of accepting or refusing the men who are to rule them" (284–85).

Whereas politics in the pluralist tradition relies on competition among groups, politics in the administrative tradition relies on competition among elites. In both traditions, citizens play the role of the consumer whose choices amount to a form of political expression. But to a much greater extent than the pluralist model, the administrative model conceives "the behavior of politicians as analogous to the activities of entrepreneurs competing for customers" (Held 1995, 174). And, significantly, this competition for customers—this appeal to voters—typically occurs only on the occasion of formal elections, which means that citizens in an administrative democracy depend as much on the state as on the marketplace for opportunities to express themselves.

Given the administrative model's emphasis on the quality of elected officials, along with its assumptions about a more or less disengaged citizenry, expectations for the media's political role tend to focus on the coverage of crises and campaigns. Rather than trying to inform citizens about issues over which they have no direct and immediate control, journalism serves an administrative democracy by alerting the community to crises, especially ones involving corrupt or incompetent leaders. Journalists also provide detailed accounts of campaign promises and platforms, especially during the months preceding a contested election.

Coverage of crises and campaigns casts news media in the role of a "guardian of institutions," a phrase Walter Lippmann (1922) used long ago to capture the limited but important contribution journalism in the United States might make if Americans agreed to the "abandonment of the theory of the omni competent citizen" (229). Vincent Blasi makes much the same claim when he argues that journalism serves society not by keeping individuals informed but by keeping officials honest. This "checking value" of a free and unfettered press neither assumes nor requires a vision of democracy in which citizens participate in any regular way in the processes of self-government: "The checking value is premised upon a different vision—one in which the government is structured in such a way that built-in counterforces make it possible for citizens in most, but not all, periods to have the luxury to concern themselves almost exclusively with private pursuits" (1977, 561). But the most elaborate justification for a more modest role for news media in democratic politics comes in the form of John Zaller's "burglar alarm" standard for mainstream news, which, like the surveillance responsibility Blasi assigns to journalism, proposes that citizens "should be alerted to problems requiring attention and otherwise left to private concerns" (2003, 121).

Building on Michael Schudson's (1998) pessimistic but arguably realistic account of how citizenship works in practice, Zaller rejects what he calls the "full news" standard, the widely endorsed but presumably untenable view of journalism that holds "that the news should provide citizens with the basic information necessary to form and update opinions on all of the major issues of the day, including the performance of top officials" (2003, 110). In its place Zaller wants a standard of news quality that honors the interests and capacity for politics of what he and Schudson call the "monitorial citizen," the individual who wants to leave ample time for the joys of private life—"appreciating a sunset, humming a tune, or listening to the quiet breathing of a sleeping child" (Schudson 1998, 312)—but who nonetheless "scans the environment for events that require responses" (Zaller 2003, 118).

This standard, which Zaller believes "is not as far from current practice as from current ideals," calls on journalists to "rouse ordinary people to action" by providing "intensely focused, dramatic, and entertaining" coverage of important issues "at irregular intervals . . . and not too often" (2003, 122). A similar logic applies to coverage of elections and campaigns, which deserve media attention only under special circumstances. Zaller expects news media to "ignore races in which the opposition party mounts no serious challenge while paying close attention to those in which it does" (125). Although Zaller claims that the "needs of democracy are met by scrutinizing the records of those incumbents whose achievements are in doubt and reelecting the rest with minimal fuss" (124), it is unclear what role journalists should play when an incumbent's record warrants scrutiny but no challenger poses a serious threat to the incumbent's reelection.

THE CIVIC MODEL OF DEMOCRACY

This model of democracy stands in stark contrast to both the pluralist and administrative models, insofar as it rejects one of the core claims of the liberal-procedural tradition: that an aggregation of personal preferences constitutes a legitimate form of popular consent. Citizens convey consent in a civic democracy through a distinctively public judgment that may or may not coincide with the sum of the private choices individuals make in a pluralist or administrative democracy. Indeed, this public judgment, understood as both a process and an outcome, assumes "that citizens are prepared to be moved by reasons that may conflict with their antecedent preferences and interests" (Cohen 1997b, 413).

Joshua Cohen, one of the leading proponents of participatory forms of democracy, prefers to describe this public judgment as a form of "public reasoning." This term better captures the deliberative nature of a civic democracy than "public discussion," which too often encompasses the negotiating and bargaining that characterizes a pluralist democracy and even the act of voting that accounts for most of the citizen participation in an administrative democracy. Public reasoning, as Cohen defines it, denotes a political process through which citizens "defend and criticize institutions and programs in terms of considerations that others have reason to accept" and a democratic outcome with which citizens will "cooperate" and treat as "authoritative" (1997b, 413). Thus citizens in a civic democracy engage each other for the purpose of discovering or establishing genuinely common interests. They work together to identify "generalizable interests" and the "general will" these interests express, which transcends and supersedes the "will of all" as that might be known through a computation of "nongeneralizable interests." In different ways but for many of the same reasons, democracies in the liberal tradition discount what democracies in the republican tradition regard as a key presupposition about the nature of reason and rationality in democratic politics: that individuals "can know a good in common they cannot know alone" (Sandel 1982, 183).

A civic democracy, it follows, depends on a civic culture that honors the importance of a robust public life and cultivates the commitment to citizenship needed to sustain it. Even when, due to the problem of scale, citizens cannot involve themselves directly and formally in the affairs of the state, their political will and therefore their sovereignty rest on their ability to respond collectively, on the basis of "free public reasoning among equals" (Cohen 1997b, 412), to questions about the community's needs and interests. Whether this collective response comes in the form of a consensus or a compromise, a public judgment arrived at through deliberation distinguishes itself from the kind of judgment individuals make in a pluralist or administrative democracy. Even "the results of voting among those who are committed to finding reasons that are persuasive to all are likely to differ from the results of an aggregation that proceeds in the absence of this commitment" (Cohen 1997a, 75).

The public reasoning that characterizes a civic democracy places a particular burden on journalism, which plays a significant role in not only keeping citizens informed but in maintaining a certain quality of public discourse. Journalism in a civic democracy promotes political participation by creating and managing opportunities for public deliberation. It provides what Nancy Fraser usefully describes as "an institutional arena for discursive interaction" (1997, 451), which benefits not only the citizens who participate in it but also the uninvolved though attentive public whose participation in public affairs might amount to little more than an occasional vote. Whatever their level of involvement, citizens in a civic democracy expect news media to play some role in "making the community work"—a popular refrain of the "public journalism" movement in the United States.

A loosely organized but widely diffused response to the increasingly cynical tone of political journalism and the alienation and apathy associated with it, public journalism posits a set of deliberative ideals for the press. It calls on journalists to find better ways of engaging readers, listeners, and viewers as citizens with a stake in the issues of the day. Public journalism emphasizes substance over strategy, especially in coverage of political campaigns, and treats problems in a manner that highlights the prospects for their resolution. True to the republican commitment to participatory forms of democracy, public journalism understands the purpose of the press as promoting and indeed improving the quality of public life—and not merely reporting on and complaining about it (Glasser and Lee 2002, 204–5, 203).

Journalism exhibits its interest in promoting and improving the quality of public life by being "thoughtfully discursive, not merely informative," and "adequately inclusive and comprehensive" (Baker 2002, 148–49). But inclusion does not mean pandering to uninformed and uninterested individuals who remain by choice at the periphery of participatory democracies. It means instead accommodating different voices, different points of view, and even different forms of expression.[4] And comprehensiveness does not imply attention to administrative and legislative details, for which elected representatives, engaged in their own forms of public deliberation, assume responsibility. Neither does it impose on the press a more general responsibility to reconcile its coverage of the community with the inevitable fact that, as Christiano observes, "many individuals know a lot more than others about the kinds of policies that are in place and their effects as well as how these policies came about." The importance of specialized knowledge notwithstanding, what matters most in a civic democracy are the application of "basic moral insights" to questions concerning the future of the community—and discussion, analyses, and critiques of these insights. "Citizens must choose the overall aims of their society in order to exercise their rights of sovereignty and political equality," Christiano explains. "It is not essential for them to know how these aims are being carried out" (1996, 193).

THE DIRECT MODEL OF DEMOCRACY

This model takes self-government literally by accentuating unmediated involvement in public affairs. In the version developed by Benjamin Barber, a widely cited advocate of "strong" democracies and the "wide popular participation in politics" they imply, direct democracy envisions a politics of cooperation and concord. In such a politics, "human beings with variable but malleable natures and competing but overlapping interests can contrive to live together communally not only to their mutual advantage but also to the advantage of their mutuality" (Barber 1984, 8, 118). This model offers a revision of the civic model of democracy, moving the republican tradition away from representative forms of government and toward forms of democratic participation in which "all of the people govern themselves in at least some public matters at least some of the time" (xiv). While this model is often linked to ancient Greece and the city-states of Italy during the Renaissance, it is important to acknowledge the narrow and exclusive conceptions of citizenship that made it easier then to involve "everyone" in politics. Beyond that history, the direct model is even more meaningfully tied to the work of Rousseau and Marx. Most modern accounts of direct democracies, like Barber's, make it a point to navigate between "nostalgia for ancient, small scale republics" and the "monolithic collectivism that can turn large-scale direct democracy into plebiscitary tyranny" (25).

Direct democracies can be best explained with reference to what impedes their success: scale, inequality, and privatism (Barber 1984, 245). By rejecting any form of representation as a violation of popular sovereignty—as Rousseau famously warned, "The instant a people allows itself to be represented it loses its freedom"—direct democracies, particularly in societies with a large territory and a heterogeneous population, invariably face the challenge of overcoming physical and social distance. One prominent solution, usually attributed to Marx (e.g., Marx 1970), involves supplanting representation with delegation:

> The smallest communities would administer their own affairs, elect delegates to larger administrative units (districts, towns) and these would, in turn, elect candidates to still larger areas of administration (the national delegation). This arrangement is known as the pyramid structure of direct democracy: all delegates are revocable, bound by the instructions of their constituency and organized into a pyramid of directly elected committees. (Held 2006, 115)

Citizens retain their sovereignty in a system of revocable delegates—or in any form of direct democracy—only, however, when each individual enjoys a full and equal opportunity to influence others.

Unlike democracies in the liberal tradition, where equality refers to the absence of any role for the state in promoting or limiting the opportunities for political participation—opportunities that individuals create for themselves—direct democracies proscribe any accumulation or distribution of resources, public or private, that would have the effect of creating unequal opportunities for political participation. This very different conception of equality affirms a direct democracy's aversion to private centers of power and the unaccountable political influence they wield. If a direct democracy, as Barber contends, "neither requires nor corresponds specifically with particular economic systems" (1984, 252–53), it nonetheless "proclaims the priority of the political over the economic" (257). And this priority calls into question the familiar liberal claim, especially popular among pluralists, that "politics is an instrument of private economic purpose" (253).

The priority of the political over the economic also calls into question the viability of a privately controlled media. While private ownership in general might not be an issue in a direct democracy, private control runs counter to the demand for public accountability that direct democracies impose on any institution that plays a public role or claims a public purpose. In a direct democracy, freedom of the press exists to serve the interests of the community, not the interests of journalists and their managers. The community, rather than market forces or even the newsroom itself, needs to be the final arbiter of journalism's quality and value. Alexander Meiklejohn put it succinctly when he rejected the popular libertarian view of freedom of expression, which regards individual liberty as sacrosanct. He embraced instead a view of freedom of speech and freedom of the press that favors what the community needs to hear over what individuals want to say: "What is essential is not that everyone shall speak, but that everything worth saying shall be said" (1960, 19). In this decidedly illiberal view of freedom of expression, collective self-determination trumps individual self-expression (see Fiss 1996; Glasser and Gunther 2005), which is to say that freedom of speech matters more than the freedom of speakers.

Meiklejohn's conception of freedom of communication, built on the model of the New England town meeting, focuses on precisely what journalism in a direct democracy needs to facilitate: dialogue. Whereas dialogue implies deliberation, deliberation does not require dialogue;[5] and this becomes one important way of distinguishing civic from direct democracies. By virtue of its commitment to provide a forum for "everything worth saying," journalism in a direct democracy plays the role of parliamentarian. Not to be confused with a common carrier role for news media, in which journalists make few or no judgments about what they disseminate (journalism often plays the role of common carrier in its treatment of advertising), a parliamentarian role calls on the press to manage debate and discussion in a way that ensures that all issues receive a full and fair hearing.

If the conditions for dialogue and direct participation "are increasingly remote from the actual circumstances in which decisions have to be taken today," as Thompson claims (1995, 254), they nonetheless exist in any number of neighborhoods and small communities and in a wide variety of organizations and associations. Where and when a direct democracy remains a viable and desirable option, journalism promotes deliberation by providing a space for dialogue.

The Media and Democracy: Key Concepts

Among the many terms and concepts that have been used over the years to develop accounts of democracy and democratic practice, six stand out as particularly relevant to our interest in understanding media roles in democratic societies: liberty, equality, public opinion, popular consent, community, and communication. Rather than describing each separately, we pair them in a way that highlights some of the tensions and differences in democratic thought.

LIBERTY AND EQUALITY

All types of democracy embrace the principle of "equality of liberty," but in practice liberty and equality often denote very different, even competing, perspectives on power, participation, and responsibility. To be exact, liberty and equality, the cornerstones of any theory of democracy, intersect in ways that distinguish one type of democracy from another.

As a general proposition, democracy in the republican tradition assigns a priority to equality, while democracy in the liberal tradition assigns a priority to liberty. Although both traditions recognize the interdependence of liberty and equality, their difference in emphasis rests on very different assumptions about how democracy works and what democratic participation demands. Specifically, liberalism celebrates individuals as separate and sovereign; the liberty of individuals protects their sovereignty and thus ensures their freedom of choice. Republicanism, to the contrary, regards the community as sovereign; equality among individuals ensures their opportunity to participate in their common affairs. By prioritizing liberty, liberalism defines basic rights and freedoms in terms of individual autonomy. By prioritizing equality, republicanism views the same rights and freedoms as enabling the formation of a community that is responsive to the needs and interests of its members.

Isaiah Berlin, in his widely cited essay on "Two Concepts of Liberty," captures a key tension in the two democratic traditions when he examines the differences between "negative" and "positive" freedom (1969, 124–30). Understood negatively, liberty means freedom-from; viewed positively, it means freedom-to. The shift in prepositions points to not only different conceptions of liberty but differences in the conditions liberty requires. Liberals understand liberty as requiring only the absence of certain conditions, typically the absence of coercion and other sources of external constraints on conduct. Republicans begin with this conception of liberty but add to it the requirement of empowerment, a requirement Hannah Arendt (1963) explains with reference to the distinction between being liberated and being free. Being liberated, according to Arendt, means being liberated from something, whereas being free implies the capacity to do other things. Although, schematically, the proposition "We are free from X to do Y" expresses the logic of positive freedom, Y in the republican tradition needs to be understood broadly and politically as the opportunity to participate in the life we live with others (MacCallum 1967, 314). This amounts to an important addendum to liberalism's emphasis on individual liberty, insofar as it moves freedom beyond merely permitting individuals to pursue their private ends and toward empowering individuals to achieve in common what they might not be able to achieve alone. For Arendt, then, freedom is not a means to individual ends but an end itself, a shared and common good, the "actual content" of which "is participation in public affairs, or admission to the public realm" (Arendt 1963, 25).

The private freedom liberalism promotes—private in the sense of being personal and idiosyncratic—celebrates the importance of freedom of choice, a type of freedom that may or may not require the assent of others. When freedom of choice involves embracing certain beliefs or expressing certain opinions, no one else is implicated. But when freedom involves the freedom to select one product over another, or one political issue rather than another, it assumes the availability of options provided by others. In either case, equality enters the equation only insofar as the state distances itself from any particular choice or set of choices and thus treats individuals equally with regard for their preferences. Even when the state intervenes for purposes of creating or improving the conditions for more or better choices, it cannot favor any particular outcome.

The public freedom that republicans embrace—public in the sense of being shared and common—accentuates the importance of self-discovery through processes of public deliberation. It implies, as Christiano puts it, "a substantive commitment to promoting the common good" (1996, 29). By defining democratic participation as an essential feature of self-government, republicans presuppose an equal opportunity for individuals to engage each other in debate and discussion. The state creates and sustains equality as a way of conferring legitimacy on the outcome of democratic participation. This is what Christiano calls an "equality in resources" (in contradistinction to the "equality in well-being" that liberalism prefers). Equality, it follows, is a principle the state affirms with its policies, rather than an ideal it supports through its inaction.

With liberty as the bedrock value, democracies in the liberal tradition—for example, the pluralist and administrative models of democracy—seek to protect individuals in their "natural state," which, following the "respectable tradition of Locke," is all that individuals need to "order their actions and dispose of their possessions and persons as they think fit" (Nozick 1974, 9, 10, quoting Locke). Liberty means the absence of interference, especially interference from an overbearing state. Accordingly, Robert Nozick rails against the "illegitimate power of the state to enrich some persons at the expense of others" (272); his language illustrates the liberal—and especially the libertarian—aversion to any redistribution of resources and other measures aimed at securing opportunities for presumably disadvantaged individuals. Equality exists only as a commitment to fair play. The state—what Nozick would prefer to see as a minimal state with little more than "night watchman" responsibilities—honors individual initiative by limiting its role to the enforcement of agreements: "contracts, prohibitions on aggression, on theft, and so on" (272). Any grander conception of equality, any larger role for the state, would impose on individuals the state's preferences, which would, in turn, limit individual liberty and restrict freedom of choice.

With equality as the bedrock value, democracies in the republican tradition— for example, the civic and direct models of democracy—seek to achieve political parity among individuals as a precondition for individual liberty. Republicans take seriously the "effects of economics and social inequalities on political equality" (Christiano 1996, 142); hence the republican emphasis on the redistribution of resources and other measures aimed at creating and sustaining the conditions for inclusive political communication. An "egalitarian approach to democracy," Christiano writes, "requires that each person's *interests* ought to be given equal consideration in choosing the laws and policies of society" (53).

COMMUNITY AND COMMUNICATION

The liberal community works as a voluntary association that furthers its members' aims and interests. It can be strictly instrumental, in the sense that its members agree to associate because an association will advance each member's interests, or it can be sentimental, insofar as individuals with similar sentiments find some advantage in their collective pursuit of common ends. In either form, community in the liberal tradition exists for individuals and is not in any fundamental way definitive of them.

One important characteristic of the liberal community, then, is an unqualified faith in the individual to understand the world and to decide how best to live within it. Communities and other forms of voluntary associations might at times aid individuals in their understanding of the world, but such associations can never be a condition for that understanding: "society is to be understood by the individual mind, not by the tradition of community" (Waldron 1987, 135). The liberal community does not present itself as a good worthy of achievement but rather as a means to ends already known.

Just as individuals in the liberal tradition can prosper without the benefit of community, meaning in the liberal tradition can exist without the benefit of communication. Meaning, like opinions, is the property of the individual mind; it is something individuals have. From Locke and the Enlightenment we inherit what Carey (1975) appropriately describes as a "transmission" or "transportation" model of communication, where meaning is to communication what freight is to a train: one simply transports the other. In a liberal community, individuals are entitled to understand the world in their own ways and to express those understandings. But there is no corollary right to communicate what is publicly expressed if by communication we mean transmission or transportation.

Communication as transportation is, logically, an aspect of commerce, which is privileged in the same way—or for basically the same reasons—as any private transaction. Unlike "free" expression, which can flourish in the absence of suppression by the state, communication can flourish only as it succeeds in the marketplace. Accordingly, individuals in a liberal society only have the right to speak *in* public; to speak *to* the public requires communication, and communication is not a public right but a private privilege.

Community in the republican tradition can be fairly termed "constitutive," in the sense that it represents an opportunity for individuals to know themselves through their association with others. It is constitutive insofar as it views individuals "as constituted by and at the same time constitutive of a process of intersubjective interactions" (Cornell 1985, 297). The community and the individuals who comprise it are in reciprocal relation to one another, a process that requires the community to be substantively democratic. Community life is not, then, what democracy brings about but what democracy is.

Communication in this tradition falls within the domain of culture, not commerce. Individuals turn to communication not only for purposes of exchanging ideas, goods, and services but to discover common goals and shared interests. Identity and political purpose are the consequence of communication. Communication thus needs protection not as a means to unknown ends but as an end in itself. The freedom to communicate is therefore best understood positively as the freedom to engage others, an individual liberty defined and defended with reference to the power of community to transform individual self-interest into a form of collective self-interest. Freedom of communication is not, it follows, simply or narrowly an individual right but more broadly a public commitment intended to cultivate, as Michael Sandel puts it, "the shared self-understanding necessary to community in the formative, constitutive sense" (1984, 93).

PUBLIC OPINION AND POPULAR CONSENT

Liberals view opinions as personal property; opinions belong to individuals. These essentially private preferences become public only through some form of *publicity,* the noun we use to denote the process through which the private becomes public. Public opinion, therefore, represents a full account, a broad summary, or at least a well-constructed composite of individual opinions. In modern times, it usually means the publication of the results of public opinion polls.

Polls illustrate, literally and figuratively, the logic of public opinion in the liberal tradition. Public opinion polls legitimize a view of democracy that celebrates the importance of self-determination, self-expression, and self-interest. They vivify the political authority of the citizenry by affirming the viability of each individual, separate and sovereign, as the locus of democratic power. To be sure, the use of polls as a measure of public opinion began, at least with the pioneering work of George Gallup, as an effort to combat the disproportionate and arguably undemocratic influence of special interest groups. Gallup applied to public opinion the techniques of consumer preference research, which he developed in his master's thesis (1925) and then refined in his doctoral dissertation (1928), as an act of social reform. He wanted to bring about a "truer democracy" by going directly to the "voice of the people." By recognizing the value of individual opinion and by granting everyone, at least statistically, an equal opportunity to be heard, polls foster an entirely open and egalitarian form of democracy (Salmon and Glasser, 1995).

In their recent defense of the use of surveys of large samples of citizens as a reasonable measure of collective public opinion, Benjamin Page and Robert Shapiro make the point that the opinions of individuals add up to public opinion in ways that transform instances of individual ignorance into a kind of collective wisdom. While acknowledging that any individual's opinion on a given topic at a given point in time might lack the rationality that Page and Shapiro believe characterizes public opinion, they argue that an individual's policy preferences over time exhibit a central tendency; and this central tendency shows that a stable, reasonable, coherent, and ascertainable opinion can be added to other stable, reasonable, coherent and ascertainable opinions in ways that yield "rational public opinion." Despite "the evidence that most individual Americans have only a limited knowledge of politics . . . and that individuals' expressions of policy preferences vary markedly and somewhat randomly from one survey to the next, collective policy preferences have very different properties" (1992, 384).[6]

Because public opinion, as Page and Shapiro understand it, can be known only through "the statistical aggregation process, in which the expressed opinions of many individuals are summed or combined into a collective whole" (1992, 15), popular consent can be known only as a measure of allegiance to one or more of the policy choices that pollsters present to their sample of citizens. In other words, if public opinion exists mainly through the polls that measure it and give it its public appearance, then consent, too, becomes an artifact of statistics. It becomes, specifically, a claim about the quantity or weight of public opinion, a claim about whether the amount of public opinion, in one direction or another, is adequate to infer consent of the governed.

Public opinion in the republican tradition requires what in the liberal tradition it might only benefit from: public deliberation. Although Page and Shapiro acknowledge that public debate often refines and enlarges public opinion, the absence of debate in no way precludes the formation of the individual opinions that, when added up, become public opinion. The principal difference between individual opinion and public opinion is measurement error. Republicans, however, view the difference in more fundamental ways; they regard public opinion as a consequence of, and thus not incidental to, public debate.

Public opinion from a republican perspective stands in contrast to the liberal presupposition, as Page and Shapiro develop it, that equates individual opinion, when properly measured and aggregated, with public opinion. Republicans do not assume, as Nancy Fraser puts it, that the public's preferences and interests "are given exogenously in advance of public discourse." Rather, republicans contend that public preferences and interests "are as much outcomes as antecedents of public deliberation" (1992, 130). Thus the republican framework for understanding public opinion rests on a conception of *public* that, first, designates the place where individuals engage each other; and, second, refers to interests that emerge from this engagement as common or shared.

By operationally defining public opinion as a compilation of individual opinions, polls defy the very publicness of public opinion that republicans want to honor. Polls accentuate the privateness of opinions by not requiring individuals to speak in public about what they want and why they want it. Individuals express themselves anonymously and without any responsibility for explaining and defending their preferences and the grounds for them. More than that, polls can frustrate and even alienate the public, as Susan Herbst (1993) found in her study of a politically diverse group of Chicago area residents, by dictating the issues that can be "discussed" and by limiting the "discussion" to responses chosen and fashioned by a pollster. If indeed the substance of political life is public discussion, as countless republicans have argued over the years, then polls not only fail to capture it but might at times inhibit it.

This connection between public discussion and public opinion underscores the role individuals play in the construction of opinions that transcend personal and private interests. The opinions of publics, in contradistinction to the opinions of individuals, focus on general or common interests. The opinions of publics represent a collective wisdom that benefits from an open and accessible discussion focused on issues of common concern, a discussion dedicated to the possibility of reaching a resolution of issues that meets with the approval of everyone engaged in the discussion. Ideally, then, public opinion reflects what Habermas calls a rational consensus, a full and uncoerced agreement on what needs to be done. In practice, of course, public opinion often signals a compromise, an agreement that fails to identify truly general interests and instead strikes a balance between competing personal interests.

Understood as a byproduct of acts of public deliberation, public opinion confers consent with the critical authority of a distinctively public point of view arrived at through an open and unfettered debate. This consent through argumentation, unlike the consent by acclamation proffered by polls, requires either a consensus or a compromise on the issues of the day. Without one or the other, no matter how abundant festering individual opinions might be, what prevails is not, properly speaking, public opinion but what Habermas calls "nonpublic opinion."

The Future of Democracy

Since the mid- to late 1980s, considerable work has been done to develop a model of "deliberative democracy," a phrase coined by Joseph Bessette in a 1980 essay on republican forms of government. Most of the work in this area focuses on methods to bring the liberal and republican traditions together in ways that will make democracy more responsive to, and more viable in, a world where global trade and communication have fundamentally altered the demands of democratic practice. Political participation now extends beyond traditional nation-states and requires forms of democracy that are sensitive to centers of power unbound by geography. Held thus calls for the implementation of a model of cosmopolitan democracy, one that extends and deepens the "mechanisms of democratic accountability across major regions and international structures [and] would help to regulate the forces which are already beyond the reach of national democratic mechanisms and movements" (1995, 283).

Held, among others, focuses on what he understands to be a new and pressing need for a global democratic order, an international arrangement aimed at sustaining "diverse and distinct domains of authority, linked both vertically and horizontally" (1995, xii). Without discounting the importance of local, national, and regional democratic orders, Held's "cosmopolitan model of democracy" envisions a framework for a "transnational structure of democratic action" (235). Cosmopolitan democracy recognizes local, national, and regional authority but also coordinates and integrates this authority in ways that build an even larger democratic community: "an international community of democratic states and societies committed to upholding democratic public law both within and across their own boundaries" (229).

More abstractly, Held's model of democracy embraces a type of democratic community built on Kant's principle of "universal hospitality," which Held develops into an argument about the importance of transcending "the particular claims of nations and states" and focusing instead on "mutual acknowledgment of, and respect for, the equal rights of others to pursue their own projects and ends." Universal hospitality, Held explains, thus entails "both the enjoyment of autonomy and the respect for the necessary constraints on autonomy"; it requires the "mutual acknowledgment" of the "equal and legitimate rights of others to pursue their own projects and life-plans," which at a minimum means not shaping or determining the "quality of life of others . . . without their participation, agreement or consent" (1995, 228).

Through the creation of a global parliament—an assembly of *democratic* states rather than the more inclusive interstate organization the United Nations functions as—Held's plan for a global democratic order begins with a legislative commitment to deal with the very conditions that threaten any effort to internationalize democracy: "health and disease, food supply and distribution, the debt burden of the 'Third World,' the instability of the hundreds of billions of dollars that circulate the globe daily, global warming, and the reduction of the risks of nuclear and chemical warfare" (Held 1995, 274). Held also anticipates "general referenda cutting across nations and nation-states in the case of contested priorities concerning the implementation of democratic law and the balance of public expenditure, with constituencies defined according to the nature and scope of disputed problems" (273). Beyond a legal infrastructure that binds together the democracies of the world, Held recognizes the need for "non-state, non-market solutions in the organization of civil society," including the creation of a "diversity of self-regulating associations and groups."

Notes

1. Indeed, *democracy* means rule by the people or popular power. But its combining two Greek words already suggests a conceptual complex rather than clear meaning. *Demos* refers to a citizen body living in a polis, but it also refers to the lower classes, "the mob." *Kratos* for its part could mean either power or rule. Regardless of the fact that the majority of Greeks were women and slaves who were not considered to be free citizens, the idea of democracy introduced the problem of wealth, as highlighted by Aristotle: "Whenever men rule by virtue of their wealth, be they few or many, there you have oligarchy; and where the poor people rule, there you have democracy" (in Arblaster 1994, 13–14). No wonder, then, that democracy has always been a controversial concept. On the other hand, it has inspired much analytical reflection, from the Greek classics until now.

2. See Cohen and Rogers (1983) for an argument in favor of a more expansive view of democracy, one that extends democratic ideals beyond the "formal arena of politics" (150) and specifically rejects as undemocratic the "subordination of the interest of workers to the interests of capitalists" (146). See Hardt (1995) for a discussion of the neglect of workers in most accounts of American journalism, including a lack of a sustained and programmatic critique of a "media environment that is determined more by commercial interests than by the professional judgments of newsworkers" (24).

3. See, for example, Baker's (2002) conception of "elitist democracy" (129–34) and Held's (2006) model of "competitive elitism" (125–57).

4. See Young (2000) for a thoughtful discussion of the criteria for "inclusive political communication" (52–80).

5. As Thompson (1995) points out, "[t]here are no good grounds for assuming that the process of reading a book or watching a television programme is, by itself, less conducive to deliberation than engaging in face-to-face conversation with others. On the contrary, by providing individuals with forms of knowledge and information to which they would not otherwise have access, mediated quasi-interaction can stimulate deliberation just as much, if not more than, face-to-face interaction in a shared locale" (265).

6. "While we grant the rational ignorance of most individuals, and the possibility that their policy preferences are shallow and unstable, we maintain that public opinion as a collective phenomenon is nonetheless stable" (Page and Shapiro 1992, 14).

5

Roles of News Media in Democracy

The first news media were newspapers, that is, regularly appearing written accounts of current events, mainly of a political, diplomatic, military, or commercial character. They claimed to offer reliable information, or at least to be an authoritative, official source of information. They primarily served the needs of a mercantile class in growing urban centers of trade and administration. While early European newspapers had only limited freedom in practice and were sometimes organs of authority, the press institution could not have developed without making some claim both to freedom of publication and to economic freedom. The newspaper press grew slowly, its fortunes bound up with economic development and the reigning degree of political freedom. It was more vigorous in northern Europe and in North America than elsewhere.

Gradually, new forms of print media emerged alongside the original models of mercantile newsletter and official gazette. Partisan presses of various types came to serve the interests of factions struggling for power or movements for political and social reform. In the latter half of the nineteenth century, the mass newspaper formed a new bridge between the established quality press and the true mass media, yet to emerge. The commercial newspaper aimed to be truly popular and universal. Its owners' primary goal was to make money; but there was often a secondary goal of exerting political influence. These developments, briefly summarized, have made it difficult to combine the various print news media under a clear concept of the newspaper press, so diverse are the forms and goals of publication. The popular press of the twentieth century claimed the rights and respect due to the earlier newspaper—but did not offer to carry out the same roles, fulfill the same social responsibilities, or observe the same norms of conduct. This tension, which in part reflects a disjunction between economic and political goals, remains at the heart of normative debate over the role of journalism in society.

There have been continuous changes in the newspaper press, with ever newer journalistic forms. The emergence of broadcast news, first by radio and then by television, has made it even more difficult to treat the news media as a single institution. In these newer media, the provision of news often takes second place to other communication tasks, especially advertising and entertainment. And journalists face entirely new pressures of space, time, and format. The more international character of television news has added to the complexity, since televised news is much more likely to circulate beyond its original context and to convey its meaning more directly than written accounts alone. Print news is largely confined to a national arena and is designed to meet local expectations. Competition between news media has intensified, often leading to a loss of product diversity and new dilemmas of editorial decision making. On the one hand, there is an increased impetus toward objectivity and neutrality, and also toward specialist news in an increasingly secular and information-hungry age. On the other hand, competition generates pressures to make news and information more homogeneous, as well as more digestible and entertaining for a wide audience. The consequences are very mixed, with competing goals and unclear prescriptions for quality and professionalism.

While circumstances vary a good deal from one country to another, the many variants that have emerged can be represented approximately by Schudson's three models of journalism: "advocacy," "market," and "trustee" (1999, 118–21). The first describes an essentially partisan press, and the second the commercially driven journalism of popular press and broadcasting. The third refers to professional journalism that aims to look after the varied informational interests of the public in an independent way. In the United States, these three models appeared more or less in sequence, with the first one largely disappearing and the second two now competing for dominance. In Europe the advocacy model, although in decline, has survived longer and with more general acceptance as one model of professional journalism. In Europe, too, the trustee model appeared in an additional guise: that of publicly regulated broadcasting, editorially independent of the state and other interests but charged with broad informational and educational tasks on society's behalf. These models may have arrived in sequence, but they can and do coexist and compete with each other for predominance.

These brief historical notes are relevant for understanding the press's position in any contemporary society that subscribes to the democratic principles of freedom and self-government. The internal contradictions, as well as divergent purposes and practices, affecting the media make it impossible to be definitive about the central characteristics of journalistic activity or the norms that should apply. Despite this uncertainty, it can be argued that the trends described, coupled with globalization of the media, have converged on a dominant type of journalism in which several loosely related features coexist. This model applies to most mainstream news media, whether in the commercial or public service systems. The main features of this type are pluralism of news and opinion; neutrality and objectivity in reporting; market orientation; and professionalization according to shared norms of practice. We might add "media sectorial identity" as a characteristic, given the large and persistent differences between news and information in newspapers, television, radio, and—increasingly— the Internet. This dominant model was favored in Western eyes to replace the extinguished communist variants of the press in central and Eastern Europe, and was exported to developing countries as well. It is typically supportive of established forms of democracy and respectful of legitimate authority whether judicial or governmental. However, in choosing a neutral or middle position, it is not very accessible to radical voices and avoids partisan attachments. In the same sense, this version of professionalism is not very open to direct social and political participation and is wary about new movements and ideas until they have clear popular support. As many critics have observed, this is a formula for caution and conservatism that limits the social purposes of journalism.

News Media Tasks and Types

Against this background, we provide an initial framework within which to locate the basic tasks of the news media, which have origins internal to the media (professional, commercial, and idealistic) and also external (in the form of various pressures and claims). Journalism has been guided by the enterprise, vision, and purpose of many individual editors, publishers, and journalists who have sought to record or influence the course of history with diverse motives. The press has also been a channel of communication for political and social activists. In addition, the press tries to meet the economic and cultural demands of owners and many different clients, including publicists and prospective audiences. This is true irrespective of the relative predominance of material or idealistic goals. From this perspective, the basic tasks of journalism in a democracy can be classified under three main headings:

1. The task of *observing and informing,* primarily as a service to the public
2. The task of *participating* in public life as an independent actor by way of critical comment, advice, advocacy and expression of opinion
3. The task of *providing* a channel, forum, or platform for extramedia voices or sources to reach a self-chosen public

For these tasks to be carried out, different requirements must be met. The first relies on the public's trust, which in turn depends on the public's perceiving the media as both independent and competent. The second relies primarily on the existence of an efficient and extensive information collection and distribution system, plus an editorial intention to give access to a wide range of sources and views. The third task arises from journalism's involvement in democratic action and debate, and depends on an active use of press freedom in the context of a healthy public sphere.

This differentiation of news media tasks can also be understood in terms of the intersection of two dimensions, as shown in figure 3. The vertical dimension contrasts the observer/informant task with that of active involvement in political and social life. At one end, the media operate as a passive but reliable mirror; at the other end, they are seen as a weapon in activists' hands. The horizontal dimension records varying degrees of neutrality or intervention in the channeling task, affecting gatekeeping, access, and processing of whatever is carried in the channels. Access can vary on a range between fully open and closed. Openness requires that no limiting criteria are applied to selection for transmission or amplification. The reverse is a situation of limited access, but usually according to restrictive criteria that are transparent. Media systems (as well as individual media) are also diverse in the way their component media perform in these respects. Figure 3 identifies four main types of news media according to the two dimensions discussed. These types can be described as follows:

1. The internally pluralist and secular media that seek to maximize circulation or audience in their chosen market (not necessarily a mass market), partly by appealing to a wide range of political and social groups
2. The externally pluralist commercial media that also seek a high circulation but also adopt a particular ideological or political line to appeal to a like-minded audience
3. The partisan media, usually noncommercial and small in scale (local or national) and dedicated to the interests and ideas of a particular (political) group
4. The minority media of opinion and debate, dedicated to the expression and exchange of new and diverse facts and opinions

We are reminded of the varied and complex character of the operating context in which media roles are performed. This typology (figure 3) is derived primarily from examples taken from such print media as newspapers and periodicals. Broadcast news media, especially television, have not shown the same range of differences. Most television news systems, whether commercial or public, still tend to have a location in the upper left area of the quadrant. They seek undifferentiated large audiences for content that is informative according to the dominant concept of news objectivity outlined above. At the same time, as a result of regulation, unwritten convention, or commercial pressure, they typically are less fully open and less editorially independent than the print media. This at least was the later twentieth-century model of broadcast journalism,

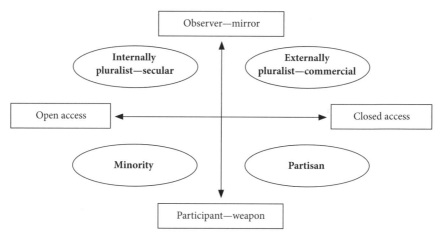

Figure 3. Typology of News Media

even if it is breaking down under the impact of channel multiplication, and the escape from regulation and format diversification offered by the Internet.

The Concept of Journalistic Role

In choosing to retain the concept of a *role,* embedded as it is in a particular history of journalism in certain Western liberal-democratic societies, we run the risk of continuing to carry much of the baggage that has accumulated over the last fifty years of research and theorizing about the media. Unfortunately we have no other term that would allow us to avoid this history, and some other terms are even more limiting, such as the words "duty," "responsibility," "task," "goal," or "function."

The term *function,* derived from sociology, is often loosely used to describe various practices, services, or objectives or the satisfaction of certain needs. However, it has little precise meaning unless embedded in some system with operating needs that are met by specialist components and elements. Thus a democratic political system can be sketched as having informational needs or requirements that are satisfied by the activities of the media. But we have no such model of a political subsystem that would be any more than a description of a complex of interrelated flows of information.

The word *task* is too narrow on its own for our purpose, but it can be incorporated in our concept of role as explained below. Ideas of duty and responsibility are also involved and can be applied readily to the news media. However, in isolation they are not very useful, since they draw on a diversity of value systems and perspectives that may not be relevant or appropriate for assessing the work of journalism in a particular case. External judgments of performance or the attribution of purpose to news media are often made on the basis of ethical, political, or cultural criteria that do not take adequate account of the constraints placed on the journalist. Such judgments and attributions are not invalid for that reason, but they do not help to construct a normative theory that is helpful for journalism itself.

The term *role* refers here to a composite of occupational tasks and purposes that is widely recognizable and has a stable and enduring form. Roles are normally located within an institutional framework, and they are regulated according to the main activities, needs, and values of the institution, in this case the mass media. A role has a dual aspect, consisting of empirical elements and evaluative dimensions. The first comprises the tasks that media journalists actually carry out. The second is understood in terms of the purposes or ends to be served and the relative value or importance attached to them. Purposes are not always declared or obvious and may be interpreted or identified in different ways. The primary source of purpose for most professional journalists is provided by their own particular location within the media system, since that is where journalists are trained, socialized, and directed.

The specific occupational tasks of news journalists are too many to enumerate, but they usually involve four basic activities: discovery, collection, and selection of information; processing into news accounts; providing background and commentary; and publication. These basic activities are translatable into more generalized role descriptions that acquire in the process a larger purpose and thus evaluative loading. This translation produces another set of terms that seem to explain what journalism is for in the wider scheme of things. There are alternative versions of these role descriptions, but the most typical list includes the following:

- Providing surveillance of the social environment
- Forming opinion
- Setting the agenda of public discussion
- Acting as a "watchdog" in respect to political or economic power
- Acting as messenger and public informant
- Playing an active participant part in social life

Although we can separate out the empirical from the normative components of the journalists' role in relation to society, there is an underlying problem in reconciling the two aspects, since the modal type of "objective" journalism described above represents the role as more or less value free. Professional journalism should not be biased toward any point of view or interest group and should aim to represent the social world, as far as possible, as it is. This is itself a normative judgment, but relates to something that is generally considered essential and thus above debate. In any case, it can be argued that objectivity is more an issue of good practice than an abstract ideal. From this perspective, it does not matter that perfect objectivity is not attainable.

As noted, media institutions are not the only source of normative purpose or of evaluation. Other sources include the authoritative views of respected figures in the wider society, sometimes expressed by way of commissions and inquiries; pressure groups on behalf of various causes and beliefs; appeals to patriotism and public necessity; and personal moral principles and conscience. Internal personal loyalties and attractions can also have a normative impact.

These observations take us to the wider question of media accountability that we discuss later in this chapter. The media are linked to the surrounding society by various ties of attachment, obligation, and even subordination that affect how purposes are determined. These influences work by way of internal lines of control and also by way of interaction with external agents. The latter include: the intended audience most of all and the wider public; owners, clients, and sponsors; other social institutions, groups, and organizations that depend on the media; and ultimately government and the state. Although the media control their own activities in detail, they are constrained and directed at many points by more remote, sometimes powerful forces.

In these circumstances, it is not surprising that research into the role conceptions journalists hold has uncovered a number of basic tensions, oppositions, and choices that confront media institutions and journalists personally, despite the protection given by the consensual or dominant version of the journalistic task, as outlined above. The main oppositions that have emerged are the following:

- Adopting a neutral versus a participant role vis-a-vis the surrounding society
- Concentrating on facts versus setting out to interpret and provide commentary
- Acting as a gatekeeper for all voices in society versus being an advocate for a chosen cause or interest
- Serving the media organization versus trying to follow an idealistic conception of the journalistic task
- Choosing between social and nonprofit purposes and the criteria of the marketplace

These dilemmas are distinct and to some extent independent of each other, but there is an underlying theme, and they also reflect the pull of divergent normative poles. They reflect the diversity of what we call journalism and the variety of forms the news media can take, each with its own purpose, self-selected public, and market niche. The arrival of new media forms, especially those based on the Internet, have added to the variety and clouded the issue of what journalism is.

News Media Roles as Normative

It is clear from this discussion that it is impossible to make any definitive statement concerning what *should* be the main tasks of the media institutions and the norms appropriate for carrying them out. There are two fundamental problems. First, there are varying, even opposed interests and expectations on the part of those inside and outside the press. Second, no formal claim can legitimately be made on a free press to carry out any particular task. Freedom of the press is a much wider concept than the freedom of the news media to act. It includes both the freedom not to publish and also the right to refuse or evade any externally imposed communication obligations. The first critiques of the early twentieth-century mass press drew on then-current ideas of appropriate standards for publication and the conduct of public life, as well as on notions of fairness and the rights of minorities and opposition groups to be heard. Principles of democracy were a basis for claims against a venal and capitalist press and also a source of norms for good practice. Critics and claimants attributed obligations to the press in the absence of any formal basis or means of enforcement.

The privately funded U.S. Commission on Freedom of the Press (1947) made the first significant move in modern times toward attributing specific social responsibilities to the press, from an established and consensual rather than a radical position (Blanchard 1977; Commission 1947; Siebert, Peterson, and Schramm 1956). The Royal Commission in the United Kingdom soon afterward offered its own views about press responsibilities to society and democracy (Royal Commission on the Press 1949). The starting point for American concerns was the excessive power of large newspaper magnates and sensationalist tendencies debasing the flow of public information. The critique of the press in Britain followed similar lines, although with more emphasis on the lack of political diversity in the newspaper press arising from the concentration of ownership.

The report of the U.S. commission spoke of several duties incumbent on the press in a democratic society, in which the press occupied a somewhat privileged social position. These duties included providing a full and reliable account of daily events; separating fact from comment; providing a forum for the exchange of comment and criticism; and providing a representative picture of the society. These obligations expressed commonly held views of the liberal political class of the day concerning good journalistic practice. They were not widely endorsed by the owners of the press or even by radicals on the left but were somewhat high-minded ideals of the bourgeois intelligentsia and were held by the Commission to arise as a moral duty, without which the claim to press freedom could not be sustained. The unwritten contract that gave the press its right to publish in the public interest and protected it even beyond the freedom of an ordinary citizen called for some services in return.

A leading member of the commission, William Hocking, referred to the "right of the people to have an adequate press" (quoted in Nerone 1994, 97). It was in effect a positive interpretation of the meaning of the press's freedom, in place of the predominant (then as now) negative sense of freedom from any particular duty and constraint. An important component and support of the Commission's views was an appeal to professionalism. The report suggested that "the press look upon itself as performing a public service of a professional kind" (92). Hallin comments on this notion of professionalism as follows: "What I mean by professionalization here is, first of all that journalism like other professions developed an ethic of 'public service.'" It was "part of a general trend, beginning in the Progressive Era, away from partisan politics as a basis for public life and towards conceptions of administrative rationality and neutral expertise" (1996, 245).

The version of the press's duties that the Commission on Freedom of the Press first put into words in an authoritative way has never been accepted as binding by the newspaper press itself, although many of the same or similar requirements have been included in various codes of ethics in many countries (see Laitila 1995; Nordenstreng and Topuz 1989). The ideas contained in this social responsibility notion of press duties are congenial enough to professionals who practice the dominant liberal mode of objective journalism following Schudson's trustee model (see chapter 6). A similar range of ideas has, not surprisingly, emerged from subsequent research into the views of journalists and editors about their own role perceptions (e.g., Fjaestad and Holmlov 1976; Johnstone et al. 1976; Weaver 1999; Weaver and Wilhoit 1986; 1996). Basically the same tasks envisaged by the Commission are still recognized by professional journalists today, although with varying views on how far they should be engaged in the controversies of the day and how far they should be neutral observers and reporters rather than interpreters and even advocates.

Research on the views of news audiences has also tended to emphasize the demand for full and impartial information (Andsager and Miller 1994; Andsager, Wyatt, and Martin 2004; Fitzsimon and McGill 1995; Immerwahr and Doble 1982; Wyatt 1991) as well as for scrutiny of government (Gleason 1994). Regarding the needs of the political system, there is also a tendency for political actors in modern democracies to concur on much the same general requirements of media performance. In the absence of dependable political support from the press, or open access for politicians to the channels (neither very professional nor necessarily in the general public interest), politicians usually want access to the news media on what they consider to be a fair basis. This usually means proportionality, with extra attention to the government in office. Politicians also want journalists to treat politics according to consistent and predictable norms of news value and of objectivity, from which politicians can benefit by doing newsworthy things. Whatever the motivation, the outcome of journalistic, audience, and political actor requirements tends to converge on a model of practice that still seems quite close to the social responsibility version of press theory as enunciated by the Commission.

The content of the roles assigned to or accepted by the modern media is derived largely from the needs experienced by different participants in the political process and from the preferred working practices of the press itself. For instance, Blumler and Gurevitch argue that citizens have needs for material to support their political beliefs; guidance in making choices; basic information about events, conditions, and policies; and affective satisfactions to promote engagement in politics (1995, 15). These needs expressed by audiences in turn call for a relevant response by the media in the form of editorial advice, plentiful information, critical attention to political events, and a manner of presentation that engages attention. In varying degrees, these needs also require the provision of direct access to political agents to persuade, inform, and make themselves known.

However, the apparent consensus that exists about how the media should go about their business in relation to politics and society conceals serious and possibly growing fissures; they largely express a socially desirable and idealized set of outlooks and practices. The media take little account of audience disinterest in politics; the calculative self-interest of politicians, press owners, and managers; the trend to marginalize the traditional press; and the rise of new types of entertainment media (see Bennett and Entman 2001). These points aside, it is not only the substance of media roles in a democracy that is problematic but also their uncertain legitimation and the lack of any accountability, constraint, or sanction in the case of nonfulfilment.

As noted, there is no shortage of typologies of possible roles for the press in relation to the wider society and to politics in particular. The most basic statements of the roles and functions of the media usually emphasize providing information, forming opinion by way of advocacy or forum, and providing critique through the watchdog function (see Nordenstreng 2000). These can be elaborated in terms of different practices and systems, for instance, public versus commercial media forms. To conclude this part of the discussion we return to Blumler and Gurevitch's (1995) summary of the main "functions and services for the political system" that democracy requires. The main elements they propose are:

- Surveillance of the sociopolitical environment
- Meaningful agenda setting
- Platforms for an intelligible and illuminating advocacy by politicians
- Mechanisms for holding officials to account
- Incentives for citizens to learn

- Principled resistance to efforts of forces outside the media to subvert their
  independence

Blumler and Gurevitch also draw attention to four main obstacles to performing these functions and services. One is the mutual conflict between some of the underlying democratic values, for instance between editorial autonomy and giving access. Second, there is usually a structural inequality between the political elite and ordinary citizens. Third, political goals cannot claim unlimited privilege vis-a-vis other claims and interests. Fourth, the media themselves are constrained by their economic and institutional contexts.

It is clear from this discussion that we have considerable latitude in choosing particular media roles for close attention and also in deciding how to define them. Nevertheless, our choice is significantly narrowed by this book's purpose and is guided by our view of the history of the normative theory of the media. The main criterion for selection is relevance to the democratic process. Next, we keep in mind the different traditions of journalistic activity as outlined in chapters 1 and 2, each of which has its own distinctive origins, theoretical underpinnings, and practical forms of expression.

Central to our concerns has been the ongoing debate about the degree to which the media have any obligation at all to serve society. From a liberal–individual or *libertarian* perspective, it may even be thought desirable that the media eschew all collective goals, whether chosen or allocated. All concepts of the public interest in this view are revealed as particular goals and end up as constraints on a free press. Only the free market and the laws of supply and demand should govern what is published. At another extreme, the perspective of communitarianism and *citizen participation* clearly prescribes that the media should adopt positive social goals and engage the community and society in which they are embedded, seeking to practice universal ethical and related values. In between, we find varieties of professionalism, which define the press's roles according to technical and professional standards or some version of the public interest as defined by expert judgment or legitimate authorities. Two intermediate cases can be distinguished, one termed *corporatist,* with social needs determined by elites acting for a supposed public good, and the other a *social responsibility* type, more open to democratic determination. The corporatist type often includes an administrative version of journalism that, although based on professional values, is quite closely engaged with the dominant social institutions and primarily serves the business and economic elite. The paradigmatic tradition of social responsibility prescribes for media a broad set of obligations to serve the common good, following an unwritten social contract. The precise terms of social responsibility have to be filled in, although the main versions of this tradition agree on certain conventional standards and values of an ordered society. The view that it is a task of the media to criticize stems from a strong notion of engagement (the participant perspective), but the pursuit of that task can also be encouraged within a libertarian tradition. Social responsibility can also embrace the duty to be critical on behalf of the public and in the interest of truth.

Four Key Roles for Journalism

To highlight the typical issues and key dilemmas that arise when the press encounters conflicting requirements and value positions in its operating environment, we have chosen to focus on four roles, which we label monitorial, facilitative, radical, and collaborative. They are displayed in figure 4 in relation to two dimensions: The vertical one between strong and weak institutional power, and the horizontal one between media autonomy and dependency.

The *monitorial* role is probably the most widely recognized and least controversial in terms of conventional ideas about what the press should be doing, as seen by the press itself, its audiences, and various sources and clients. It refers to all aspects of the collection, processing, and dissemination of information of all kinds about current and recent events, plus warnings about future developments. Some comment and interpretation is appropriate as an offshoot of editorial selection, on grounds of relevance, but is subordinated to representing reality and giving objective accounts. There are different versions of the scope of the monitorial role, and it varies according to involvement of the media in society. It can range from the more or less passive channeling of information to carrying out a watchdog role ostensibly on behalf of the public. However, this role stops short of partisan advocacy and is restrained by precepts of pro-

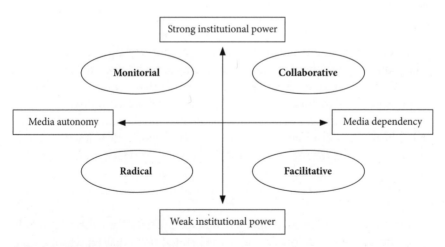

Figure 4. Four Media Roles

fessional journalistic practice, in particular those that require opinion and attitude to be distinguished from facts that can be supported by evidence. The modal version of professional journalism described earlier is expressed most fully in this role.

The *facilitative* role—as we have chosen to conceptualize it—is not prominent in the literature, although it is implicit in functionalist theories of media and society. It draws on several elements in social responsibility theory and on notions of the press as a fourth estate in democratic societies that support debate and people's decision making. The theory of the public sphere has also identified the media as an essential element. That theory refers primarily to journalism that is deliberately practiced as a means of improving the quality of public life and contributing to deliberative forms of democracy as opposed to procedural and constitutional liberalism. It is designed to widen access and promote active citizenship by way of debate and participation. Aside from deliberative democracy, the media facilitate civil society and promote the cultural conditions conducive to democratic life (Taylor 1992a). They promote inclusiveness, pluralism, and collective purpose. According to the concept of the facilitative role, they help to develop a shared moral framework for community and society, rather than just looking after individual rights and interests. The latter are treated as subordinate to a larger good, which itself must not be manifested by decree but developed by way of public communication. The facilitative role is not only in tension with individualism but also hard to reconcile with many of the practices of a press driven by profit and competitive instinct. It may require some subordination of typical professionalism.

The *radical* role is also familiar in accounts of normative expectations from media, even if it has been downgraded in the typical development of press institutions because of its potential clash with journalistic professionalism and market forces. In fact, radical journalism is not inconsistent with professionalism or market criteria. In its fully developed form, however, the radical role cannot be subordinate either to professional norms or to market considerations. It stems ultimately from social and political purposes that lie outside the range of the press institution. It focuses on exposing abuses of power and aims to raise popular consciousness of wrongdoing, inequality, and the potential for change. The radical role is distinguishable from the occasional critical attention given within the scope of the surveillance role and involves systematic and principled engagement according to clearly stated values. The goal is fundamental or radical change in society. Under conditions of authoritarian government, the need for a critical press role is apparent, but the conditions for its practice are limited. In more normal conditions of liberal democratic society, the radical role tends to be fulfilled by a minority sector of the printed press that represents some social or political movements and advocates radical opinions and policies along partisan lines. It is a role less represented in broadcast journalism because of a mixture of public regulation and commercial pressure. Nevertheless, on occasion this role is fulfilled by documentary films and television shows that can have a high impact.

The *collaborative* role specifies and values the tasks for media that arise in situations of unavoidable engagement with social events and processes. Typical situations where this role is appropriate are those of new nations, with their intense pressure toward economic and social development under conditions of scarce resources and immature political institutions. However, collaboration between media and the state is often advocated, if not mandated, under unusual conditions of crisis or emergency, or threat to the society, from external or internal causes. Terrorism and war are obvious examples of such situations, but natural disasters and crises of crime, health, and safety lead in the same direction. Even under normal conditions, there is usually a latent or partial system of cooperation between the media and organs of government and the state that produces voluntary collaboration. Collaborating meets the needs of both parties, recognizing the fact that the media possess an essential societal resource—the public information network—though authorities often control the supply of "news." While collaboration of the kind described almost inevitably impinges on the independence of the press and other media, it can usually be legitimated on grounds of immediate necessity. The collaborative role, however, is scarcely represented at all in the literature on press roles, largely because it goes against the libertarian and professional journalistic grain and expresses some truths that many would rather leave unsaid.

It should be clear that although this selection of roles is limited, it is not arbitrary, and these four take us directly to the dilemmas and complexities that lie at the heart of any body of normative theories of the media. The main omission in the set of roles relates to the press's role as either a tool of partisan advocacy or a platform for advocating opinions. However, elements of advocacy appear in relation to a facilitative role, since advocacy could not be fulfilled without a flow of articulated positions on controversial issues affecting community and society. Adequate information also implies the availability of diverse relevant standpoints and alternative choices and solutions for problems. Even more strongly, advocacy is central to the radical role of the media, since effective criticism is typically based not on evidence and expert analysis but rather on alternative visions of what is right and good.

Roles in Context

Whether or not the roles are chosen and the constraints placed on their exercise depend on a number of general factors that we describe in the following pages.

The main dimensions of these factors are community, the distribution of power, and issues of legitimation and accountability.

DIMENSION OF COMMUNITY

Social contexts for journalism vary according to the quality of collective life in a given place. The term *community* is used as shorthand for several key elements, although it has itself a complex etymology and carries considerable baggage. While it is now frequently used to refer to any set of individuals sharing some interest or outlook, its fuller meaning refers to an ideal of belonging, shared identity, cooperation, forms of solidarity, cohesion, and continuity. As such it contrasts with a condition of individualism, isolation, competition, anonymity, and flux. National societies are usually internally differentiated in terms of potential for community formation, from the most local to the most extensive sphere of action. Conditions of community in the ideal sense are more likely to be found in neighborhoods and small towns, but also in certain collective movements bringing together like-minded people. The differences are reflected in various kinds of politics and thus in different expectations from relevant media. The more intense the community attachment, the more likely are the media to be active participants, as well as partisan, since this is what audiences want and expect. At the level of large-scale and society-wide political activity, we can expect a more detached, diverse, informative, and balanced mode of media practice. Other things being equal, in the latter circumstances, the monitorial role and the modal concept of professional journalism are likely to predominate.

However, there is also a variation between societies in democratic traditions and the historical circumstances of the moment. If one considers the case of internally divided societies or those that are mobilized for development, or in economic decline, oppressed, misgoverned, or externally beleaguered, there are many deviations from the norm of prosperous, secular democracies. Some societies are more individualistic, secular, and market or consumer oriented, with little evidence of strong public institutions and weak notions of any common good. Elsewhere ideology, religion, ethnicity, class, or regional identity still exert a major influence, and the notion of interventionist political action on behalf of the public good is deployed even if intensely contested. The norms for the way media should work will not be the same across these various cases, but more detached in the prosperous, secular versions and more participatory and adversarial in the latter.

Under the same heading of community, we have to consider freedom of access to information, as well as the freedom to publish and disseminate it. What concept of freedom to publish, within what limits, is dominant? Is it absolute, subject only to the rights and essential interests of other individuals? Must the media accept any responsibility for wider or unintended consequences of publication that is in itself lawful? Can the community legitimately act to suppress, limit, or punish publication on the grounds of furthering the general welfare in conditions other than that of pressing danger? Is serving public life with informational channels something that should be entirely left to the market? These and other questions are likely to be answered differently in different societies. Of course, it is quite clear that there is a general principle involved, one that pits advocates of liberalism against those of collectivism. This opposition is reflected in the debates about press theory we discussed in chapter 2. However, those debates do not settle the issue, and the daily operation of any media system in matters important for public life inevitably stirs up the same issues. This point is of particular relevance to the adoption or rejection of both the facilitative and the collaborative role.

The issue of equality also arises in relation to community, although the relationship is an ambiguous one. Most relevant here is the question of equal rights to speak out and express views, to participate vocally. The more community-like the setting for operating a medium, the more equal should be the chance for access and the stronger the claim for fair representation of differences and variations within the community served. Egalitarian ideals impel societies toward universal access and set norms for media performance and informational outcomes. Such ideals go beyond what equal opportunity requires, what the media market would support, or what the owners and controllers of the media choose to dispense. The question of ownership takes us beyond the dimension of community to that of power, but it is relevant to note that communal values are violated in situations where the capacity to publish on any large scale is limited to the very rich (whether individuals, organizations, or firms). The issue that arises in terms of the press's role is whether the media belonging to those with large financial interests can be trusted to carry out their tasks in a way that is both fair and sympathetic to the needs of the wider community. If not, how are the interests of the community to be looked after?

THE DIMENSION OF POWER

It is very common to refer to the power of the press. Often the media apply this epithet to themselves when they refer to the press as a fourth estate. Power in this context usually has a dual meaning, referring both to direct media influence on the information and opinion in circulation and to the fact that the otherwise powerful in society (government, business, or others) have to take account of the press in various ways. The press as a fourth estate is analogous to the other three branches of government: legislative, executive, and judiciary. This concept recognizes the essential point that the press in a democracy is normally expected to act in some sense (and thus to exercise its power) on behalf of the people or the general public interest. Its power is not that of law or force but either the power of truth and of influence with respect to truth, or the capacity of publicity to achieve chosen ends for those who have access to the media.

There is a general assumption that in a democracy, power is ultimately in the hands of the people and the press is, in some sense, independent of the state and government and able to mediate between various power blocs. However, in everyday practice, there are quite a few deviations from this assumption that affect the media's role. A realistic assessment of the working of the media does not entirely support the simple fourth estate model. The principle of editorial independence is both a consequence and a mark of press freedom. Where it obtains, true independence secures the possibility of information and opinion being circulated in an impartial form and therefore not necessarily serving any particular interest but supporting the publication of diverse views.

Perhaps the most obvious deviance from the ideal of a democratic press is not a deviation at all. The fact is that the free press is generally owned by commercial firms with material interests of their own that are not the same as those of the general public or society as a whole. An extensive literature of theory and evidence shows that the media often protect certain sectional economic interests. There is even more reason to believe that the mainstream media frequently serve the interests of government and the state, with varying degrees of enthusiasm, reluctance, or awareness. The collaborative role we have described is often only a more transparent and accentuated case of what goes on much of the time. At least there is enough ground for concluding that the media cannot be assumed to be disinterested—even when they claim to be neutral and impartial.

Another deviation from independence is that of public broadcasting, where a branch of the press is actually employed by a publicly owned body and subject to government rules and regulations about purpose and content. While satisfactory degrees of editorial independence and transparency have usually been achieved in most day-to-day matters, the strategic position of public broadcasting in relation to the state is always potentially problematic.

More in keeping with the ideal of how the media should be related to power in a democracy is the notion of the media as a watchdog in relation to abuses by those with power, especially governments and their agencies. Thus the media are conceived as not so much having power themselves as having the means to place a check on those who really have power by way of sounding warning signals and publishing revealing information and criticism. Zaller (2003) writes of the "burglar alarm" model of the press in public affairs. The ideal of an adversarial press (e.g., Rivers and Nyhan 1973) elevates the notion of independent critic and tends to neglect the many ties that bind an established and successful branch of the media to a variety of other interests, including that of the state itself. A more recent gloss on the watchdog role has pointed out that it can as easily become a guard dog role, with the press looking out for the interests of its sponsors or chosen heroes (Donohue, Tichenor, and Olien 1995).

Often missing in discussions of the power of the press are the powerless in any society. There are extensive constituencies in any society who are not formally disenfranchised but are excluded or marginalized (thus lacking power) by their level of education, income, place of residence, health, race, social problems, criminalization, or combinations of these factors. Generally, sets of people identified in this way do not participate actively in social and political life and are not well organized or represented. Generally also the media do not view them as a significant or even potential part of their audience. The mainstream media do not usually try to express their views, and when they are visible at all it is in terms of social problems for the rest of society, occasionally treated with sympathy.

These remarks should be sufficient to indicate that any role chosen by or assigned to the press must be examined or specified according to power relations in society. In a more detailed version of democratic theory, as well as in day-to-day media practice, there are many ways power relations shape the role the media play in society.

THE DIMENSIONS OF LEGITIMATION AND ACCOUNTABILITY

The main issue here is the degree to which the various roles can be justified by taking account of their performance and consequences. The starting point for considering the question of legitimacy is the quality of what is published and the many possible consequences of publication. Relevant consequences for others include, inter alia, reputational harm, breach of property rights, offense to decency, and violation of privacy or confidentiality. There is another range of issues concerning the presumably unintended harmful effects often attributed to the media regarding violence, sexual morality, and other issues.

Formal answers to most questions of potential harm are found in law and convention, but underlying these answers are more fundamental issues. There are few answers to questions about societal obligation, but also numerous fundamental issues. There are alternative, sometimes competing, grounds on which legitimate claims can be made that the press should fulfill one or another of the various roles. What principle of right or authority can be cited or appealed to in calling for the performance of some role? The original *Four Theories of the Press* located legitimacy somewhere in the ruling ideology or spirit of the overall social system, whether this was permissive or restrictive, prescriptive or proscriptive. In a liberal social system, there could be no legitimate appeal to state authority to guide or limit the media, and obligations were not spelled out. In a Communist society, the interest of the working class was supposed to justify actions of and restraints on the media. Moreover, it has been argued that the position and sometimes privilege enjoyed by the media in a liberal society involves an unwritten contract to make "good" use of the freedom it enjoys, not as an unfettered right but as a trustee of the general good.

Appeal can also be made to majority opinion as to how the media should behave. However, while it is easy to conduct opinion polls on media standards or obligations, the results carry no particular authority, and it would be tyrannical if they did. In a liberal society, the main basis of legitimacy is de facto the market system, which supports the idea that audiences should be given what they are willing to pay for, within the law. Besides the market and the popular will, there are some organized means for expressing relevant (sometimes partisan, sometimes expert) opinion that provide intellectual, moral, or philosophical support for claims for and against the press, even if there is no power to compel. For public broadcasting, there are specific instruments for legitimating intervention to secure certain services and maintain quality. Even so, it is difficult to see how this particular source and form of legitimation for press roles could be extended. Its scope of influence has been contracting, as broadcasting itself is in relative decline. However, it does exert some influence on standards by example and prestige.

Accountability refers to the willingness of the media to answer for what they do by their acts of publication, including what they do to society at large, and refers as well to the feasibility of securing accountability where there is unwillingness. Being accountable is normally linked to accepting, or being given, certain responsibilities, tasks, or goals. It implies some constraint on freedom, and enforced accountability is a denial of freedom. However, some forms of accountability are quite compatible with media freedom as generally understood—especially where freedom does not extend to permitting harm to others (Bertrand 2003; McQuail 2003; Plaisance 2000). For present purposes, the central question of accountability might be formulated as follows: To whom are the media accountable for carrying out a given role, and by what means is accountability achieved?

There are several alternative means by which the media may be called to account, with varying relevance for the roles under discussion. The foremost form of accountability for institutional conduct that affects others and other interests in society is law and regulation. Despite their extensive freedom, the media are typically hedged in with restrictions—especially where there is potential harm to personal reputation or financial interests or to public order and the state's security. For the most part, these restrictions do not entail any positive obligations. Media are sometimes governed by regulations that require them to behave in a certain way and to give an account of their record, especially when there is a question of granting or renewing licenses. Many broadcasting systems, public and private, are regulated, and the once free Internet is increasingly faced with calls for legal control, derived from public demand and the needs of effective and profitable operation. None of the four roles under discussion—leaving aside public broadcasting—are legally enforceable, and the media are not formally accountable to society for carrying them out. A rare exception arises where emergency situations or legislation require cooperation from the media for protecting vital interests of society and the state.

The second main form of accountability (i.e. the market) works as a "hidden hand" to bring society's needs, as expressed by individuals, into balance with the interests of media communicators. There is no enforcement, but the market can be considered reasonably effective in ensuring the performance of the monitorial role (since it meets a clear audience demand) and only intermittently relevant to the other three. Neither facilitation nor collaboration are much within the scope of market forces, although in some circumstances collaboration receives strong public approval. The radical role is usually independent of the market-place, despite the fact that critical journalism may also be popular or at least have a niche market.

The third main means of accountability is that of public pressure, either in the form of general public opinion or by way of organized pressure groups and lobbies. While normative pressure from society and communities can be very effective, it is mainly so in relation to negative aspects of press performance on which there is a high degree of consensus. Such pressures do not do much to produce positive results. Tendencies of the media toward facilitation and col-laboration in these matters can be encouraged by public pressure, but there is no question of accountability. Despite these remarks, we cannot exclude the possibility that the media are encouraged in the performance of their more altruistic roles by public esteem and enhanced status.

The fourth main form of media accountability is professional self-regulation, which may either emerge from within the media or be requested from outside by society as it were. Adherence to professional standards of conduct and ethi-cal norms requires voluntary acceptance of the need to answer for failings and to promise improvement. This willingness may lead to better fulfillment of the facilitative and monitorial roles; it is largely irrelevant to the radical role, which generates its own internal dynamic toward fulfillment.

Media Roles and Models of Democracy

In chapter 4, four models of democracy were identified under the headings "pluralist," "administrative," "civic," and "direct." Here we need only point to the relative prominence of the roles identified earlier in this chapter in relation to the models.

The monitorial role is required under all four models, but in different vari-ants. In pluralistic democracy it is the dominant role, since competing interests vie for support on the basis of freely available information and opinions. The main variations are between polarized forms of pluralism (Hallin and Mancini 2004) and moderate or less contested forms. In the former case, the monitorial role has to be carried out from a particular perspective on behalf of a particular group. This requires a vertically segmented form of media system, with different media channels for different political groups. Journalists are committed to reporting a particular selection of events and to offering a particular interpretation of the world scene, rather than just recording it. Journalism reflects the antagonisms of the society, and there is little chance for neutral, objective reporting. By contrast, under conditions of liberal or moderate pluralism, without sharp conflicts of ideas, we are more likely to find internal forms of media pluralism. This means that informing the public does take the form of neutral, objective journalism, plus varied commentaries reflecting different perspectives and allegiances.

The administrative model of democracy requires a flow of information but has less need for reflecting different opinions. The information provided by the media derives mainly from official, independent, or professional sources. Public trust in the media is encouraged by credible claims to accuracy and fullness of information provided, even if the flow does often come from official sources that may be suspect. The chief professional virtue of journalism in this model of democracy is a cultivated reliability. The news media pay less attention than they do under pluralism to minority sources or those perceived as deviant. The supposed national or general interest determines the criteria of news selection and prominence, as well as the frames within which news is reported.

Under civic and direct democracy, the monitoring role has to be performed in more fragmented ways and under less objective forms. There is no central claim to truth as an independent and verifiable attribute of news accounts. There is no way of determining objectively what is more or less relevant. This is a matter for citizens to choose and determine for themselves.

The collaborative role is not very prominent under normal conditions of pluralistic democracy, aside from the situation of a partisan press in its relation to its own party or a government of its own color. The media do not typically seek to help society directly or to cooperate closely with authority, although under the administrative model there is a degree of collaboration with authorities for reasons of supposed national interest. However, the collaborative role is compatible with the media operating in terms of the deliberative model, according to which service designed to meet social needs is a basic feature of democratic society. Under direct democracy, a somewhat theoretical condition in modern times, the media are likely to be subordinate to rather than to cooperate with the elected authorities. These remarks do not, of course, say anything about authoritarian tendencies that can show up in democracies, especially under crisis conditions. A collaborative role may then be either hard to avoid or democratically legitimated by popular demand and even democratic decision.

The radical role also appears in different guises in different models. Under conditions of contested pluralism, it is very prominent, whether there is strong or weak contestation. Without the critical voice of the media, citizens are less able to choose between alternative parties and candidates: partisanship cannot operate without strong and opposed critical voices. The administrative model does not in principle require a strong media adversarial voice, although the claim to legitimate authority does entail processes of public accountability in which independent media scrutiny plays an important part, albeit without rancor or self-interest. A deliberative model of democracy clearly needs critical journalism. Direct democracy needs critical voices, but not necessarily stemming from a media institution that is somewhat remote from the people. The operation of direct democracy may also involve intolerance of what is perceived as unconstructive criticism for the purposes of selling newspapers or the electronic equivalent.

The radical role is characterized by the perspective of power, whereas the facilitative role is focused on citizenship, the collaborative role is defined in terms of the state or other powerful institutions, and the monitorial role falls between citizenry and institutions. While the distinctive feature of the monitorial role is to *expose,* that of the facilitative role to *deliberate,* and that of the collaborative role to *mobilize,* the keyword for the radical role is to *oppose,* to contradict. Thus the radical role causes the media to be partisan by definition— a medium of advocacy. It also suggests changing things for the better, and this strong normative tone justifies its being called ameliorative.

Conclusion

It should be clear from this account that the very notion of a media or journalistic role remains open to debate and alternative versions are inevitable. Expectations from the media are often inconsistent and also open to continuous change, redefinition, and negotiation. No certain claim can be made upon journalism, under conditions of freedom of publication, to perform a task on behalf of some notion of the public good. Conversely, it is also the case that the media, with all their faults and freedoms, can hardly operate successfully without making commitments to their own audiences and to the many others with whom they have dealings. These commitments inevitably give rise to persistent expectations, which cannot lightly be denied, even if they are not strictly obligatory. Quite aside from this normal feature of all social interaction, whether private or public, the media as an institution have a long history of voluntary engagement with society and have always displayed contradictory tendencies that include strong elements of altruism alongside self-interest.

PART THREE

Roles

6

The Monitorial Role

Harold Lasswell (1948) gave the media's monitorial role a theoretical basis, describing a basic function of all communication as *surveillance*. This idea has been generally adopted in communication theory to refer to the process of observing an extended environment for relevant information about events, conditions, trends, and threats. It conjures an image of a watching post, a lookout tower, or the crow's nest of a ship, which gives a longer and wider view and early warning of developments on the horizon, both natural and human. Surveillance is sometimes used as a shorthand expression to cover processes of observation, collection of information, and the informational content itself.

In fact, Lasswell's term *surveillance* suggests not only looking out but doing so in a planned and systematic way, guided by criteria of relevance and reliability. Sometimes it includes a process of reporting back to authorities or interested parties. In some uses, the term also refers to intelligence gathering and to watching for purposes of control, as in the expression "under police surveillance." In its most negative meaning it translates as spying. Foucault's panopticon, or model prison, in which inmates are under constant vigilance from a control point, is based on this sense of surveillance. In recent times, in the context of a "war on terror," this meaning has even come to predominate, especially with the extension of possibilities for electronic eavesdropping. Therefore, the term is no longer suitable to describe the function of news, because of its somewhat sinister connotations and implications of hidden purposes of control. We use instead the more general and neutral term "monitorial." This label emphasizes the open character of the activity and its intention to benefit the receiver of information rather than the agents of information or control.

The monitorial role largely fits within an early model of mediation in which the news media intervene between events and sources on the one hand and individual members of the public on the other. In this sense, reporters act as double agents of communication, serving their sources as well as meeting the informational needs of the public (Westley and MacLean 1957). News is selected according to the anticipated informational needs of the audience. The intervention extends to providing sources with feedback about public response, which also serves as a guide for the media organization in its decisions about news priorities.

The most basic meaning of the term *monitorial* is that of an organized scanning of the real world of people, conditions, and events, and of potentially relevant sources of information. A subsidiary meaning is that of evaluation and interpretation, guided by criteria of relevance, significance, and reigning normative frameworks for the public arena. This element differentiates monitoring from the now familiar model of the omnivorous electronic search engine that assembles information more or less blindly. A third element of meaning that still lurks somewhat in the background is that of vigilance and control, with some negative implications.

A free press, given minimum conditions of independence and transparency, can legitimately operate according to all three of these elements in its informational activities, subject to the judgment of its own audience. Regarding its contribution to the democratic political process, the underlying basis for the monitorial role is the notion of the monitorial citizen—one who actively seeks information in order to participate in this process (Schudson 1998). In short, the news media in their monitorial role are acting in conjunction with a body of social actors and providing them with an essential resource. We return to this matter later in the chapter.

The Origins of the Monitorial Role

The function of public information dates far back to the military and administrative needs of governments, as well as to the needs of international commerce in predemocratic and premedia times. In its early days, most news gathering and distribution confined itself, in part as a safeguard against censorship, to factual reports of events and could be subsumed under the notions of observation and information. Early newsletters carried information along trade and postal routes about foreign events affecting commerce, especially within Europe. From the early seventeenth century onward, this form of press information, when converted into a saleable commodity, was assessed and valued according to its reliability as a guide to distant events and possible future conditions (Dooley and Baran 2001).

Reports that interpreted events were left to potential users, mainly those engaged in trade and commerce, but presumably also in governmental and religious circles. These early press activities were part of a larger range of information collecting and reporting activities, which were engaged in by agents of church and state for propagandist purposes, as well as by many other kinds of travelers and commentators. In fact the activity of informing the public by way of the printed press was part of a much wider pattern of activities intrinsic to cultural and social diffusion and change.

Not only were facts relevant for business and politics in demand but so was news of all kinds—about ideas, art and design, fashion, food, architecture, crafts, and technologies. The search for and retransmission of certain kinds of news has often been singled out as the key role of journalism and of the press. But this focus neglects many other peripheral reporting and publishing activities, especially in social and cultural matters not directly connected with political or economic affairs.

The Monitorial Role among Others

In clarifying the meaning of the monitorial role, it is useful to see it within a wider framework of media roles. One of the first typologies of such roles was based on a study of American foreign correspondents (Cohen 1963). These journalists tended to see their own role as acting as a link between (government) policymakers and the public but also as involving various degrees and kinds of engagement or neutrality. These could range from the role of informer and educator of the public to the role of advocate of policy, as well as critic. The basic tension at the heart of the journalist's work between neutral mediation and active participation has been a constant theme of subsequent research on the organization of journalistic work up to today (see Patterson 1998).

In the context of the struggles and conflicts of Western society in the 1960s, ideological virtue came to be attributed to active engagement by journalists on behalf of the public and even to some partisanship—contrary to the norm of objectivity that had been more or less established as the proper journalist stance. Nevertheless, professional virtue was still ascribed to those journalists who strove not to take sides but to provide the information the public needed for forming its own opinion (Janowitz 1975). There were and remain differences in the balance of valuation between these two views of the journalistic role, with significant variations between countries (Hallin and Mancini 2004).

Research evidence from the role definitions offered by journalists themselves shows some shifts over time (Johnstone, Slwaski, and Bowman 1976; Weaver and Wilhoit 1986), along with the changing spirit of the times. But the role of the neutral reporter has remained the predominant emphasis—essentially the basic task of surveillance—supported by the values of objectivity. Weaver and Wilhoit's (1996) evidence indicates that American journalists have consistently emphasized "getting information quickly to the public." A value has continued to be attached to interpretation and investigation, the latter mainly with respect to activities of government and business that are perceived to be against the public interest. The additional roles of adversary, critic, and participant have attracted much less endorsement, although they have retained a minority following. This is consistent with the secular and commercial nature of the press, and its reduced ties with political parties, governments, and even campaigning proprietors. In other parts of the world, the predominance of neutrality as the desirable stance of journalism is less pronounced. However, it is still the most typical mode of journalistic operation (see Weaver 1999) and it has found its way into the reformed press systems of the former Communist world (for example, Wu, Weaver, and Johnson 1996).

It is tempting, when interpreting the work of journalism, to focus on the central activity of collecting and disseminating reliable information about real-world events—and to equate this with the monitorial role and with the idea of journalistic objectivity. However, this is too restricted a view. Media information does entail this core element, but it has an interface with other, less neutral activities and perspectives.

First of all, information is unlikely to be adequate without judicious selection and some direct or implied interpretation, which inevitably opens the door to subjectivity. It is hard to gather and publish information without making value judgments or applying criteria of relevance that have no objective basis. Second, the monitorial role overlaps with the familiar press role of watchdog or guardian of the public interest (Gleason 1994), since one of the criteria for selective monitoring is the wish to protect the public. This opens the way for a potentially critical or even adversarial stance. Third, monitorial activity also extends into the practice of investigative reporting that requires the identification of some problem and an active search for evidence rather than simply collecting and disseminating what is readily available. This can hardly be accomplished without personal engagement and without deploying some clear value judgments, even if not advocating them (Ettema and Glasser 1998). These remarks help to place the vigilance and control elements of monitoring in a positive light, since the "good" forms of surveillance are justified by the motive of public enlightenment. This is especially true when the media monitor on behalf of an uninformed public or of a victimized group and against the misuse of power or the negligence of elected authorities.

Finally, the related role of the news media as a forum for diverse views reminds us that our information environment includes not only data but also expressions of opinions, values, and beliefs relating to public issues. Contents of this kind are also factual events when they become part of the public record.

Despite the breadth and elasticity of the monitorial notion, we can differentiate it from certain other press roles. One of these is partisan advocacy or commitment. In this case, any information offered is likely to be biased, since it does not claim to give a full account of reality and openly seeks to select and interpret news according to one predominant perspective and on behalf of some cause or group. Similar remarks apply to mobilization or campaigning functions of the press on behalf of a self-chosen objective. Two other distinct roles are those of entertainer and forger of social consensus (Fjaestad and Holmlov 1976); the latter refers to the many ways the media promote social cohesion and identity, sometimes deliberately, more often implicitly. Although information is usually distinguished from entertainment, there is no doubt that the satisfaction of general curiosity and the stories the news tells often have a diversionary and potentially entertaining character. There is no clear dividing line between hard information and other kinds of messages about reality.

Theoretical Underpinnings

It is clear from the description so far that the provision of information to the public has been a defining feature of journalism since its beginnings. In some respects, it is the essential task of the news media as defined by the press itself, that is, the very core of journalistic professional practice. For this reason, we do not have to look far beyond the press institution for justification and legitimation of this role. We could say that journalism offers its own theoretical foundations expressed in the various formulations of norms for the profession (see, e.g., Laitila 1995; Meyer 1987), which not only indicate lines of desirable action but also sometimes prescribe various responsibilities and lines of accountability: to the public served, to society, to those who are reported on, to journalists themselves, and to employers.

Nevertheless, there is no universal agreement on what is entailed by the central practice of monitoring and then reporting on events and circumstances. There are many acceptable variants and styles, as well as gaps, in the corpus of professional ethics. There are also failures and weaknesses that arise from the fact that journalism is not independent of its masters—the owners and managers who typically have other goals besides those of professional journalism. It is also arguable that journalism is too important to society to be left to journalists alone to decide on the appropriate normative principles. They see what is desirable or not from their own perspectives, which do not necessarily reflect the perspectives of others with an equal interest in the outcome of public communication.

For this reason, the monitorial role has attracted the attention of extrajournalistic media theorists. Historically, the first relevant theory was that of democratic politics itself, even if it is hard to find, before relatively recent times, any clear and agreed-on statement about the press's role in the democratic process—apart from the belief that freedom of expression and the press were cornerstones of political liberty. Certainly during the nineteenth century and even earlier, the press acquired a key task of reporting on proceedings in parliaments and similar assemblies, without which their democratic credentials would have been much reduced. This aspect of the press's role gave rise to the notion of a fourth estate, which attributed power to the press as at least equivalent in principle to that of other branches of government (Schulz 1998).

While the claims made to fourth estate status have often been criticized for arrogance or lack of credibility, the key role played by the press in contemporary politics, even as neutral carriers of information, keeps this idea alive. At its best, this role is essential to maintaining the independent accountability of government to the public and wider society and securing the health of the public sphere. Democratic election procedures all take for granted that the media will freely circulate information about government actions, problems, issues, and politics affecting the public, as well as about candidates for office. Democratic theory tends not to dwell on such obvious matters, but they are necessary conditions of democracy, and they provide a source of criteria for judging the press and urging it to do better.

Arising at least indirectly from the same source is another body of relevant theory: that on the social responsibility of the media formulated in the report of the Hutchins Commission (Blanchard 1977; Hutchins 1947). In a famous phrase, it called on the press to provide "a truthful, comprehensive, and intelligent account of the day's events in a context which gives them meaning." The press was asked to separate fact from comment and present both sides of disputed issues. Both of these points are aspects of monitoring, although not named as such. Taken together, they go well beyond what journalistic ethics require, since the latter are focused more on the avoidance of harm than on service to some wider public good.

The standards of fullness and fairness that the Commission proposed were echoed in numerous subsequent assessments and inquiries and appeared in many of the declarations that were formulated to define the informational task of public broadcasting in many countries (Nordenstreng 1974). The requirements for broadcasting, especially with respect to fairness and objectivity, went beyond the original formulation of social responsibility. They became part of a regulatory framework that largely ruled out partisanship and the unlimited expression of editorial opinion that newspapers were allowed. The reasons for this lay mainly in the shortage of channels and sometimes the monopolistic position of broadcasters.

Despite all the positive arguments just advanced, critical theory has generally spoken against rather than for the monitorial role of the media as described. Critical theorists question the very notion of objectivity (Hackett 1984) and thus the desirability as well as the viability of any satisfactory conduct of the monitorial role. These theorists have typically viewed the provision of news information as a practice that does little more than reinforce the dominant and basically ideological interpretation of the world circulated by power holders and elites in their own interests. Neutrality in news is said to protect the essentials of the established system. At the same time, critical theory has usually stopped short of condemning the whole enterprise of objective journalism and called instead for greater awareness of its limits, for measures to secure true journalistic freedom, and for a diversity of news channels and perspectives on the world. A more radical branch of critical theory would still tend to view mainstream mass media as inevitably tending to the maintenance of an unjust social order. This is especially the case where critics adopt the perspective of marginal or disadvantaged groups and classes or simply of the developing world in its relations with dominant countries. In the postcritical era that arguably we have entered, normative theory has generally withdrawn from totally negative judgments and focused more on identifying the requirements of civil society and the public sphere for diverse and voluminous flows of information and expression (Curran 1996).

Informational Practices

The monitorial role involves any or all of the following practices in various forms and degrees:

- Keeping and publishing an agenda of public events, as notified by cultural institutions
- Receiving and screening notices and messages intended by external sources for further public dissemination; here, media act as an agent both of voices in society and of the public or intended audience as the latter presumably search for information
- Maintaining a reportorial presence at the main forums where political, social, and economic decisions are made or new events are announced and set in motion; this includes routine coverage of parliaments, assemblies, law courts, press conferences of significant bodies, and so forth
- Publishing reports on significant current events and reproducing key factual data on a continuous basis (ranging from financial data to sports results)
- Providing the public with warnings of risks, threats, and dangers that might have consequences for it, ranging from weather reports to travel disruptions and foreign war and disorder
- Providing a guide to public opinion and to attitudes and beliefs of key groups and figures on major issues
- Offering an agenda that signals current problems and issues according to criteria of relevance and significance to the audience and society

- Providing analysis and interpretation of events and opinions in a balanced and judicious manner
- Acting as a fourth estate in political matters by mediating between government and citizens and providing a means for holding government accountable at the bar of public opinion
- Adopting an active watchdog stance by "barking" when some major social actor is perceived to be acting against the public interest, especially in an underhanded or disguised way
- Initiating and pursuing self-chosen inquiries, when the information obtained suggests major deviance from the moral or social order; this may involve keeping track of gossip, rumors, and unofficial or personal information

There is an implied continuum of initiative and activity in this list of tasks, ranging from a purely observational and transmission role to a stance of readiness to take preemptive warning actions and finally to active investigation and actual pursuit. At this point, the monitorial role gives way to the critical and dialectical mode, which is essentially different. This continuum of activity is summarized below:

INFORMATION TASK AND DEGREES OF ACTIVITY

Receive and transmit notices of events (*passive*)
Selectively observe, report, and publish (*active/passive*)
Signal deviance and warn the public (*active*)
Seek, investigate, and expose transgressions (*active and engaged*)

As we have already shown, there are several tensions at the heart of the monitorial role, quite apart from the related issues of the perceived independence of the observing journalist and the degree of trust that can be earned from an audience. The most salient tension develops when informing moves along the continuum indicated above and finds a more active expression, for instance in investigative reporting, which acts as "custodian of the public conscience," in Ettema and Glasser's terms (1998). However, these authors draw attention to the paradox of journalists claiming to do this without applying their personal moralities. In keeping with the principles of objectivity, investigative reporters claim to apply news judgments rather than value judgments when they identify victims and wrongdoing. They see themselves as pursuing the culprits on behalf of the victims and society at large, not acting out of ideology or bias. At the very least, this indicates one of the main tensions in carrying out the monitorial role.

The problem of separating facts from values lies at the heart of the critique of objectivity and threatens to undermine the integrity of the monitorial role. When values and opinions guide the selection of facts, even when they are claimed to stem from a demonstrable concern of the audience or public, the basic understanding of the role as we have described it is violated to some extent.

There is no general solution to this dilemma, but it looks as if the information provision can only extend to active pursuit when there is a high degree of consensus on some widely agreed violation of the moral order or some compelling source of danger for the society as a whole. Beyond that, it becomes partisan advocacy or propaganda.

There is no single way of carrying out the monitorial role and no sure way of recognizing relevant practices. A diverse media system has numerous variants of form, format, and purpose. There are quite different media genres involved, although all share some element of "reality-orientation"; fiction and entertainment are largely excluded from consideration, if only by convention. But this still leaves a wide range of types of performance, including talk shows, heavyweight editorials, stock market reports, weather forecasts, and published gossip concerning any one of the many social worlds that the media bring into view for the private citizen.

Even within one format there can be distinct alternatives. For example, Campbell and Reeves (1989) studied the U.S. television documentary program *60 Minutes* and identified three different modes of doing what is essentially the monitorial task. One is the model of the "detective," another that of the "tourist," and a third that of the "analyst." The terms correspond approximately to the journalistic activities of investigation, observation, and interpretation, respectively. The terms also give a vivid indication of quite different purposes, practices, outcomes, and criteria. While these three different modes were found within the title and format of one television series, it is more common to find the variations distributed across different publications and formats, designed for different kinds of audiences.

JOURNALISTIC OBJECTIVITY

Most agreement can probably be found, especially among professional journalists, on the idea of the "neutral and objective reporting" of events as they take place. Here *neutral* means balanced and disinterested, unbiased, without an axe to grind. *Objective* refers to verifiable facts, and *reporting* means telling an unvarnished story in a nonemotive manner. In this view, the observer-reporter is no more than an extension of the senses of the members of the public on whose behalf the press acts. Those who hold this view do not want their press to do more than tell them what is happening in social reality, without value judgments, emotion, or interventions.

There is more to be said, but the idea of a monitorial role in this dominant meaning can be seen as delegitimating journalism activities that go too far in the direction of expressing opinions, conveying ideologies, or taking too active a part in the wider affairs of society as an involved and partisan actor. Emphasis is placed on information quality in terms of accuracy, fullness, relevance, and verifiability. The information provision also seems to require the reporter not to be selective in observation when selection might serve some particular interest or have a distorting effect. So the requirement is to report as much of the truth as possible and nothing that is not believed to be true and open to verification.

The concept of the neutral reporter recognizes that there are many competing interests and warring parties in society but insists that the news media do not have to take sides or have any vested interests of their own. Society is also understood, despite its conflicts, as fundamentally united—sharing the same basic values and a common interest in survival. The perceived capacity of journalism as an institution to identify possible harm and to expose deviance presupposes a large measure of consensus on norms and values. Whatever the political system, when it comes to basic welfare or warfare, there is almost always, as noted above, the possibility of an ultimate appeal to a national interest.

Theories of pluralistic democracy of the kind formulated by Robert Dahl (1967) and others in the mid–twentieth century, especially in the United States, are most consistent with this view, even if some of its assumptions may be illusory, especially the notion of a basic shared interest between social classes. The more one parts company with such an individualistic and liberal view of society, the more the monitorial role seems either impossible to fulfill according to its own implicit norms or at risk of becoming a mystification concealing certain special interests.

According to contemporary thinking about the public sphere, the monitorial role of the news media is a dual one. First, it serves to define the boundaries of public space and the actors, issues, and events that lie within these boundaries and on which public opinion forms and collective decisions are taken. The news media are continually constructing and reaffirming the shape and contents of the public sphere. What is not noticed or not published is essentially invisible and cannot easily be made the stuff of politics or public deliberation. The second aspect of public information is the detailed work of filling in the foreground and background of the social world and identifying the figures within it. The boundary between what is and is not public has to be maintained and policed. The news media do this task without specifically choosing it.

If one accepts the main assumptions concerning the possibility and desirability of the information provision—defined as objective reporting—as the dominant press paradigm, then it seems to be the role most appropriate to democracy. The monitorial task is appropriate to liberal and individualistic democracy, but particularly to deliberative or participative forms. Both types of democracy presuppose that citizens as voters need to know enough to make informed and rational decisions, especially at periodic elections. The press has to be a major source of such information, since no other institution is able to offer enough ostensibly disinterested knowledge on such a scale and in so timely a manner. Members of the public served by a press in this role are deemed to be capable of learning whatever they need to know about "reality" and in a position to act in their own self-interest. If the press is true to the informational ideals as outlined, there are no favors to special interests, lobbies, power holders. In some respects, those with power may even seem more restricted by the application of media information than other groups or interests, since the press knows who they are and is organizationally geared to keeping an eye on them. But such an impression is very misleading, since there are many legitimate as well as illegitimate ways available to those with power or financial resources to manipulate news media norms and practices for their own advantage.

Accountability

The press in its monitorial role is primarily accountable to its own audiences, clients, and sources for the way it carries out this role. The flow of information is largely self-regulating, with professionals motivated to serve their audience, and the audience considered able to judge for itself the quality of information or warnings it receives. A news medium that fails in the quality of the information offered, on any of several dimensions relevant to monitoring, will eventually lose the trust of its audience and have no value as a service. Moreover, freedom of the press in democratic societies gives strong protection to this version of accountability.

Nevertheless, a good deal of observational evidence suggests that the media can fail, both on a case-by-case basis and more systematically at an institutional level, in delivering an adequate survey of the environment. At the institutional level, there are numerous examples of the demonstrated failure of general public newspapers and the broadcast press to give adequate coverage to international events, their lack of diversity in news reporting as a result of media concentration, and a general failure to pursue any critical line of inquiry that offends the powerful.

The first trend has been described as affecting the United States to an increasing degree in the past decade or longer. The second has been identified in different countries as a result of market conditions, and the third also occurs widely because of risk-avoidance behavior. Overall, many if not most systemic failures can be traced to market conditions. As the media become increasingly valuable commercial undertakings, economic profit goals replace political or professional objectives.

Among the principal means of accountability that have been identified (e.g., in Bertrand 2003; Gillmor, Dennis, and Glasser 1989; McQuail 2003; Pritchard 2000), the market offers the least satisfaction as a remedy for failure, since the market is part of the problem. This leaves three main alternatives. One is professional self-regulation and an appeal to journalistic ethics. This matters a great deal, but cannot achieve much in the way of remedy in the face of corporate power and in light of its own internal weakness. There is also relatively little that governments can do by law and regulation when the media fail to offer quality information.

There is an exception in those countries where a public broadcasting system still exists, governed by requirements to provide full and balanced information services. But even this is vulnerable to commercial and political pressures. Indirectly, governments can do more to encourage adequate structures of media and information. The time has passed, however, when direct intervention to protect or raise press standards, as occurred in Europe in the latter half of the twentieth century, would be possible. There remains the pressure of public opinion, as distinct from the audience and advertising market, as a potential force for accountability. While this is effective on certain issues of media performance, it does not promise a great deal, except in the most egregious cases of media failure.

Power and the Monitorial Role

The media's relationship to power (social, economic, and political) inevitably shapes role performance. Criteria of news relevance are partly determined by the power of sources or the power of those who are featured in news. A central issue for democracy is that of the press's independence from the holding and exercise of power in society. In general, the West identifies a free press as necessarily detached from the State's power and with some independence from agents of economic power. Without this, the monitorial role could not serve the people but only the interests of power holders. Nonetheless, varying degrees of separation are found, ranging from complete separation and neutrality to full cooperation with authority.

The venerable notion of the fourth estate offers a kind of solution by crediting the press with its own power, distinct from that of the state. The control of information creates a power base in itself and is a very common feature of contemporary media. A question involving both daily choice and the institutional positioning of the news media is how much opposition or criticism media can engage in without appearing to undermine legitimate authority or challenge democratic norms.

Of course, there is more to the situation than this, including flaws in this optimistic line of reasoning. It is true that the press continuously spotlights existing power holders, special interests, and advantaged groups as it performs the monitorial role. But the same interests can also use this visibility to their advantage. The information provision not only puts a check on some interests but also can differentially advantage them. It is a question of manipulating free publicity to the best advantage, and the skills and occasions for doing this are available. Leaving aside the issue of which concept of democracy one prefers, the idea of the press as watchdog has been supplemented by the notion of its being a guard dog for many vested interests (Donohue, Tichenor, and Olien 1995).

The activities we have presented as carrying out the media's providing of information inevitably lead to journalism serving as a conduit for information, ideas, and images that are far from evenly accessible to all because of differential access and the knowledge gap. The conduit is designed mainly for a vertical flow downward. The more powerful the interest, the more it claims the channels of publicity, on the very ground that it is powerful and therefore relevant for the public to know about. It has been argued that an objective press, as in the United States, only accepts responsibility to report the main streams of opinion about events and perhaps cannot legitimately go much further. The result is to restrict the reporting of very critical, radical, or minority views and to give extra weight to the power of the state over the media (Bennett 1990).

In the balance between benefit and harm from the media's informational activities, it is far from certain that the balance is always positive. And any assessment must account for the fact that the press is rarely a neutral observer. It is also a social actor, an economic interest in itself, and perhaps also a voice for some political or economically powerful proprietor. The example of the press reporting on issues affecting itself (for example, regulation, monopoly, or criticism) demonstrates the news media's partisanship, even when ostensibly detached from party politics.

Despite criticism along the lines indicated, and the vulnerability of the whole paradigm of objective reporting, the definition of the press as essentially an instrument for conveying information in the wider public interest has shown a certain capacity to survive and to propagate itself, even against the odds. As noted, a journalism that claims to observe and report reality but patently fails to do so loses credibility and any raison d'être at some point. Where such a press is preserved by superior power, it still needs to maintain some semblance of connection with reality.

Even its failures to report can be a source of information about what is going on, as experienced readers of Communist newspapers learned at the height of censorship. During wartime, propagandists and controllers of information tell as much that is true as possible by way of the news media in order to maintain some credibility and at least the possibility of influence. There is an ultimate contradiction between very idea of the press (as understood here) and its gross failure to report on reality; seeing these as contradictory sustains faith in the monitorial role as the press's most basic task.

The Monitorial Role and Types of Democracy

As noted, the monitorial role seems most adapted to liberal-pluralist democracy, in which all citizens are presumed to need information relevant to their particular circumstances and to be in a position to generate a demand for it, which it is in the interest of a free press to supply. The market also promotes the appearance of news channels and publications that are directed at special interests, by whatever criterion these are defined. In the liberal-pluralist model, ideologically tinged news also can be purveyed.

Other models of democracy cannot operate without some version of the monitorial role, but with differences of emphasis and outcome. The administrative type of democracy puts weight on the informational quality of news and deploys a hierarchical notion of performance that deviates from purely market criteria. An adequate supply of information is only possible on the basis of a highly professionalized journalism that has an elitist orientation. By implication, this version of journalistic quality sets a high value on officially validated reporting or on information that of its nature is precise and capable of being verified. The highest quality of information is likely to be in authoritative statistical form. Facts count for more than ideas, values, or opinions.

Civic democracy values information differently and attaches more weight to the search for and supply of information. Service to the particular community matters most, and in this mode the monitorial role of the media is likely to be more directed or selective than under conditions of libertarianism or administrative democracy. Much the same can be said of direct democracy, where the ideal of objective news reporting can be challenged for its failures to promote democratically chosen values.

Barriers to Performance

The media's role of informing is well established and even protected in many countries by constitutional and other legal provisions. The press often has certain customary or even legal privileges, for example, allowing criticism of public figures, protection of sources, access to the sites of news events. However, even in well-ordered and relatively open societies, there are barriers to fulfilling the monitorial role; some are internal to the media and some external.

One obstacle concerns access to information that is not in the public domain, whether held by governments or private organizations. The rights of journalists to pursue observation and inquiry are limited by claims to confidentiality or economic interest in protecting certain information. The full and unhindered exercise of the monitorial role is rarely possible, although legal efforts have been made in many countries to extend public access to information. There has been progress, although the news media are not always the beneficiaries. As recent experience has shown, under conditions of even limited warfare or threats to internal security, government and military sources usually control information tightly; access is granted only when the information predominantly favors the authorities, as distinct from the public. And information highly relevant to the public may not be made available because it is expensive to collect or sensitive enough to expose the publisher to legal risks. Judgments on such matters can usually be made only when there is full disclosure, which is itself the issue. In addition, limits are set to what can be published without potential harm to individuals.

A second general problem arises from the constraints on publishing information that arise from the economic conditions of media operations. Most news media operate according to commercial principles, seeking profit from the sale of news or advertising space. This puts pressure on the resources available for collecting information and a premium on large audiences. The selection of news for publication is influenced in two main ways: readily available information is more economical, and news that interests a majority is more attractive.

The first of these tendencies is likely to favor the reproduction of news from sources that are best organized to supply what the media want: news agencies, public relations firms, official sources, or other well-financed organizations or lobby groups. The general effect is to limit journalism's independence and critical thrust, as well as preventing a full and balanced monitoring of what is going on. Often this factor plays into the hands of the would-be managers and manipulators of news and news events, increasing the chance of news being propaganda.

The second tendency is likely to have consequences for the quality of news that is offered, especially its depth and fullness. Many complaints about the increased brevity, superficiality, and sensationalism of news content can be attributed to the imperative of gaining and keeping an audience. The term *infotainment* has often been used to specify the intrinsic inadequacy of much contemporary news from this point of view. The charge is especially launched against the neglect of more serious and complex public issues of the kind that, according to all versions of democratic theory, should form the subjects of political debate.

It is sometimes argued in return that making the news attractive is a way of gaining an audience. Information without delivery is obviously useless, whatever its intrinsic quality. It is also arguable that trying to please and interest an audience does not necessarily reduce journalism's critical edge, since political scandal and its exposure can have important accountability value while also engaging the public's interest. It is certainly true that the success of the monitorial role depends not only on relevant information but also on the public's attending to it. In that sense, the particular failing under discussion cannot be blamed entirely on the media.

Aside from commercial pressures for audience maximization, there is another factor at work, stemming from the culture of news production and its wider media setting: mediatization, whereby the criteria of newsworthiness and manner of presentation are more and more governed by a media thirst for a good story or good television. Central to this rationale is a strong attachment to dramatic narrative, to compelling characters and personalities. There is a premium on action, surprise, excitement, and emotional involvement, as well as on whatever can be visualized in the most compelling way. Such criteria put the form of presentation before content and inevitably distort the balance of choices made. There is likely to be a bias against length; wordiness; complex, abstract, or unfamiliar ideas; memory; and explanation. The existence of this "media logic" in turn affects those who seek access to news coverage, transferring the same criteria to the sources and shapers of public information.

There are other consequences of subordinating information gathering and publication to the influence of a dominant news culture and the requirements of news organizations in a very competitive market environment. One well-attested factor is the enormous regard for the scoop among journalists, which gives relatively greater value to unique ownership of some information than to its deeper significance. The citizen looking for warning or advice could certainly be ill served by this custom. Of particular relevance to the monitorial role is the well-attested custom of all news media in a given market to follow the same story (one held to have high news value) and pay continuing attention to it well beyond any informational value. This phenomenon has sometimes been referred to as media hype (Vasterman 2005). One of its features is the creation of news with a limited basis in reality, as when a few prominent incidents are made to look like a crime wave and promote a self-generating moral panic. All this reduces the value of news to the citizen as a "burglar alarm" that we describe below.

The net effect of mediatization, arguably, is a distortion of public discourse and a flight from substantive information. We have noted on behalf of news-making an argument that at least gains an audience, but it loses its force if the information loses most of its potential value. There is no certain way to settle this debate, since the outcome turns on what precisely is to be expected from the monitorial role, and in turn, what needs it is supposed to fulfill.

In a contribution to this discussion, Zaller (2003) advanced the proposition that for healthy democracy, news only has to serve a burglar alarm function. In his view, it does not need to meet the criteria of news encouraged by social responsibility theory, what he terms the "full news standard." In his perspective, news should be feasible as well as useful. According to the burglar (or fire) alarm standard, the essential value of news in a democracy is to enable concerned citizens to maintain a routine vigilance regarding political issues and problems that are arising, without needing deep knowledge. On occasion, citizens need to know more and be more active, but not continuously.

Zaller's view is based essentially on the notion of the monitorial citizen invoked by Schudson (1998). It can also be supported by reference to Downs's (1957) economic theory of democracy, which sees the consumption of political information as guided by the personal need of individuals and the cost in time or money they are prepared to pay. A good deal of empirical research from the long tradition of news learning research also shows that the general public appears to learn rather little from even extensive and good-quality news, when it is routinely received by way of television or other mass media (e.g., Robinson and Levy 1986). At the same time, Doris Graber (2001; 2003; 2006) over a number of years has made a strong case for the view that the general public can understand and learn the essentials on important matters without needing a great volume of information. From the point of view advanced, most news consumers would seem to be sufficiently served as citizens by minimal, but well-chosen and presented, news provisions most of the time.

This line of argument is open to critique, especially on the ground that it simply tends to endorse current media trends of soft news, personalization, sensationalism, and scandal, which have been seen as diverting citizens from political participation. More specifically, Bennett's (2003) response to Zaller points to the problem that the news as a burglar alarm often sounds false alarms or fails completely when there are real problems. He also notes that although the full news standard and the burglar alarm model should be in tension in the newsroom, the burglar alarm model tends to be preferred.

The accumulated literature on press practice and performance does seem to support the view that the monitorial role is carried out only selectively and imperfectly (McQuail 1992). However, we have shown that there are various and sometimes alternative explanations for this weakness—especially in terms of media economics. It is not necessary to resort to totalizing theories that condemn the whole idea of press surveillance to the realm of ideology, propaganda, and mystification. Different media have different remits and goals. In fact, media institutions as a whole have become specialized according to their own choice of market sector. This means that in one sense, each medium can justify being selective in its own surveillance, on the grounds that other media will cover other events. But in practice, the whole spectrum of events is not covered, and there is excessive repetition as the media try to please the same news consumers. In its monitorial role, the media are usually a business first and a social institution second.

Although the monitorial role varies in its type and efficacy from media system to media system and from case to case, some general points from communication research indicate the factors that shape the monitoring process. The most relevant points are as follows:

- The range of the environment that can or will be monitored by a given medium or system is limited by geographic and cultural (including linguistic) factors, as well as by the medium's technical and organizational capacity. The periphery is typically viewed from a notional center, and the gaze is inevitably ethnocentric.
- The focus of attention is determined by economic and political criteria, according to the interests of the source of monitoring.
- Other things being equal, the large size and high status of objects, persons, and events is a guide to attention, plus what is believed to be of consuming interest to an audience (sports, popular culture, and so forth).
- More attention is attached to objects who seek publicity and wish to be monitored and less to those who wish to avoid it. The use of power and money by the objects of monitoring often shapes the difference. The environment is not evenly open to observation.
- Monitoring is not simply a matter of observing and recording isolated facts but of viewing the world from a limited number of interpretive frames. The choice of frames is likely to be limited by the range and strength of elite and popular opinion, and by considerations of national or sectional interest. Bennett (1990) has posited a process of indexation by which the media typically reflect the dominant and authoritative interpretations and marginalize deviant or minority views.
- Observation by the media is often guided and structured by a changing issue agenda that provides an initial guide to further monitoring.
- The probable effects of the monitorial role on the public are not a direct one-way transmission of information or views but a dialogic process. The media signal what sources the audience seems to want, and audiences develop an interest in, or familiarity with, what the media highlight. There is mutual adaptation.

Conclusion

In a democratic society with a free press, the news media in performing their monitorial role are vulnerable to numerous failures. In this respect, to a large extent, the quality of journalism is determined by society's general quality, especially regarding citizenship, the vitality of civil society, and the health of the democratic process. There is no special or certain remedy for this situation. At the same time, it should be recalled that there are strong natural supports for the monitorial role, both in the information needs that are continuously and widely experienced and in the traditions of reporting that have survived many unpropitious times and threatening circumstances. The monitorial role is at the heart of journalistic activity, and this is what the profession has learned to do best. It is unlikely to fail completely or to lack some self-provided remedies, given the necessary freedom. The entire press system does not have to perform perfectly for essential needs to be met.

7

The Facilitative Role

The facilitative role of the news media is rooted in the democratic tradition of civic republicanism (chapter 4). The media reflect the political order in which they are situated, and the logic and rationale for their facilitating public life is primarily that of civic democracy. In this perspective, only within active communities do we discover goods together that we cannot know alone. Public opinion arises from deliberation and is not antecedent to it. Rather than an aggregation of personal preferences generated by the innermost self, public opinion is collective wisdom based on open debate. Civic democracy understands community as constituted by interaction, and therefore public communication cultivates shared interests and common goals. In James Carey's terms, journalism only makes sense in relation to the public. Therefore, it ought to

> preside over and within the conversation of our culture: to stimulate it and organize it, to keep it moving and to leave a record of it so that other conversations—art, science, religion—might have something off which they can feed. The public will begin to awaken when they are addressed as a conversational partner and are encouraged to join the talk rather than sit passively as spectators before a discussion conducted by journalists and experts. (1987, 17)

In their facilitative role, the media promote dialogue among their readers and viewers through communication that engages them and in which they actively participate. In facilitative terms, the news media support and strengthen participation in civil society outside the state and the market. Consistent with the normative character of their roles, the media do not merely report on civil society's associations and activities but seek to enrich and improve them. Citizens are taken seriously in clarifying and resolving public problems. The aim of this interactive mode is democratic pluralism. Instead of insisting on artificial consensus and uniform public opinion, the media in their facilitative role promote a mosaic of diverse cultures and worldviews. In meeting this challenge, the media are accountable to the widely shared moral frameworks that orient the society in which they operate and give it meaning. In order to elaborate how deliberation, civil society, pluralism, and the moral order work in concert, the facilitative role of the media needs to be understood in its historical, sociological, and theoretical contexts.

Deliberation

The facilitative role of the news media is both rooted in and promotes deliberative democracy. In deliberative politics, the public articulate their claims in terms accessible to one another rather than holding them "in the privacy of one's own mind" or "appeal[ing] only to the authority of revelation" (Gutmann and Thompson 2004, 4). They must "reason beyond their narrow self-interest" and use arguments that "can be justified to people who reasonably disagree with them" (Gutmann and Thompson 1996, 55, 2; see 255). The media facilitate the process of negotiation over the social, political, and cultural agenda. Deliberation is open to a "wide range of evidence, respectful of different views," rational in weighing available data and willing to consider "alternative possibilities" (Macedo 1999, 58).

The deliberation facilitated by the press frames the democratic process in normative terms as interactive dialogue in which citizens engage one another on both practical matters and social vision. In this approach, "norms and institutions are open to challenge and debate, and derive their legitimacy from the actual agreement of citizens" (Deveaux 2000, 141). The public is more likely "to take a broader view of the issues" when moral reasons are exchanged rather than using "political power as the only currency" (Gutmann and Thompson 2004, 11).

Social conflicts are a major component of democratic life, and in deliberative politics they remain the province of citizens rather than of judicial or legislative experts. Affirmative action, environmental protection, health care policy (Gutmann and Thompson 2004, ch. 5, 139–59), global warming, gun control, arms trade, welfare reform, and doctor-assisted suicide (Gutmann and Thompson 1996) raise moral conflicts that the public itself must negotiate. Zygmunt Bauman (1993) defines postmodern sensibility as awareness that there are human problems without good solutions. When agreement is not forthcoming, channels of continued interaction are kept open by acknowledging "the moral standing of reasonable views" opposed to one's own (Macedo 1999, 123). Rather than taking for granted a consensual society, the presumption of unresolved disagreement appreciates the inevitably multidimensional character of community.

The Hutchins Commission understood the media's facilitative role essentially in these terms. The Commission went beyond news as accurate information and argued that the press should provide "a truthful, comprehensive and intelligent account of the day's events in a context which gives them meaning" (Commission on Freedom of the Press 1947, 21). Put in different terms, the news media ought to provide "full access to the day's intelligence" (28). The Hutchins report called for news reporting that makes available "the opinions and attitudes of the groups in society to one another" (22). The report recommended that the media serve "as a forum for the exchange of comment and criticism" (23). Recognizing the complicated character of democratic life, the major mission of mass communications, the Commission argued, is to raise social conflict "from the plane of violence to the plane of discussion" (23). Socially responsible news is defined by its obligations to the community. Instead of individual rights to publish, the press's rationale was centered in a healthy society.

For more than four decades, development communication models have taught us about the facilitative role as well.[1] But as Robert White argues, from the beginning development theory and practice have been "caught in a fundamental contradiction regarding the principle of participation" (1994). On the one hand, participatory communication has been emphasized, stretching from "local theater groups to participation of farmers' organizations in the formulation of agricultural policy." But all the while, scientifically based social engineering, and in some cases the primacy of state planning, have guided the logic of development practice, reserving for the "professional elite the initiative and control of development processes that deny the possibility of real participation" (95–96, 101). Early on, development journalism became anchored in monologic, positivistic, technologically oriented media theory (see Servaes 2001; 2007). The mechanistic modernization theories of Lerner and Schramm became development journalism's scholarly foundation, with "modernization at bottom an euphemism for Westernization" (Dare 2000, 167). The seemingly beneficial transfer of modern technology and organization has come to be recognized as "in reality an extension of the North Atlantic nations which implied a continued dependent linkage and a division of labor benefiting the industrialized nations" (White 1994, 104).

In contrast to the modernization model favoring political and entrepreneurial elites, participatory media in the republican tradition build and sustain a democratic constituency. Andrew Moemeka argues for a "facilitative strategy" in which development communicators "lead from behind." Derived from an ancient African tradition, leading from behind is a Socratic process of identifying together "what is appropriate to do and how to effectively and efficiently do it" (2000, 119). Ideas and plans are not imposed by outside experts, but communities build up their own knowledge and experience through interactive learning. This dialogic version of development communication depends on collaboration within the grass roots rather than a top-down approach to problem solving. Looking closely at the "complex process of constructing meaning in everyday life," White identifies a "ritualistic cultural dramaturgy" distinct from the diffusion paradigm. "The focus is on the grass roots construction of meaning, the generation of common cultural symbols, and projection of a public conception of historical development that evokes wide identification and participation" (1994, 113–14).[2] The role of the state is not to command the efforts of local and regional groups, but to respond to and facilitate their initiatives.

Breaking with the Western ideal of objective and detached reporting, development communication identifies the ways citizens can act on their own. According to Galtung and Vincent, development-oriented news media give people a voice, allowing them to talk, letting them "run more of society," and then reporting on what happens (1992, 146, 163–64). Such media promote participatory communication among ordinary people and respond to the peoples' concerns rather than the interests of the governmental elite and powerful nations. Journalists are seen as active community participants committed to understanding the concrete life of their community from the inside out.

The social narrative we call news is an agent of deliberation. In Glasser's conversational model of journalism, publicly told stories engage others by creating shared experiences and fostering mutual understanding (1991; see 1999b). In these terms, public journalism has made the facilitative role the most nuanced and explicit. Also called civic or community journalism, public journalism follows in the tradition of social responsibility theory and development communication, but is more up front with its citizen-based values and is more ambitious about actually understanding the community.[3] From this perspective, journalism is an avowedly democratic practice that "stimulate[s] citizen deliberation and build[s] public understanding of issues, and . . . report[s] on major public problems in a way that advances public knowledge of possible solutions and the values served by alternative courses of action" (Lambeth, Meyer, and Thorson 1998, 17). Such journalism differs from conventional journalism in seeing people as a public rather than individual consumers, "as potential actors in arriving at democratic solutions to public problems." Public journalism goes "beyond the limited mission of telling the news to a broader mission of helping public life to go well" (Merritt 1995, 113–14; see Merritt and McCombs 2004).[4]

In the midst of weakening demand for serious news, political news losing its credibility, and flagging interest in civic affairs, media professionals and academics began searching in the 1990s for a new kind of journalism. "They set out to understand democracy in a new way, so they could see journalism from another angle: as democracy's cultivator, as well as its chronicler" (Rosen 1999b, 8). Public journalism was born from the need for a more robust public and greater citizen involvement. Edmund Lambeth describes this form of journalism as listening sympathetically to the stories and ideas of citizens and choosing frames for them that best stimulate the people's deliberation and build public understanding of the issues (Lambeth 1998, 17).

While the movement spawned by public journalism has its roots in the United States, similar "experiments [are being] carried out by media houses around the world," attempting to engage citizens in interactive democracy. In Latin America, "more public journalism projects have been carried out than in any other continent" (Mwangi 2001, 24–25; 2007). *El Nuevo Dia* and *La Razon* have identified corruption as the main threat to democracy in Bolivia and are highlighting citizens' responsibility to come to grips with it. In Costa Rica, Radio Reloj, the leading news radio station, and San Jose's Channel 6 television station are engaged in community forums. Journalists in Kingston, Jamaica, involve citizens in serious efforts to take on health problems such as HIV and prostate cancer (Mwangi 2001, 26; 2007). Since the mid-1980s, "many Guatemalan newspapers have enlarged and invigorated the public sphere by reporting and commenting on the peace process, and by opening their pages to a variety of public opinion" (Crocker 2000, 113).

James Fishkin (2007; see 1992; see Fishkin and Laslett 2003; Ackerman and Fishkin 2005) of Stanford University's Center for Deliberative Democracy has carried out successful experiments in facilitating democratic deliberation. He advocates deliberative polling, in which citizens inform themselves on the issues ahead of time and then discuss them together before a national television audience, with the conclusions reported in the major newspapers. In October 2007, a European Union–wide deliberative opinion poll was held in Brussels from a Friday afternoon through a Sunday evening. A total of 362 citizens from all twenty-seven EU countries deliberated in twenty-two languages on key social and foreign policy issues, under the title *Tomorrow's Europe* and hosted by Fishkin's "deliberative poll" and *Notre Europe,* with twenty cosponsors across Europe. The delegates were chosen by country in proportion to their representation in the EU parliament, from a random sample of thirty-five hundred citizens who took a comprehensive questionnaire to qualify for final selection. The pre- and posttests indicated that as the event concluded the participants were dramatically more informed and changed their views about a number of important issues relating to the European Union's future. Participants from the twelve newer and fifteen older member states generally started with different opinions but tended to converge on such issues as economic reform, international trade, enlargement, and the European Union's role in the world (see www.tomorrow.stanfo.eu; http://cdd.stanford.edu/polls/eu/index/html).

"We the People Wisconsin" (WTPW) is a facilitative project operating in Madison, Wisconsin, since 1992—the oldest civic journalism enterprise in the United States. The rationale for WTPW is deliberation. Television, newspapers, and radio collaborate to air to the community town hall meetings, hearings, debates, and citizen juries on policy issues and elections (see www.wtpeople.com). For the principals of WTPW, its basic mission is "to facilitate conversations and to help reestablish the link between people and politics. . . . ["We the People"] views [itself] as a catalyst for stronger community conversation and therefore for stronger public life" (Friedland, Sotirovic, and Daily 1998, 202; see Friedland 2003; Sirianni and Friedland 2005, ch. 5). The longevity of the project gives it notoriety, and the quality of its televised deliberations makes it credible. It has generated coalitions across a wide range of economic, religious, political, and voluntary grassroots groups. However, as the project's scope is statewide, it has been less successful at generating local problem solving. This project demonstrates how media-driven deliberation can be institutionalized cooperatively, though it self-consciously uses a strategy of weak deliberation (Barber 1984; see 1998; 2007) in which "there is no intention to organize deliberation beyond the presentation of individual projects" (Friedland et al. 1998, 206; see Friedland 2004).

In journalism's facilitative role, media practitioners do not reduce social issues to financial and administrative problems for politicians but enable the public to come to terms with their everyday experiences themselves. They aim for "writing that moves a public to meaningful judgment and meaningful action"; they exhibit a "form of textuality that turns citizens into readers and readers into persons who take democratic action in the world" (Denzin 1997, 282; see 2003, 106–30).

Civil Society

The media facilitate civil society. They actively support and strengthen democratic participation in neighborhoods, churches, and organizations outside the state and the market (Arato 2000; 2005; Cohen and Arato 1992; Edwards 2004; Sandel 1998; 2005, ch. 5). Since Habermas, theorists of deliberative democracy have disputed the proper range of deliberation. Rather than being limited to conventional government institutions, as Joshua Cohen (2002) and others would restrict it, deliberation here includes all civic, professional, and cultural associations. This is a normative claim, in that the media do not simply report on civil society's activities and institutions but seek to promote and improve them. The civil society argument is considered a "strategy to remedy a number of the political ills that plague contemporary politics" (Fierlbeck 1998, 148; see Miller and Walzer 2007; Walzer 1995; 2004, 66–89).

The pivotal historical figure in developing the concept of civil society was G. W. F. Hegel. In the early nineteenth century, he identified self-supporting citizens with their own centers of gravity as entities distinct from the political state on the one hand and from the family on the other. Fierlbeck (150) refers to Hegel's *Philosophy of Right*. Taylor (1991) puts Hegel's notion in the context of other political theorists, principally Locke and Montesquieu. Reidel (1984) describes civil society in terms of Hegel himself. For Kaviraj and Khilnani, Hegel also is "the pivotal figure in shaping contemporary understandings" of civil society (2001, 23), while they remind us that it is an old term that "entered into English usage via the Latin translation, *societas civilis,* of Aristotle's *koinonia politike*" (17). In addition, their comprehensive review locates other traditions besides the German strand running through Hegel and Marx, such as those of the Scottish and French Enlightenment (chs. 4 and 5). Kaviraj and Khilnani also describe how intellectuals in various non-Western countries are "infusing new and complex life" (12) into the concept—in India, Latin America, the Middle East, China, Africa, and Southeast Asia (chs. 8–14).

Habermas describes civil society as "nongovernmental and noneconomic connections and voluntary associations that anchor communication structures of the public sphere in the society component of the life world" (1996a, 366–67). A precondition of civil societies is that members have transient character, are mutable, "able to choose political loyalties and public affiliations," and thus have "the capacity of being open to discursive persuasion and deliberation" (Kaviraj and Khilnani 2001, 28). In this sense, healthy democracies depend on an "energetic civil society which is able to force issues and perspectives onto a public agenda" (Stevenson 1999, 43).[5] The Sudanese Council of Churches has broadcast its *Radio Voice of Hope* (www.radiovoiceofhope.net) to millions of displaced persons in southern Sudan during years of war, mistrust, and political conflict (Herfkens 2001, 6; see Lippman 2007). The League of Women Voters has advocated a wide variety of civic innovations in child care and the environment. Authoritarian states insist on a quiescent and depoliticized civil society instead.

The public sphere is located in civil society. Therefore, among contemporary North American philosophers such as Charles Taylor, Michael Sandel, Michael Walzer, and Robert Bellah, the concern is not the overwhelming power of the state but "the nature of citizenship itself" (Fierlbeck 1998, 153; see 2006). For Sandel, liberal freedom in the Lockean tradition presumes "a neutral framework of rights within which people can choose their own values and ends." The civil society is built on "republican freedom," which "requires a formative politics, a politics that cultivates in citizens the qualities of character that self-government requires" (Sandel 1998, 58; see 2005, ch. 5). In Taylor's terms, advocating the ideal civil society pushes us toward the "norm of self-determination" rather than marginalizing the political. Retrieving a rich and complex understanding of civil society gives us a framework for moving forward on human rights (Taylor 1991, 131; see Benhabib 2006, 13–81; Fierlbeck 1998, 173).

At the last World Conference on Human Rights, for example, in Vienna in the summer of 1993, 171 states were represented, but 800 nongovernmental organizations (NGOs) were also—two-thirds of them at the grassroots level. The UN General Assembly, not the NGOs, set the agenda and endorsed the resolutions. Moreover, the committee drafting the final declaration excluded the NGOs, and their three thousand representatives were largely sealed off on the first floor of the Austria Center from the official delegates of participating governments. Despite these limitations, human rights agencies and organizations exercised enormous influence. The voice and expertise of NGO delegates explicitly shaped the assessment of how much had been accomplished since the 1948 Universal Declaration of Human Rights. New ground would not have been broken, extending the definition of human rights to children, indigenous people, and women, without the presence of the NGOs Human Rights Watch, Amnesty International, the International Human Rights Law Group, and the Global Campaign for Women's Human Rights, among others. United Nations mechanisms for defending human rights would not have been strengthened without their presence either.[6] Meanwhile, the NGOs' knowledge of human rights history, specific abuses, UN machinery, additional resources, and strategies were indispensable to the news media in their coverage of the convention. The voices of civil society were crucial in developing an understanding of the ways democratic participation and sustainable development must be integrated.

Civil society is not merely "those human networks that exist independently of, if not anterior to, the political state" (Isaac 1993, 357; see Fierlbeck 1998, 154; Taylor 1991, 117). The "composition of state and civil society" is a "complex relationship rather than a clear opposition. . . . Politicians, military officers, and bureaucrats belong to churches or clubs or cultural associations" and thus do not always make "decisions on behalf of the state that are purely divorced from the interests of civil society" (Fierlbeck 1998, 155–56). Civil associations lobby the government; and trade unions, for example, galvanized democratization in South Africa. In terms of civil society's genealogy, some versions of the concept are concerned about authoritarian states, "while those in industrial democracies tend to focus on the political apathy and nihilism of modern urban life" (162).

Gordon White accounts for these complexities by adopting a broad definition of civil society but insisting that each manifestation be understood in its particular context. Civil society, in his terms, is "the intermediate associational realm between the state and family populated by organizations which . . . are formed voluntarily by members of society to protect or extend their interests or values." All such associations must be explained in terms of their "relationship to the broader socio-economic structure" in which they are embedded (White 1994, 378, 386). Deliberation is never free of power (Cohen and Arato 1994, 23). The civil society is not an ideal arena absent of coercion. It includes such nongovernmental international associations as Doctors Without Borders, Friends of the Earth, World Peace Federation, World-Watch on Deforestation, Stockholm International Peace Research Institute, the International Red Cross, the Roman Catholic Church, Human Rights Watch, Greenpeace, Amnesty International, the Coalition for an International Criminal Court, and the International Campaign to Ban Land Mines. Women's movements and organized labor also are civil society associations. All of them of any consequence "contain inequalities and domination," and their "internal balances of power" typically determine their effectiveness as agents of democratization (White 1994, 385).[7]

Cultural Context

The media facilitate the cultural conditions of democratic life. Through communication, human beings not only exchange goods and services but vivify their beliefs and presumptions about the world. A "secure cultural context" is increasingly recognized as resisting the individualizing forces of liberal democracy (Taylor 1992b; see 2007). For Benhabib, Rawls's political conception of democracy is rooted "in the state and its organizations, including first and foremost the legal sphere and its institutions" (2002, 109). She argues that his model of public reason gives us a restricted agenda. It pushes too many issues that involve our cultural lives "into the private sphere and precludes them from public consideration" (110). Her version of civic republicanism—what she calls deliberative democracy—includes a second, cultural track, though not as a separate and isolated "background culture" (111; Rawls's label); dualism is "analytically untenable." The noncoercive political process to which democracies subscribe cannot be isolated from their religious, philosophical, and moral dimensions: "gender equality, bodily integrity, freedom of the person, education of children," and the practices of minority subcultures (111). There is no "baseline of a nonpolitical culture in a liberal society" (120). A "vital interaction" exists between the formal institutions of liberal democracies like legislatures, the courts, and the bureaucracy and the unofficial processes of civil society as articulated through the media and social movements and associations" (121). In the discourse ethics that undergirds Benhabib's multicultural democracy, a society's members are required to create "public practices, dialogues and spaces" for "controversial normative questions in which all those affected can participate" (114; see 2006, 13–44).

In other words, culture provides the environment in which autonomy and rights are meaningful. Human identity is constituted through the sociocultural realm. Cultures are the collective beliefs and customs within which we communicate, and therefore the fundamental "context within which we make our political choices" (Tully 1995, 5; see Brett and Tully 2006). While the political, economic, and cultural dimensions of public life are thoroughly intermixed, cultural practices and institutions also need to be understood and critiqued on their own terms. Exclusion from housing or employment is political and economic but is simultaneously infected by racism, gender bias, and what Thorstein Veblen called conspicuous consumption. "Economic deprivation, political marginalization and cultural disrespect" operate in and through one another (Stevenson 1999, 50). A concern with poverty involves struggling with dependency and a lack of dignity. Since Raymond Williams and Walter Benjamin, we have recognized that culture must be both democratized and politicized. Widely shared public culture is a major arena for both antidemocratic oppression and social transformation.

Global broadcasting represents these entangled dimensions. Ownership structures, policy, content, and technology need to be understood in themselves and together (see Vincent, Nordenstreng, and Traber 1999). Cultural issues are also crucial. The technological enterprise is a human process, value-laden throughout. Valuing penetrates all technological activity, from selecting what needs to address and what materials to use through the processes of design and fabrication and to the resulting tools and products. Technology proceeds out of our whole human experience and is directed by our ultimate commitments. The problems of one group are addressed, but not all. Certain resources are used and not others. Arnold Pacey (1992; see 2001) reminds us that today's technologies, including the media, are rooted in deep-seated beliefs about expertise, unlimited natural resources, and progress. As a result, the values of magnitude, power, and efficiency direct the technological process as a whole at present, and global broadcasting specifically. And if we want to see a revolution toward more humane technologies that meet society's basic needs rather than serve productivity and technical virtuosity, then a revolution is needed in the cultural context in which technologies are embedded. When we turn the mythologies of industrial progress, engineering expertise, and neutral reality on their head, new forms of technology will emerge as a result. In fulfilling its facilitative role, the news media must represent the cultural values underlying the industrial world—not only its mechanics and functions on the surface.

In their facilitative role, media professionals do not merely emphasize cultural institutions such as libraries, museums, concert halls, educational systems, and public broadcasting. Their focus is not limited to electronic music, cinema, television, feature magazines, theatre, and the arts. They do not cover only national holidays and institutional anniversaries. Culture is also a crucial dimension of our citizenship that requires nurturing and reflection. As cultural beings, the verbal and visual symbols of everyday life, images, representations, and myths make social relations meaningful for us and locate us in time and space. This semiotic material needs to be woven into our news narrative.

When we enact the facilitative role in reporting on human activities and institutions, we examine a creative process whereby people produce and maintain forms of life and society, as well as systems of meaning and value. This creative activity, the process by which humans establish their heritage in time and space, is grounded in the ability to build cultural forms through symbols that express the will to live purposefully, and the reporter's first obligation is getting inside this process. Creativity is unique to the human species, and narratives that are valid pay circumspect attention to this distinctive aspect of social life. Knowing local languages in their nuance and complexity is crucial for representing communities and intermediate associations. Understanding religious language and ritual, for example, is essential. Symbolic forms are a critical element in our total humanization, and the evils of starvation, inadequate housing, health hazards, and unemployment cannot be solved in a culture of silence.

People arbitrate their own presences in the world. Human beings are not puppets on a string but live actors on a stage who improvise as the drama unfolds. They do not merely respond to stimuli but rather live by interpreting experience through the agency of culture. This is as true of microscopic forms of human interaction (e.g., conversation and neighborhood celebrations) as of the broadest human initiatives (e.g., attempts to build religious systems of ultimate meaning and significance). Communication is the catalytic agent, the driving force in cultural formation; therefore, the media are not neutral purveyors of information but agents of acculturation. All symbolic modes are culture builders—the dramatic arts, news discourse, literature, and electronic entertainment.[8] We are born into an intelligible and interpreted world, and we struggle to use these interpretations imaginatively for making sense of our lives and institutions. The ability to plan one's life, to choose commitments and pursuits, makes a community's existence worthwhile. "On this account, planning one's own life is not valuable because it promotes some further valuable end, but rather . . . the self-directed life is intrinsically good (Reaume 2000, 246). The concept of humans as cultural beings gives us the "starting hypothesis" that "all human cultures . . . have something important to say to all human beings" (Taylor et al. 1994, 66–67). Thus the media's facilitative role is dedicated to understanding the possibilities and contentions of language in human existence.

In Rousseau's terms, democracy is not an aggregate of atomized interests but the collective determination of what is best for the society as a whole. The moral framework of a society is the basis for respecting the moral worth of its members (Fierlbeck 1998, 89). In that sense, communally shared conceptions of the good have priority over individual rights. Appealing to rights tends to justify selfishness. Insisting on rights makes citizens' choices arbitrary—the expression of one's personal preferences that have no more validity than any others. Rights provide us no framework when communities face emergencies and crises. As societies fragment and break down, rights language is mute. For individual rights to matter beyond oneself, they cannot be separated from shared meanings and mutual belief in their importance. The common good is the axis around which communities have identity and purpose.

Social entities are considered moral orders and not merely lingual structures. Societies are not formed by language alone. There are no selves-in-relation without a moral commitment. Our widely shared moral intuitions—respect for the dignity of others, for instance—are developed through discourse within a community. A self exists within "webs of interlocution," and all self-interpretation implicitly or explicitly "acknowledges the necessarily social origin of any and all their conceptions of the good and so of themselves" (Mulhall and Swift 1996, 112–13). Moral frameworks are as fundamental for orienting us in social space as the need to "establish our bearings in physical space" (113). According to Charles Taylor, "Developing, maintaining and articulating" our moral intuitions and reactions are as natural for humans as learning up and down, right and left (1989, 27–29). Freud argued in *Totem and Taboo* that societies create taboo boundaries to distinguish themselves from others. But they also raise up totems to give themselves aspiration and identity. The news media as facilitator promotes discussion of these social characteristics and ideals.

Public life cannot be facilitated in technical terms only; journalists must speak of moral issues in appropriately moral discourse. And when they critique vacuous or unjust relations, they must do so in terms of common values that have wide acceptance in the community as a whole. In this sense, media professionals participate in a community's ongoing process of moral articulation. In fact, culture's continued existence depends on identifying and defending its normative base. Therefore, public texts must enable us "to discover truths about ourselves"; narratives ought to "bring a moral compass into readers' lives" by accounting for things that matter to them (Denzin 1997, 284; see 242–62). Communities are woven together by narratives that invigorate their common understanding of good and evil, happiness and reward, the meaning of life and death. Recovering and refashioning moral discourse help to amplify our deepest humanness.

Moral issues are concentrated in the proceedings of truth and reconciliation commissions (see Hayner 2002; Truth and Reconciliation Commission 2006). Nelson Mandela appointed South Africa's Truth and Reconciliation Commission in 1995 "to discover the dark facts of apartheid . . . [and] report them to South Africa and the world." Whereas most of such earlier commissions—including those in Uganda, Bolivia, Argentina, Zimbabwe, Uruguay, the Philippines, and Chile—did not hear testimony in public, "for fear that it might be too inflammatory or arouse retaliation from the ousted military officers (who were still around) or their patrons, the South African Commission . . . insisted on public as well as private testimony, and the public interrogation of accused perpetrators by victims as well as prosecutorial figures from the Commission's staff, and by the commissioners themselves" (Rotberg 2000, 5). The Commission, chaired by the Anglican archbishop Desmond Tutu, also facilitated public involvement by gathering testimony in various locations throughout the country, making the proceedings accessible, maintaining a website, and responding fully and readily to public criticism. Radio and television "in many of the country's languages extensively covered" the Commission's activities, "especially the hearings on individual human rights violations and amnesty applications" (Crocker 2000, 101).

In the spirit of civic republicanism, the Commission's activities educated South African society generally, even before its official findings could be presented to the president and the parliament. "Widely disseminated verbatim accounts became the content of an ongoing national drama. . . . Unlike a trial, or a series of trials," the Commission expressed the range of behavior and issues "that society needs to judge and condemn, and to which it needs to be reconciled" (Rotberg 2000, 5, 9). Actual murders and murderers were unmasked and unmarked graves located. In its facilitative role, the press recognized that "proper remembrances fulfill the collective needs of badly damaged societies. . . . Forgetting reinforces losses of self-esteem among victims and even among victims as a group" (7).[9] In fact, public communicators played a crucial role. They endeavored to "lay bare the mind of even the worst perpetrators, while sensitively seeking to understand the suffering of victims and/or survivors in as comprehensive a manner" as professionally possible. It was said that citizens could not make intelligent and informed decisions about the reconciling process without "honest, blow-by-blow reporting which conveys the emotion, the atmosphere, and the angst of the moment." This kind of exposure of the victim or survivor to the perpetrator and vice versa is indispensable for "creating a climate within which reconciliation can occur" (Villa-Vicencio 2001, 31, 36).

As the cases of Argentina and Chile make clear, the work of truth commissions "can be compatible with trials and punishments" (Crocker 2000, 104). However, their rationale is not criminal justice per se but the morally ambitious goal of providing restorative justice. When done with depth and sophistication, while having no power to execute punitive justice, systems of communication institute "corrective moral justice by putting the record straight" (Villa-Vicencio 2001, 36). "Truth commissions have struggled with basic questions about what justice requires. . . . Out of these struggles are emerging new vocabularies of truth and justice as well as a new institutional repertoire for pursuing them." Truth commissions "direct a national morality play that places victims of injustice on center stage" while pursuing "profound and nuanced moral ends" (Kiss 2000, 70).

Pluralism

The media facilitate pluralism. For Hannah Arendt, the defining characteristic of democracy is plurality (Bohman and Rehg 1997, 401). Likewise, Nancy Fraser argues for a plurality of publics to prevent a unitary Other from dominating the political order. Already in the nineteenth century, John Stuart Mill identified "the tyranny of the majority" as an endemic problem for democratic societies. Even with today's demands for global thinking, citizenship ought to be what Held (2004) calls "multilevel and multidimensional" (114). For democracy to be deliberative, "decision-making should be decentralized as much as possible, maximizing each person's opportunity to influence the social conditions that shape his or her life" (101). The principle of inclusiveness "requires diverse and multiple democratic public forums for its suitable enactment" (102).[10]

The contemporary drive for cultural pluralism is potentially an obstacle to deliberative democracy, and therefore the media's challenge is to make "democratic life more vibrant"—that is, diverse—by improving "the public use of reason" (Bohman 2000, 72). The media's facilitative role under modern social conditions is not to be directed toward uniform public opinion but toward a multicultural mosaic and multifaceted governance.[11] The aim is a "public of publics" rather than "a distinctively unified and encompassing" aggregate of all individuals (140). Nation-states are composed of a variety of "polycentric and decentered" (148) communities, within which the interactors are reflexive and participatory.[12] Democracy is a "union of social unions" constructed of trade-offs and accommodation through "concessions of one's own for equal ones by others" (79–80).

The media's task in facilitating cultural pluralism cannot be reduced to settling political disputes (see Macedo 2003). When American citizens debate tax cuts or Europeans debate monetary policy within the European Union, they typically do not question the role of private property within the nation-state or the validity of elected governments. In addition to a shared framework, there is general agreement about the democratic procedures for settling differences politically (Bohman 2000, 73). But fostering cultural pluralism operates on a deeper level. Dealing with the political status of minority cultures, for example, often involves fundamental differences in moral assumptions and political processes. Some dilemmas are created by "irreconcilable values"—using Rawls's term—and raise a basic question about the role of reason and information, "if standards of rationality are themselves subject to deeply conflicting interpretations" (73). As James Bohman argues, the singular, procedural view of public reason Rawls advocates is not adequate for facilitating such pluralism. Rawls presumes a liberal constitutional state and "a common human reason," that is, "the capacities and procedures of reason, such as drawing inferences, weighing evidence, and balancing competing considerations" (79; Rawls 1993, 200). Habermas's more dynamic and complex understanding of public reason, where the "pluralism of convictions and worldviews" is not bracketed "from the outset" (Habermas 1995, 118–19), is closer to the way dilemmas and conflicts can be addressed fruitfully in pluralist democracies.[13]

Most democratic theorists since Rousseau have considered deep moral conflicts intractable. As Bohman notes, "moral and epistemic diversity often go hand in hand" (2000, 86). Differences in moral outlook are entangled in different assessments of the evidence, varying data, and disagreements over appropriate public language. In these instances, "appeal to a common human reason can still fail to produce agreement even when agents are not irrational" (86). And Rawls's "method of avoidance" in such cases is typically counterproductive. Certainly pragmatic strategies, such as a "gag rule" or "self-binding" device to remove some issues from public discussion, obviously do not enable deliberation but contradict it (74). Therefore, a dynamic and pluralistic framework does not seek a singular, impartial standpoint that every citizen is expected to endorse (Rawls 1993, 217). Rather, the media facilitate a public discourse that takes all interpretations into account, without aiming toward the convergence of an abstract point of view. No single norm of reasonableness is presupposed, and deliberation goes beyond trade-offs and making concessions that compromise people's beliefs. In a pluralist democracy, "agents can come to an agreement with one another for different publicly accessible reasons. . . . The ideal of public reason . . . permits rather than denies or avoids, moral conflict and differences in democratic politics" (Bohman 2000, 83–84).

Ronald Dworkin (1993) proposes a pluralistic agreement on abortion to which each side assents for different reasons. In his framework, "the intrinsic value of human life" is recognized without contradicting the "procreative autonomy" of women. Dworkin's proposal is public and pluralistic. "Each side can find its moral reasons represented, interpreted and assessed. . . . Citizens' values and conceptions of the good life are put up for public debate. . . . It is far from the method of avoidance" and in fact provides an "expanded framework for deliberating about differences" (Bohman 2000, 92). The terms of the debate are widened beyond the values of individual rights in procedural liberalism, with the expectation that original moral beliefs need not be abandoned in the continuing search for compromise or a new moral framework. When moral disagreements are reflected on dialogically, a larger universe of discourse emerges or, at a minimum, "deliberators may achieve mutual respect and accommodation as they exercise plural public reason" (Habermas 1996a, 411). Those who are morally prolife could conclude they can be coherently prochoice politically, and both sides can learn to tolerate each other's position, given the inconclusive biological debates over the exact origins of life.

Christian Scientists refuse to allow conventional medical treatment of their treatable diseases on the grounds that diagnosis or medical invasion will cause disease to occur. The conflict is not over medical facts but different assumptions about mind and matter. Adult Christian Scientists can exempt themselves from the healing process on the grounds of adult autonomy, but for their children no legislative compromise is possible. Christian Science could conclude that living with this disjunction in a democratic society provides enough other benefits to make withdrawal unwise, as long as they can continue to contest the system as a cultural minority (see Bohman 2000, 76–77, 262). Pluralist and administrative liberalism (see chapter 3), in Joshua Cohen's terms, appeal to "nothing but the truth but not to the whole truth" (1993, 283). However, when deliberation is inclusive and dynamic, agreement in the broader arena enables cultural pluralism to prosper. And sometimes within that larger domain of agreements, a mutual belief emerges to move democratic life forward. Debates over pornography, for instance, ordinarily revolve around the rights of free expression versus moral offensiveness. However, deliberation focuses on a common framework of discrimination against women.[14] When both sides agree on gender equality, it becomes obvious that brutalizing women in hardcore pornography subordinates them, dominates them, and denies them equal opportunity. And on the same principle of gender equality, erotic realism in art is acceptable—that is, sensuality within a context of affinity could be aesthetically authentic and not exploitative.

The media also have a strategic role in facilitating dynamic and pluralist deliberation regarding minority subcultures. This aim is legitimate, despite the near intractability of persistent inequality that results from the history of conquest of the first peoples of Australia, Canada, and the United States, among others. Clearly political conflicts over mineral rights, taxation policies, education, and governance need careful and comprehensive press coverage. But what are the public bases of pluralism when fundamental differences exist over the very meaning of inclusion and citizenship (Kymlicka 1989; 2001)? Guaranteeing equitable and accessible voting does not in itself promote cultural identity. "Monetary solutions tend to benefit each member of the tribal group while providing no real protections or benefits for the cultural goals of the group as a whole" (Bohman 2000, 78).

Recognizing the dialogic, interactive structure of deliberation, in fact, is important in understanding correctly the media's facilitative role. The requirements of dialogue are "the mutual recognition of the deliberative liberties of others," "openness of one's own beliefs to revision," and "continued cooperation in public deliberation even with persistent disagreements" (Bohman 2000, 88–89). The interaction is a process of reflection on conflicting values, with the ongoing goal of creating a common framework and opening new avenues. As Monique Deveaux argues, cultural pluralism requires a thick conception of democracy. Deliberative versions "encourage respect for one another's social differences and cultural identities." They emphasize "reciprocity, political equality and mutual respect—all crucial to meeting basic justice claims" made by a nation's minorities. National and cultural minorities have the "right to challenge and help shape the public and political culture of the society in which they live," and deliberative democracy makes such interaction a sine qua non (Deveaux 2000, 4–5; see 2007, ch. 4).

One such possibility is reconciliation, not as a singular abstraction with the content known in advance but as a negotiation text that suggests alternative ideas and policies. Breaking with the logic of hatred and revenge, in reconciliation new times and spaces are created for dealing with past grievances." The Canadian Charter of rights adopted in 1982, recognizing Quebec and tribal groups as distinct societies, is a rare political example of giving native peoples equal deliberative standing in constructing policy. As we have described, truth and reconciliation commissions can serve as another model of pluralistic deliberation, with reconciliation their axis and inspiration.

As Charles Taylor observes, one dimension of pluralism—what he calls "the politics of recognition"—is a troubling issue for democratic politics. Democratic societies are committed by definition to equal representation for all. Each counts for one; in principle every person is given equal access to the procedures of democratic institutions. Therefore, the crucial question: "Is a democracy letting its citizens down, excluding or discriminating against us in some morally troubling way, when major institutions fail to take account of our particular identities?" (Taylor et al. 1994, 3). In what sense should our specific cultural and social features as Albanians, Buddhists, Jews, the physically disabled, or children publicly matter? Democratic citizens in principle share an equal right to education, police protection, political liberties, religious freedom, due process, and health care. Shouldn't our public institutions treat us as free and equal citizens without regard to race, gender, or religion? Should universities and colleges that are circumspect about fairness and equal opportunity in admissions and the classroom also provide cultural centers and specialized curricula for underrepresented students of color?

The contemporary challenge of recognizing multicultural groups politically has no easy solution—especially in immigrant societies such as the United States and Canada. Perhaps there is a way for democracies to operate on two levels at the same time. While insisting on political neutrality in minimal terms at the polling booth and in taxation and legal protection, in other areas such as education, democratic institutions are free to reflect the values of one or more cultural communities.

Globalization makes the promotion of pluralism a demanding challenge these days (Bohman 2007). By *globalization* is meant a broad set of processes that have "intensified and accelerated" the "movement of people, images, ideas, technologies, and economic and cultural capital across national boundaries" (McCarthy et al. 2003, 444). Modern capitalization drives globalization, as well as the interests, needs, and desires of ordinary people everywhere, with the result that it is sweeping all corners of the contemporary world. These processes are rapidly shrinking spatial relations between hitherto far-flung parts of the planet and deepening "the imbrication of the local in the global and the global in the local" (Giddens 1994, 181–89). The media are generating an explosion of new images, identities, and subjectivities in aesthetic culture generally. But these expanding representational technologies and capacities mean that many people "now express their sense of past, present and future" in terms of popular culture. Humanity cultivates its "interests, needs, desires, and fears in the landscape of the new media." The placeless language "of moral panic and its obverse, the language of panaceas and quick fixes," of e-commerce and technicistic discourse are deluging the modern subject, disempowering ordinary people, and eroding the efflorescence of everyday life in media-saturated societies (McCarthy et al. 2003, 455). A pluralist public realm is being challenged by this hybridization of culture and fragmentation of identity.

A study of government websites in sub-Saharan countries found that they reflect Western interests. Citizens are constructed as exotic others who can be marketed to foreign investors and tourists. The technological logic and aesthetics of the World Wide Web privilege affiliation with Western host institutions, and African authority over and local involvement in the text is ill defined. "Identification can be activated only by acceptance of problematic colonial representations and mostly Western forms of knowledge production" (Furisch and Robins 2002, 203–4). In more general terms, societies of the global South are typically considered cultures with agents. Even in well-meaning accounts of imperialism and colonialism radiating from Europe and North America, there is little recognition of resistance, indigenous struggles, and local alternatives. Non-Caucasians come through as dependent, with minimal talent and limited capacity for self-determining democracy. Therefore, the media ought to represent the voices of justice in children's theatre, aboriginal art, folktales, teen music, poetry, and people's radio (McCarthy 1998, 39–48).

Pluralism presumes a dynamic democratic form in which the public sphere is not a structure but a process of changing and emerging collectives. In order to remain democratic, societies need to be open to popular renewal and new social movements—green networks, ethnic organizations, educational reform, feminist campaigns, and so forth. Pluralism as a normative ideal uncovers the voices of the excluded and marginalized. Difference is discovered against the outpourings of centralized media. TV Globo is a virtual monopoly in Brazil. More than a hundred groups are active in video, developing an alternative communication system from below that allows users to control their own production and distribution. These video groups are spread throughout the country in both rural and urban areas, linked to labor unions, their churches, neighborhoods and cultural associations. Such grassroots movements for pluralism are an educational strategy for social change.

The facilitative role is a response to the fact that human lives are culturally complex and loaded with multiple interpretations. First-rate ethnographic accounts possess the "amount of depth, detail, emotionality, nuance, and coherence that will permit readers to form a critical consciousness. Such texts should also exhibit representational adequacy, including the absence of racial, class, and gender stereotyping" (Denzin 1997, 283). The Global Media Monitoring Project (GMMP) has established the world's largest research and advocacy network, systematically studying in 102 countries the way women's identity and contributions are represented in the news—radio, television, and newspapers. In seeking gender equality in public discourse, the GMMP recognizes that sexism has been embedded long-term in cultures around the world. The project insists on representational adequacy out of concern that old ideas of authority with diminished news-voices for women get in the way of new ideas of community and leadership (see Media and Gender Monitor 2005; Spears, Seydegart, and Gallagher 2000; Turley 2004).

The fundamental challenge for the media in their facilitative role is to foster conscientization—helping citizens gain their own voices and collaborate in their culture's transformation. "The semiotic struggle from below offers an ethics of resistance against the incorporation of people into dominant ideological categories" and media narratives ought to reflect these complexities (Stevenson 1999, 10).

Notes

1. For an overview of the long and complicated history of development communication see Moemeka (1994) and Gunaratne (1998, 292–302). Development journalism was a significant facet of the New World Information and Communication Order debates (cf. Gerbner, Mowlana, and Nordenstreng 1993; Nordenstreng 1984; Traber and Nordenstreng 2002). For a description of the way development journalism has been confused with authoritarian government-controlled media, see Gunaratne (1995).

2. For an elaboration of the various dimensions of authentic participatory communication for development in terms of Paulo Freire and Martin Buber, see Thomas (1994).

3. Lambeth (1998) summarizes these strategies as including but not limited to: "citizen polling to identify major issues on the public's mind; resource panels of both citizens and specialists to help journalists understand the basics of an issue before they immerse themselves in reporting; focus groups with citizens to deepen and give reporters first-hand knowledge of key facets of an issue; open forums to allow the public to begin to engage and work through public issues; and, finally, studies to discover how well media performed" (18).

4. For a thoughtful overview of public journalism's history and rationale, see Rosen (1999b). For an examination of the foundational issues raised by public journalism, see Glasser (1999b). For the most reflective account from a news professional, see Merritt (1995; Merritt and McCombs 2004).

5. Lewis Friedland speaks of civil society as social capital—"those stocks of social trust, norms, and networks that people can draw on to solve common problems. Networks of civic engagement, such as neighborhood associations, sports clubs, and cooperatives, are essential forms of social capital. The more dense these networks, according to social capital theory, the more likely that members of a community will cooperate for mutual benefit" (Friedland, Sotirovic, and Daily 1998, 195–96; see Friedland 2003; 2004; Sirianni and Friedland 2005).

6. For the "Official UN Report of the World Conference on Human Rights," see www.unhchr.ch/huridocda/huridoca.nsf/(Symbol)/WCHR+En?OpenDocument. For the "Documents of the World Conference on Human Rights," see www.unhchr.ch/huridocda/huridoca.nsf/FramePage/WCHR+En?OpenDocument. For information on the Office of the UN High Commissioner for Human Rights, see www.unhchr.ch/map.htm.

7. OneWorldOnline of the One World International Foundation is a civil society space on the Internet devoted to issues of human rights and sustainable development around the world. Launched in 1995, it has a thousand partners, including two hundred community radio and some video/TV members. Partners share their material without cost, making more than 2 million texts available for approximately a million users from over 125 countries. For a description of the OneWorld.net supersite, see Vittachi (2001).

8. Like that of Jacob Burckhardt (*Force and Freedom: Reflections on History),* this definition of culture is semiotic—in contrast to anthropology where culture refers to entire civilizations as complex wholes, and in contrast to traditional parlance, which identifies culture as refined manners. Most definitions of culture are expansive, encompassing virtually all social activity. Culture is thus said to involve technologies, customs, arts, sciences, products, habits, political and social organizations that characterize a people. Such a broad definition is not invoked here, but culture is distinguished from political and social structures, from direct experimental efforts to understand nature (such as chemistry, physics, and astronomy) and from religious institutions. Culture thus is defined as essentially human communicative activities, and refers primarily to the products of the arts and language.

9. Gutmann and Thompson analyze this therapeutic purpose in terms of restorative justice and democratization. "Many citizens (including the victims themselves) may reasonably believe that it is morally inappropriate to forgive people who are unwilling to be punished for their crimes, or unwilling to offer their victims restitution" (2004, 172; see 177–87).

10. Cultural pluralism in civic republicanism, diversity that is both ideological and ethnic, differs fundamentally from pluralist liberalism (see chapter 4). Pluralism in the facilitative role is rooted in positive liberty, whereas in procedural liberalism, pluralism assumes negative liberty, and equality of opportunity is basically a private matter. For the challenge of pluralism transnationally, see Bohman 2007.

11. Held (2004) properly insists on integrating the cultural and political: "De facto status as members of diverse communities needs to be matched by a de jure political status, if the mechanisms and institutions that govern these political spaces are to be brought under the . . . principle of inclusiveness and subsidiarity" (101).

12. Bohman holds out the hope that computer-mediated communication can expand deliberative interaction across national boundaries, thus enabling a more transnational cosmopolitan democracy than the traditional literary national public spheres (2004, 138–51; cf. 2007). For a thoughtful review of the major issues regarding the internet and democracy in a globalizing age, see Hilde (2004).

13. Building on Habermas' more dynamic view, Bohman advances his own complex "plural conception of public reason" for "working out reasonable moral compromises," and Bohman's perspective frames the argument here (2000, 75–105).

14. While not using this example, Charles Anderson calls this "meliorative reason" (1990, 174–76). He seeks to enhance this form of reasoning among public communicators, but does not mean producing a self-evident solution agreeable to all. Journalists skilled in this discourse are suggestive, point to different courses of action rather than reporting false dilemmas or conflict in itself (see Lambeth 1999, 30–31).

8

The Radical Role

The radical role of the media and journalism insists on the absolute equality and freedom of all members of a democratic society in a completely uncompromising way. Too often, in societies based on the competitive market principle, great imbalances of wealth, education, and access to information and communication are accepted as simply the rewards of personal initiative. Journalism in the radical role makes every effort to ensure that no injustice is ever tolerated. The radical democratic commitment works for the continual elimination of concentrations of social power to enable every person to participate equally in all societal decisions. Professionally, journalists are called on to encourage not just superficial changes, such as voting procedures, but changes in the core of the existing social institutions. There may be a focus on particular forms of discrimination and defense of particular groups of the voiceless and disenfranchised, but the long-range goal is a society of universal recognition of human rights for all.

The monitorial role typically takes a given power structure for granted and provides the systematic information needed to make such social configurations work. However, the radical role recognizes that power holders impede the flow of information and that it is necessary to change the system of public communication so that less powerful groups can get the information they need. Radical journalism seeks to help minorities articulate an alternative set of goals that represent the needs and just moral claims of all, especially the marginalized, the poor, and the dispossessed. The role of journalists is to challenge the injustices perpetrated by hegemonic alliances and to propose instead a new order and support movements opposing these injustices.

The radical role attempts to expose the conflict of interest between those who dominate the political-economic conditions and cultural values of a society and those who have little influence over these conditions. Journalism in the dominant media may try to obscure these conflicts of interest; radical journalism not only exposes them but points out the injustices and contradictions in these conflicts. It also sides with those who are developing forms of resistance and advocacy against the dominant power holders. Thus, the radical media are by definition partisan.

The radical role rests on the view that there is a political-economic power structure in society that tends to produce a hegemony of the privileged few over the interests of the majority of ordinary people. The underprivileged may or may not be concerned about this structural imbalance. Whenever they are concerned, they constitute an active social force for emancipation and empowerment—either a moderate force for systemic reform or a revolutionary force for overturning the system. If the underprivileged are not concerned and are indifferent to change, according to this view, they have been socialized into passivity or a false consciousness. In this case, the process of emancipation must be triggered by activists and minority movements. Accordingly, the radical media support activist and avant-garde movements that try to liberate intellectually repressed or indoctrinated people, helping them to participate in the process of democratic governance.

From the seventeenth to the nineteenth centuries, a radical or revolutionary role for the press was part of political and religious reform movements that created the conditions for contemporary democratic societies. In the twentieth century, the politically focused press was transformed into mass-distribution commercial media that operate as a capitalist enterprise responding to the hunger for profits of investors who may care little for the media's responsibilities in a democratic society. These predominantly commercial media have been integrated into a market-driven mainstream that has less and less space for traditional radicalism spearheaded by political movements or political parties.

Since the collapse of Communism in Eastern Europe and with the globalization of market logic, the radical role is no longer tied so much to institutional parties but rather to new movements based on excluded social identities, such as feminists, ecologists, and ethnic and racial minorities. This shift of radicalism's main locus from institutional politics to issue and identity oriented movements has its parallel in the evolving theories of civil society (Cohen and Arato 1992) and of postmodern politics (Pulkkinen 2000) and in such concepts as emergent publics (Angus 2001).

These new centers of radical empowerment resort to alternative media (Atton 2004), community media (Howley 2005), and other forms of oppositional expression, outside the orbit of mainstream media (Couldry and Curran 2003). Less challenging versions of alternative media are supported by national or international media policies, giving minorities (ethnic, linguistic, cultural, and political) access to and means for informational and cultural expression. In such cases it is no longer self-evident that we are talking about truly radical media, since after all they are integrated into the sociopolitical system at large. In that sense, there is a continuum of degrees of opposition by the media to the prevailing power structure. In fact, some of the alternative and community media represent such mild versions of radicalism that they could fit equally well in the facilitative category. Admittedly, there is a gray area of mixed roles between the poles of facilitative and radical, but it is still worth upholding the ideal types at the conceptual level.

In general terms, the rationale of the radical role is to expose to public opinion the concentration of social power, especially regarding the democratic procedures of collective decision making. This implies a persuasive dimension, with attempts to mobilize public opinion and public action toward the redistribution of social power. Much of this mobilization is to point out the harmful effects of the concentration of social power and, conversely, the benefits of a redistribution of social power.

Such consciousness-raising regarding power structures requires media that are more participatory and dialogical than the conventional media—even beyond the level reached by the facilitative role. In a truly democratic system the media must expose not only abuses of power but also the causes and consequences of power concentrations, helping the public to see avenues of action to redistribute social power. It is not enough to have brave but isolated voices to do this; the target is ultimately society at large, with prospects for structural change.

Therefore, "radical" refers here to a perspective that literally goes to the roots of the power relations in society, challenging the hegemony of those in power and offering an alternative vision not just for some building blocks but for the whole structure of society. We do not use the term "critical" to denote this oppositional role of the media, because a degree of critical distance from power structures is also presupposed by the monitorial and facilitative roles. Moreover, "critical" has come to carry so many meanings that it easily misses the point of fundamental challenge, which is better described as "radical." Yet it is important to acknowledge the general axiom that science is basically a reflexive critique with "no place for the absolutist mind," as Cees Hamelink points out in his contribution to the opening issue of *Communication, Culture and Critique* (2008, 3). Slavko Splichal reminds us that being critical is the essence of what the public sphere means, and it ultimately leads to the universal right to communicate (2008, 29).

In this context, journalism in the radical role seeks to redistribute the social power from the privileged (typically few) to the underprivileged (typically many). In a rough classification of ideologies into three—conservative, reformist, and revolutionary—we are dealing here with revolutionary ideology: journalism as an instrument for challenging and changing political and economic systems. The monitorial and facilitative roles represent reformist ideology: the media as instruments for improving the system. The collaborative role represents conservative ideology: the media as active instruments for preserving the system. Radical journalism was a departure from both bourgeois elite journalism and from the emerging commercial mass press. It was typical of the nineteenth century in most of the Western world, with revolutionary movements in each country with its own particular conditions and timetables. As Jane Chapman has demonstrated (2005, 11), radicalism, along with political repression and economic change, emerges as one of the basic elements in comparative media history.

Indeed, radical journalism constitutes a crucial chapter in media history. Even the United States has a rich tradition of media radicalism—not so much in the form of revolutionary media as such but more as radical criticism of the mainstream commercial media, as documented by McChesney and Scott (2004) and by Berry and Theobald (2006). But the closer we come to the contemporary world, the less there is left of original radicalism in the media landscape. Radical journalism has been more and more integrated into a nonradical or even conservative mainstream. In general, the revolutionary movements and their radical journalism present a history of "rise and incorporation" (Conboy 2004, 88).

However, radical journalism still is to be found also in today's media—not only in minority media but also in sections of the so-called mainstream media that choose an independent line and provide platforms for radical criticism of established power on specific matters. Accordingly, we have to distinguish between radical media and radical journalism and acknowledge the fact that although in the contemporary world there are few truly radical media, radical journalism as a phenomenon has survived and is manifested in certain forms of public debate.

Radical Tradition

Historically, the idea of a radical role leads us to Marx and his evolution from reformist social democrat, striving for freedom, including press freedom, to revolutionary communist, striving for hegemony of the working class (see Hardt 2001). In this respect we are indeed dealing with a "Marxist theory of the press." On the other hand, it is fundamentally misleading to associate the radical role with the communist system, especially that of the former Soviet Union, as *Four Theories* did. The countries that used to call their regimes "real socialism" actually could hardly be said to have realized the original Marxist project. The theoretical roots of the radical role generated both the precommunist societies of the nineteenth century and the Western ideologies of the twentieth century.

An essential aspect of radicalism is captured by the phrase "ruthless criticism," which the young Karl Marx introduced in the 1840s to highlight his view that the true social criticism of the day "must not be afraid of its own conclusions, nor of conflict with the powers that be" (Solomon and McChesney 1993, 1). The same approach has inspired the so-called neo-Marxist schools, which gained prominence in the media scholarship of the post-1960s (Hardt 1992; Pietilä 2005; Schiller 1996). This intellectual movement—known by various names, including "critical theory" and "political economy"—had many variants but always remained faithful to the idea of ruthless criticism, in the sense of exposing what most people fail to see.

Actually the idea of the media's radical role is best captured by tracing the evolution of this approach rather than trying to establish a simple textbook definition. This can be done conveniently with the assistance of collections such as Durham and Kellner (2001): the evolution begins with Karl Marx and Friedrich Engels and their thesis that "the class which is the ruling *material* force in society, is at the same time its ruling *intellectual* force" (39–42). Next came Antonio Gramsci and his notions of ideology, hegemony, and counterhegemony (43–47), and the Frankfurt School of Theodor Adorno, Walter Benjamin, Max Horkheimer, and others, who introduced the concept of "culture industries" as vehicles for diverting creative human energy into the service of soulless commercialism (48–101).

While Marx and Engels, and Gramsci, developed the perspective of a dominant class opposed by an energetic radical movement that inspired class struggle, the Frankfurt School instead promoted the gloomy prospect that "media culture simply reproduced the existing society and manipulated mass audiences into obedience" (Durham and Kellner 2001, 9). Jürgen Habermas, the post–Frankfurt School critical theorist, went on to conclude that a progressive bourgeois public sphere, which in the time of the early newspapers enabled democratic debate, had perished under the colonizing influence of corporate powers (1989). The same line of thought was pursued in France by Louis Althusser with his notion of "ideological state apparatuses" (1984), suggesting that the media and journalism are forms of an ideological machinery determined to serve class interests—especially those of the bourgeoisie.

Thus neo-Marxist thinking emphasized the evils of capitalism—a perspective that could seem to leave little hope of changing the world. In reality, it fueled radicalism by promoting a critical consciousness of the structural obstacles existing in Western societies. A radical approach to media—including the radical role of journalism—came to be known above all as a proactive movement for change, far from defeatism. An illuminating example was presented in Germany by the post-Frankfurt, post-Habermas approach of Oskar Negt and Alexander Kluge (1993), who advocated the possibility and necessity of a "proletarian public sphere," despite all the sociopolitical system's cooptation of passive mass audiences. It was such an intellectual climate in the 1960s and 1970s that gave rise to theories of political economy and later to cultural studies.

POLITICAL ECONOMY AND CULTURAL STUDIES

In order to understand later developments of the radical tradition, it is vital to recall the broad landscape of communication research. It was dominated until the late 1960s by what Veikko Pietilä in his historical overview of the field calls "classical behavioral mass communication research" (2005, 105–26). This school of thought, dominant particularly in the United States, was rich in empirical findings and research techniques, spurred on by the advent of computers, but poor in wider theoretical approaches and more profound ethical perspectives. It was a typical case of logical positivism at the time—so dominant that it gave rise to critical reactions, especially outside the United States (see Nordenstreng 1968). Marxism in general and political economy in particular came to fill this vacuum of theories and values, with scholars such as Dallas Smythe and Herbert Schiller in North America and Armand Mattelart and Nicholas Garnham in Europe paving the way for a whole generation of radical researchers. This was by no means a uniform approach but subsumed several streams, some of which focused on economy and class structure, while others were concerned with ideology and subjectivity (Pietilä 2005, 221–44; Schiller 1996, 132–84). Yet the approach had a common core in "the recognition that the mass media are first and foremost industrial and commercial organizations which produce and distribute commodities" (Murdock and Golding 1974, 205–6) while it also perceived the media industry as involved in capitalist commodity production in many ways other than by manufacturing media products and audiences (Mosco 1996).

By the early 1980s, the entire field of communication research was profoundly affected, and in some countries even dominated, by the radical tradition—at least in its milder critical variants. A good reading of the situation is the special issue "Ferment in the Field" published by the *Journal of Communication* in 1983. It was typical of this period that this journal's editor, George Gerbner, concluded, after presenting an impressive panorama of research paradigms and their challenges, "if Marx were alive today, his principal work would be entitled *Communications* rather than *Capital*" (Gerbner 1983, 358). This rhetorical remark was not intended to undermine Marxist emphasis on capital and class but to highlight information and communication as equally crucial factors in any theory of postindustrial society. Connecting Marxism with communication also signaled an emerging new line of research inspired by notions such as "cyber-Marx" (Dyer-Witherford 1999) and "digital capitalism" (Schiller 2000), with the perspective that "the information commodity has become the prime site of contemporary expansion—such as it is—within and for the world market system" (Schiller 2007, 16).

Parallel to these developments, cultural studies emerged as another strand of the radical tradition by the 1980s. Its roots go to the British school of cultural studies, built on the 1960s and 1970s work of Richard Hoggart, Raymond Williams, E. P. Thompson, and Stuart Hall. Cultural studies had a fairly positive perspective, counting on the potential resistance of working-class culture in the face of capitalist domination (see Barker 2000). In this version of the radical tradition, popular culture was seen to be full of contradictions, and the media were not understood to operate under a totally deterministic order. On the contrary, youth culture especially, with its rock music, was seen as a liberating force leading toward emancipation and empowerment (see Grossberg 1992).

Cultural studies expanded rapidly and while gaining worldwide recognition became so diversified that much of it could no longer be taken as critical, let alone radical. Although cultural studies, like political economy, can be seen as an intellectual child of antipositivism, these two streams diverged and by the 1990s were in frequent conflict with each other. While cultural studies welcomed the arrival of a host of scholars from the humanities—often frustrated by their original surroundings—those pursuing a political economy approach were surrounded by an increasingly hostile academic environment, especially after the collapse of communism. Robert McChesney describes this part of his journey as a radical media scholar as "the rise and fall of political economy of communication" (2007, 37). However, that stage was soon followed by a "historical turn," with a lot of potential for change. In general, the development of the field can be seen as a series of "ferments," with a more or less visible presence of the radical tradition (Nordenstreng 2004).

Summarizing the ups and downs of the radical tradition, James Curran situates it against the liberal tradition and pays special attention to the "new revisionist movement" that emerged in media and cultural studies during "the conservative 1980s" (2002, 107). He admits the "mid-life crisis of radical media studies" (x) but presents a program for revitalizing the radical tradition, with a conclusion that is highly relevant to scholarship on media roles:

> The radical tradition was weakened by self-referential revisionist argument, while the liberal tradition expanded relatively unchecked by criticism. Yet, the traditional radical perspective offers important insights that need to be retained. . . . Radical analysts are entirely right to insist that the media are, in general, subject to strong elite pressures which propel the media towards the sphere of established power. However, the media can also be exposed to countervailing popular influences. . . .

> In sum, a reconstituted radical perspective needs to be championed against the
> advancing tide of revisionist argument, which overstates popular influence on the
> media and understates the media's influence on the public. (Curran 2002, 165)

GLOBAL PERSPECTIVE

A worldwide prospect for radical thinking was opened up by the idea of a new international order in the 1970s, aiming at the decolonization of national economies as well as cultural and media systems in the developing world. This was no mere academic orientation but a powerful trend in international relations, spearheaded by the Non-Aligned Movement (Third World), with the support of the socialist countries (Second World), and leading to reform initiatives at the United Nations known as the New International Economic Order and the New International Information Order. The latter was further developed by UNESCO into the concept of the New World Information and Communication Order (NWICO) and was highlighted by the so-called MacBride Report (see Mansell and Nordenstreng 2006; Nordenstreng 1999). All this was only partly radical and revolutionary; mostly it stood for a reformist improvement of the media systems in the world. Even as such, it was considered a threat to Western political and corporate interests, which began to push it back under the conditions of changing power constellations in the 1980s fostered by the Reagan administration in the United States. Accordingly, a completely different "new world order" advocated by a United States–led Western coalition in the early 1990s replaced the Third World–driven new order, which had earlier inspired such concepts as NWICO.

By the turn of the millennium, this new world order was understood typically in terms of globalization, and its United States–driven market orientation gave rise to an antiglobalization movement embodying the same political and intellectual elements that had rallied around NWICO earlier. So ruthless criticism has not disappeared from the debate on the nature and role of media in society—particularly regarding the "information society" (Webster 2006) and "postmodern culture" (Best and Kellner 2001). According to Durham and Kellner, "a postmodern turn in culture and society would correspond to an emergent stage of global capitalism, characterized by new multimedia, exciting computer and informational technology, and a proliferation of novel forms of politics, society, culture, and everyday life" (2001, 26). The elements of radicalism at this "postmodern turn" offer a number of intriguing perspectives, beginning with the replacement of class by information as the determining factor in understanding societies (Castells 1996; Poster 2001) and ending with the emergence of hybrid cultures (Canclini 1995; Martin-Barbero 1993) as well as new approaches to morality and ethics (Stevenson 1999) and to critical pedagogy (Giroux 2004; McLaren and Kincheloe 2007).

RADICALISM IN THE DIGITAL AGE

The turn of the millennium has opened up contradictory perspectives for the radical role of the media in general and journalism in particular. First, the traditional left in the industrialized West, previously mobilized by the socialist and communist parties, has been largely integrated into the welfare society, while their century-old social and economic programs have been more or less established. Second, the new dissident movements that have emerged, particularly in the developing world, and are fueled typically by religious fundamentalism, are important, though this variant of radicalism does not fit within our definition of democratic radical media. The process of globalization, accompanied by neoliberal doctrines that challenge the humanitarian and communitarian values that used to fuel traditional radicalism, has provoked the formation of a third perspective of contemporary radicalism: a reaction in the form of the antiglobalization movement, with a strategy of employing new information and communication technologies (ICTs), particularly the Internet.

The result has been so-called indymedia, with its own global network organization (www.indymedia.org/). It was nurtured by the movement created during the demonstrations at the 1999 World Trade Organization (WTO) conference in Seattle, "for the creation of radical, accurate, and passionate telling of the truth." Indymedia has given rise to a worldwide movement of independent media centers related to the tradition of socialist anarchism (Downing 2003) and has inspired a new type of journalism (Platon and Deuze 2003). The latest version of alternative media is largely based on individually run weblogs.

These developments are also fueled by new approaches to intellectual property in computer-based media. The commercial software industry, notably Microsoft, is challenged by a worldwide movement of free software designers known as open source systems, notably Linux. For these computer programs, digitally transmitted communication should not be sources of capitalist gains but should be freely placed at people's disposal. In so doing, a commodity economy is replaced by a gift economy—essentially the same perspective that was raised by the political economy tradition of media studies, which on one hand exposed the undemocratic nature of capitalist media industry and on the other hand advocated a democratic order for public good.

Jay Rosen, one of the builders of the public journalism movement, lists "ten things radical about the weblog form in journalism" (http://journalism.nyu.edu/pubzone/weblogs/pressthink/2003/10/16/radical_ten.html). He begins with the point that "the weblog comes out of the gift economy, whereas most (not all) of today's journalism comes out of the market economy," and ends with the point that "journalism traditionally assumes that democracy is what we have, information is what we seek. Whereas in the weblog world, information is what we have—it's all around us—and democracy is what we seek." In the same spirit, Douglas Kellner and Richard Kahn suggest that blogging leads to "a vision of the democratic future of the Net" (www.gseis.ucla.edu/faculty/kellner/essays/internetsubculturesoppositionalpolitics.pdf).

Others claim that weblogs are no longer a predominantly radical force but rather have become a new means of feeding established media (Singer 2005). For example, Chantal Mouffe is not enthusiastic about the new media, because many people are not using "this incredible possibility of choice." Instead, according to Mouffe, the new media "perversely allow people to just live in their little worlds, and not be exposed anymore to the conflicting ideas that characterize the agonistic public space. New media are making it possible to only read and listen to things that completely reinforce what you believe in" (Carpentier and Cammaerts 2006, 968).

Obviously there are both optimists and pessimists—the latter calling themselves realists—about the future of journalism in the digital age. An important category of optimists are the new advocates of critical pedagogy (see McLaren et al. 2005). Among them are those who see a huge potential in free software and open source technology, with applications such as Wikipedia: "If Gutenberg's revolution was about making printed media more abundant, the Wikipedia has the same effect multiplied to a different order of magnitude" (Suoranta and Vadén 2007, 146). Although the main focus of these scholars is a paradigm shift in education and the challenge to literacy, their discussion is also relevant to media and journalism: "When the self-organizational nature of hacker communities is combined with the observation that the digital code is not a scarce resource, we get a cybercommunist utopia where volunteer organizations and communities of non-alienated labor manage themselves in a post-scarcity economy" (153).

In short, the digital age has contributed two kinds of elements to the radical tradition. First, ICTs have been integrated into existing movements. Although they are called indymedia, they do not represent an independent force but are merely a new platform for traditional political struggles. Second, ICTs may also provide some genuinely new sites for radical thought and action. The open source approach is still at an exploratory stage, but it has intriguing potential for radical thinking broadly and radical journalism specifically. Curran (2003) concludes from the British-based Internet magazine *openDemocracy* that despite its elite connections, open source "has made a significant contribution toward building a global civil society" (239).

VARIANTS OF RADICALISM

After this excursion into the tradition of critical/radical media studies, it is clear that one simple definition of the radical role of the media in general and journalism in particular is impossible. What *radical* means is a typical "it depends," in this case not only on the nature of the media in question but also on the nature of the society—indeed the nature of the world—that one is talking about. On one side is the traditional notion of radical media as instruments of significant revolutionary movements directed at the power structure at large. On the other side are those later forms of radical media defined by John Downing as "media, generally small-scale and in many different forms, that express an alternative vision to hegemonic policies, priorities, and perspectives" (2001, v).

Today a mainstream use of the word "radical" no longer suggests predominantly Marxist perspectives of the political left but increasingly suggests those fundamentalist approaches that in the Western ideological framework are typically connected to extremist Islamist movements and international terrorism. The radicalism of extremist political and religious movements is indeed one variant of radicalism, but in this connection it would be misleading to speak about the radical role of journalism. Whenever media serve as instruments of such extremist movements, they perform, according to our typology, a collaborative rather than a radical role. This applies to movements on the extreme right as well as the extreme left—fascist as well as Stalinist. Downing (2001, 88–96) lumps the two extremes together under the category *repressive* radical media, in contrast to *democratic* radical media. In our terminology, *radical* refers to a democratic rather than a repressive role for journalism. Although the border between repressive and democratic forms of radicalism is often unclear and sometimes impossible to draw, at the conceptual level it is still important to make—and to problematize—this distinction.

Accordingly, a radical role for journalism in our typology does not mean that the media serve any type of oppositional purpose. They serve those people in society who are opposed to the establishment because they do not have a fair share of the national public sphere—because they are underrepresented and disenfranchised. Thus the radical role, in our case, has a popular—even populist—undertone, and in this respect it is closely related to the concept not only of power but also of citizenship.

The radical role, in this sense of the term, is far removed from big institutional structures such as the state. It is typically pursued through various alternative media run by different elements of the civil society outside the established political parties, trade unions, and professional associations. For such new social movements and grassroots elements, the media are not just instruments to promote their causes but vehicles to articulate their oppositional ideas and activities. Accordingly, alternative media are an integral part of the movements or groups they represent—as the press organs of the early political parties and liberation movements used to be. In this respect, alternative media pursue advocacy journalism.

Actually advocacy journalism is pursued not only in alternative media but can be found also in conventional media that are not radical as such. Indeed, an important variant of the democratic radical role is constituted by critically engaged journalists working within the mainstream with reference to fundamental issues, including social justice and human rights. These radical voices appear as exceptions from a more or less conservative line of the mainstream media, and often these exceptions make a big difference within the overall climate of opinion. Thus a radical role should not be defined according to a medium or a whole media system, but rather according to a specific form of journalism that may even have a minority position within a conservative or liberal mainstream.

The facilitative role, on the other hand, provides dialogue and participation for the democratic process and thus fulfills an instrumental role. Both the facilitative and the radical roles operate at the level of civil society and promote the people's power, and in this respect there is little difference between them. What distinguishes them from each other in our typology is the purpose they are supposed to serve—promoting dialogue among citizens (facilitative) versus mobilizing opinion against the power structure in society (radical).

Alternative media as radical media—both in theory and practice—are thoroughly presented and discussed by Downing (2001) and by Atton (2002; 2003). Since around the turn of the millennium, the phenomenon of alternative media has gained more and more attention, because of developments in both the political and media worlds. In politics, established institutions, including old political parties, have lost their credibility among the electorate, calling for alternative ways to do politics. In the media world, the landscape is characterized by two contradictory tendencies: concentration of ownership and the decentralization of operations based on digital technology, particularly the Internet.

Clemencia Rodriguez (2001) carries the story further from alternative media to citizens' media, inspired both by global perspectives of NWICO and by various examples, notably in Latin America, of indigenous people and other grassroots groups taking media into their own hands and creating what can be seen as a worldwide movement of community media. Rodriguez avoids a dualism lurking behind the alternative media concept—between top-down institutional media (bad) and bottom-up popular media (good)—by reverting to these ideas: the "sense-making" of Brenda Dervin and Robert Huesca (1997), the "hybrid cultures" of Jesus Martin-Barbero (1993), and the "radical democratic citizenship" of Ernesto Laclau and Chantal Mouffe (1985; see Mouffe 1992). A crucial lesson of these reflections is that neither alternative nor citizens' media should be seen mechanistically as a binary phenomenon but dynamically as a hybridized phenomenon made up of multiple elements.

A similar paradigm, known as "subaltern studies," emerged in the 1990s in South Asia, notably India, and in Latin America—the latter motivated by the

United States–based Marxist Literacy Group inspired by Frederic Jameson (I. Rodriguez 2001, 1–2). This is a truly radical school of thought, in a spirit of academic militancy "placing our faith in the projects of the poor" (3). Although it has not produced a specific variant of radical media theory, it provides an example of the relevant intellectual environment surrounding those who pursue a radical role for journalism.

Last but not least are feminist studies, focusing on the structural inequalities embedded in the social relations based on patriarchy. Since the 1960s, this school of thought has been a vital part of radicalizing the media's context. With classics such as Nancy Fraser's *Unruly Practices* (1989), feminist studies has developed a distinct brand of media studies (van Zoonen 1994). However, this is by no means a homogenous school and is divided into several streams more or less radical.

Dimensions of the Radical Role

The foregoing history of radical thinking about the media has provided an overall profile and the main elements of what the radical role of journalism means. Next we focus on the dimensions we presented in chapter 5 as central factors in determining the journalistic roles.

POWER

Social-political power is the most crucial concept in defining a radical role. The media in enacting this role fundamentally depart from what is given by the state and other power structures in society. The radical role sustains an oppositional and antagonistic relation to the dominant forces, offering alternative channels and perspectives to those reflecting the political, economic, and cultural hegemony. While media in the collaborative role support the dominant institutional power typically represented by the state, and can be seen to enjoy minimal autonomy, the media in the radical role are located at the other end of the continuum, standing on the side of autonomous social movements and people's power directed against exclusivist powers.

The next question for understanding the media's radical role concerns the nature of power, and this question takes us back to the contradiction between radical and liberal traditions discussed earlier. As shown by Curran (2002), the variant of Marxism that sees power as directly determined by economy is too simple and even misleading. But it is equally misleading to undermine economy as a source of power and to take the view, as many postmodernists in cultural studies do, that power is so highly fragmented and widely diffused that, in effect, economy need not be taken seriously any longer. Such an approach represents the liberal paradigm of more or less independent individuals hanging in the thin air of abstract society.

It is important to see that there are two fundamentally different notions of power: an Anglo-American view and a Hegelian-Marxian view. The Anglo-American tradition, based on Thomas Hobbes, follows the Galilean metaphor of a universe of freely moving objects, including human beings with free will and the absence of external impediments. In this tradition, power means intervention against free movement; power is the capacity to block free movement. The Hegelian-Marxian tradition follows Kantian philosophy: human beings are determined by the laws of nature and also by moral reasoning. Freedom in this tradition means autonomy from nature and is based on the rational and moral capacity of human beings. Freedom "is not the ability to act according to one's will and interest without being intervened with, but rather is almost exactly the opposite—it is the placing of natural desires and interests in a position in which they are governed by moral judgments" (Pulkkinen 2000, 12). In the Hegelian-Marxian ontology, power is not an obstacle distracting natural movement but an essential instrument to ensure morality and order in civil society and ultimately in the state.

A radical approach to media typically belongs to the latter, German tradition, although the complicated intellectual history involved is not always made clear. Power in this ontology is far from a simple and mechanistic concept, as was the case in the Anglo-American tradition, which served as the springboard for a libertarian theory of politics and democracy, including modern classics such as the works of Robert Dahl. Libertarian theory defines politics as a game between atomistic individuals, whereas the Hegelian-Marxian tradition understands politics as an organic part of society, where power is not the relation between two individuals but "an instrument of justice in the process of the self-control of society" (Pulkkinen 2000, 94).

Michel Foucault (e.g. 1982) is a typical example of this second way, while he is also in general a very important source of inspiration for contemporary theorizing about social power. As summarized by Geoff Danaher, Tony Schirato, and Jen Webb, "Foucault doesn't think of power as a thing to be owned or held by somebody, but as a ubiquitous, and ever-changing flow" (2000, 80). Thus power is dispersed and mobile but is still very much present and influential. Moreover, the Foucauldian thesis suggests that power is more effective when hidden from view. In those terms, there is a trend in (post)modern societies away from the brutal and public exercise of power to "hidden coercions" (81). This perspective is pursued by Schirato in his Foucauldian introduction to the role of communication in a "panoptical society" (Schirato 2000; Schirato and Webb 2003).

Such a notion of power opens up a challenging perspective for the media's radical role. The traditional Marxist concept of social power is typically associated with a class-based political and economic hegemony, which for its part fuels class-based opposition with its own radical media. But the Foucauldian notion of power cannot be ascribed to a particular social position. Radicalism under such conditions does not mean to expose a clearly identifiable source of power but to see an omnipresent structural condition, that is, a built-in bias in the sociopolitical fabric.

This perspective is not completely new. It was already partly present in the thinking of Gramsci, the Frankfurt School, and later social critics such as Jacques Ellul, Stuart Hall, and Herbert Schiller. What they had in common was a holistic view whereby (Western) societies have a structural bias based on a power system that needs to be challenged by radical analysis and action. Those who pursue the radical role in journalism belong to the same intellectual tradition, with a holistic view of society and a notion of power as omnipresent.

COMMUNITY

Power is typically exercised in a community, but the two main traditions just discussed have fundamentally different views of the nature of community. The Anglo-American tradition conceives of a community as made up of individuals pursuing personal interests. The German tradition conceives of a community as a collective of individuals who are bound together by the exercise of reason, morality, and a common interest. The former notion of community is quite loose; the latter is very strong—with a Hegelian state representing a collective interest. Society in the libertarian tradition consists of individual subjects; society in the German tradition is composed of a collective subject: the community. The former tradition holds the community almost as fiction; the latter holds the individual almost as fiction.

In practice, community is mostly understood as a mixture of these traditions. Nowadays it is especially rare to meet a purely libertarian notion of community. This is true despite a worldwide trend of economic liberalism, the so-called neoliberalism. With all the talk of global governance and ecological crises, it is impossible to claim that there are no general interests beyond individuals. Accordingly, ideas of communitarianism and so-called strong democracy have gained more and more ground in the United States. This departure from the Anglo-American tradition does not introduce a new wave of radicalism; it is just a variant of libertarian doctrine, but a reminder of the impasse that classical liberalism has reached (discussed in chapter 1).

As for journalism's radical role, community is a very receptive site for it, as community is for the facilitative role. Most radical media are created or supported by a community—geographic or interest-based—but as Downing (2001, 39) points out, it is a fuzzy concept that raises more questions and dilemmas than it answers. Still, community media cannot be omitted when listing new centers of radical empowerment, as in the introduction of this chapter. Indeed, there is a worldwide movement to capitalize on it (Fuller 2007; Rennie 2006) and even

the World Association of Community Radio Broadcasters does so (www.amarc
.org/). Nico Carpentier, Rico Lie, and Jan Servaes (2007) distinguish four approaches: (1) media serving a community, and (2) community media as alternative to mainstream media, (3) as part of civil society, and (4) as "rhizome"
embedded in flexible social movements. Each of these approaches may accommodate radical as well as other media types, but with an overall direction
toward greater participation and wider access, they fit quite well within the
radical role of journalism.

These ideas notwithstanding, some forms of radicalism do better without a
community's collective support. Dissident voices and anarchist ideas may even
be repressed by the stifling influence of a community—however radical it may
be. For postmodernists like Lyotard (1988), respecting and supporting difference is the key for getting beyond the dualism of individual and community as
suggested by the two main traditions.

LEGITIMATION AND ACCOUNTABILITY

Being radical in society means to break free from the bonds of mutual trust of
others, except for others belonging to the same radical group. Thus the radical
role of journalism does not enjoy overall legitimacy in society; it is viewed by
many as unsettling and subversive. However, the radical media and journalists
themselves consider their own oppositional position to be highly legitimate,
while society at large is seen as illegitimate.

This situation means that the radical role accepts no accountability to society
at large and none to the state. However, conceptually the radical role is still a
reaction to hegemonic power; such radicalism is unthinkable in the absence
of the dominant power structures at which it is directed. Therefore, radical actors cannot totally delink themselves from the rest of society; an accountability
relationship between the source and the target of radicalism always remains.

The very nature of radicalism, with its oppositional approach to the prevailing
social system, is alien to the idea of legitimation and accountability. Therefore,
it is not surprising that the four types of accountability presented in chapter 5
do not apply very well to this role. Radical journalism sees the legal frame as a
threat to freedom instead of a regulatory safeguard. After all, the radical often
aims at precisely changing the law and even the constitution. The market frame,
for its part, represents the corporate power and bourgeois control that are typical targets of radicals' struggle. The public frame may fit within the radical role
in cases when radicals are supported by elements of the civil society against the
official levels of society, for example in labor disputes. The professional frame
is likely to be counterproductive for the radical role, because professional self-
regulation tends to jealously guard the profession's own values and indirectly
the existing power structures in society.

Conclusion

How does the radical role relate to the four traditions of normative thinking presented in chapter 2? Obviously, it fits best within the tradition of citizen participation. The social responsibility and libertarian traditions may also have a radical dimension under certain circumstances. But there is little room for radicalism in the corporatist tradition, which is geared toward consensus and organic unity, whereas the radical role builds on conflict and division.

Relating the radical role to the four models of democracy introduced in chapter 4, it has a natural place within the two models of deliberative democracy, civic and direct. Both models count on a lively exchange of contradictory views based in civil society rather than in institutional structures. On the other hand, the pluralist and administrative models of democracy leave little space for a radical approach, since both are based on a logic of preserving rather than challenging the prevailing order.

While the radical role of journalism as specified in this chapter can be seen to enrich deliberative democracy, one can ask whether a really ideal democracy any longer needs radical journalism. After all, a democratic social order means that mechanisms such as political parties, professional associations, and trade unions channel various interests in society so that conflicts are negotiated in open debate and settled through legitimate institutions. Such democratic processes, if fully employed, do not allow any particular interests to occupy a hegemonic position that needs to be challenged by radical media. Indeed, under ideal conditions, the democratic order is supported by the monitorial, facilitative, and collaborative roles, leaving the radical role practically out of the picture.

However, an ideal theory of democracy seldom works, and there is constant need for a radical role for journalism. Even in a well-functioning democracy, it is important as a reserve mechanism to ensure that minorities and powerless segments are not marginalized and that a lively debate is carried on throughout society. Accordingly, the radical role can be seen as a safeguard for democracy, and radical journalism remains a vital element in democracy.

9

The Collaborative Role

Perhaps because the very idea of collaboration implies a relationship with the state or other centers of power that clashes with the libertarian ideal of a free and autonomous press, a collaborative role for journalism seldom receives the attention it deserves. In many parts of the world, the media exist as a check on power, not as a conduit for it. Lee Bollinger makes just this point when he describes American journalists' self-image with reference to a "model of journalistic autonomy" that "breathes life" into "a press conceived in the image of the artist . . . who lives (figuratively) outside of society, beyond normal conventions, and who is therefore better able to see and expose its shortcomings" (1991, 55). By conferring on journalists unfettered power and virtually no accountability, the reigning model of journalistic autonomy promotes what Bollinger views as "a posture toward the world that says, in effect, no one will tell you what to do" (57). Whatever can be said of the actual performance of the media, journalism often views itself in ways that effectively exclude cooperation or collaboration.

Without discounting the values of freedom and autonomy and the media roles they might imply, a collaborative role for journalism is too pervasive and too historically important to be swept aside by ignoring it or downplaying its significance. In democracies everywhere, collaboration not only describes instances of press performance but sometimes prescribes it as well. As reluctant as journalists might be to acknowledge it, at times collaboration distinguishes itself as a genuinely normative role for journalism—not merely an empirical claim about what the press is or does but an ideal that captures what the press should be or what journalists ought to do.

Collaboration characterizes any number of relationships in which the media willingly, sometimes even enthusiastically, participate. When the media agree to withhold information about the location of troops during times of war, few journalists dismiss collaboration as inappropriate or without justification—many in fact view it as an obligation or a patriotic duty. When a television network agrees to cover a presidential debate, no one looks askance at the network and its decision to cooperate with the debate's organizers. Journalists ordinarily view it as a public service the networks should provide. In other instances, however, acts of collaboration might be considered a sign of weakness and a lack of commitment to the principle of independent news judgment. Whether in the end collaboration distinguishes itself normatively and democratically depends on whether a public justification can be made for it.

Collaboration with the state does not, of course, exhaust the collaborative roles the media might play, as the "public journalism" movement in the United States makes clear with its call for a reinvigorated relationship between the press and civil society (see Glasser 1999; Merritt 1995; Rosen 1999a, 1999b). Centers of power other than the state—from advertisers who subsidize the media to community activists who want access to the public—regularly appeal to the media for cooperation and sympathy. But collaboration with the state stands out as a special case, for only the state can intervene in the affairs of journalism in ways that fundamentally alter the nature of everyday news. Through its laws, policies, and directives, the state—and only the state—provides a legally permissible infrastructure for the media. C. Edwin Baker puts it succinctly when he reminds us that the state, however laissez-faire its approach to journalism might be, inevitably assumes some responsibility for ensuring a public purpose for a private press. Even in countries like the United States, Baker writes, where almost everyone equates a free press with free enterprise, legal support for a free press, including constitutional protection from an overbearing state, "should be read to allow the government to promote a press that, in its best judgment, democracy needs but that the market fails to provide" (2002, 213).

Among the democratic media roles we discuss, a collaborative role is unique in that it deals as much with the needs and expectations of the state as the needs and expectations of the press. Defined in relation to the state, a collaborative role for the media implicates government(s)—locally, regionally, nationally, and at times even transnationally—in the mission of the press. Collaboration represents an acknowledgment of the state's interest—to which the media accede either passively or unwittingly, reluctantly or wholeheartedly—in participating in the choices journalists make and the coverage they provide. This participation does not necessarily involve censorship. And when it does, censorship does not always run counter to the freedom and responsibility journalists want for themselves. But, invariably, participation by—or deference to—the state, no matter how benign or even positive its effect on media performance, raises important questions about the meaning of autonomy in journalism.

Autonomy and agency vary considerably across the range of relationships that defines the scope of a collaborative role for the media, and we allude to this variance in the next section, where we sketch out the contours of various forms of collaboration. But the bulk of this chapter examines a collaborative role for the media by focusing on particular instances of it. We begin with a brief look at the idea of "development journalism," which stands out as one of the few efforts, by practitioners and academics alike, to transform collaboration into a genuinely normative theory of the press. We then turn to examples of collaboration between the media and the state. The first involves the application of the principles of development journalism to Singapore's press, which is expected to assist the state in building and sustaining a national agenda for progress and prosperity. The second focuses on military censorship in Israel, which cultivates a certain bond between the media and the state. The third deals with public safety measures in the United States, where an agreement between the state and the media led to the publication of a terrorist's manifesto.

Conditions for Collaboration

Understood normatively, a collaborative role for the media implies a partnership, a relationship between the media and the state built on mutual trust and a shared commitment to mutually agreeable means and ends. In practice, collaboration between the state and the media often falls short of this ideal. A collaborative role for the media comes in many forms, depending on the grounds and motives for it, and more often than not it fails the test of "mutual trust" and "mutually agreeable means and ends." As outlined in table 2, the conditions for a collaborative role for the media range from coercion to full acceptance of the particular arrangements and outcomes that collaboration implies. Extrapolated from the work of David Held (1995, 160–62), table 2 divides the conditions for collaboration into three broadly distinguishable categories—compliance, acquiescence, and acceptance—and then expands these into seven analytically distinct forms of collaboration. While "these distinctions are analytical," Held reminds us, "in ordinary circumstances different types of agreement are often fused together" (161). These categories and distinctions nonetheless provide a useful framework for discriminating among various types of collaboration and a vocabulary with which to assess the legitimacy of a collaborative role for the media.

Collaboration through compliance offers the weakest and least compelling rationale for a collaborative role for the media. Collaboration achieved through coercion is collaboration in appearance only. The very idea of "coercive collaboration" is an oxymoron; any effort to compel journalists to collaborate preempts the very partnership on which a truly collaborative role rests. While apathy and tradition do not involve coercion, they amount to an uncritical acceptance of

Table 2. Conditions for a Collaborative Role for the Media: From Compliance
to Acceptance

Collaboration as Compliance	
Coercion:	No choice in the matter; a law or some other form of overt control compels the press to cooperate
Apathy:	Indifference or ignorance; cooperation exists in the absence of any serious attention to it
Tradition:	Custom dictates action; journalists accept history as a justification for cooperation
Collaboration as Acquiescence	
Pragmatic:	Cooperation is unappealing but inevitable; journalists avoid coercion and accept their fate
Instrumental:	Cooperation is unappealing but instrumentally useful; journalists accept some kind of trade-off
Collaboration as Acceptance	
Practical Agreement:	Given what is known about particular circumstances, journalists judge cooperation to be right or proper
Normative Agreement:	Given all that needs to be known about these circumstances, journalists judge cooperation to be right or proper

prevailing arrangements; they conserve the status quo by leaving it unquestioned. In the case of apathy, a collaborative role for the media exists in the
absence of any attention to it; through indifference or ignorance, journalists
assume a role they neither endorse or perhaps even understand. In the case of
tradition, the past justifies the present; with history as its foil, a collaborative
role for the media resumes as a matter of custom or habit.

Collaboration through acquiescence involves a reluctant acceptance of arrangements. The commitment to collaborate is based on either a calculation
of the consequences of not collaborating or a consideration of arrangements
and outcomes unrelated to collaboration. The media acquiesce for pragmatic
reasons when, in their judgment, a lack of collaboration will result in coercion;
journalists "accept their fate" and avoid the ignominy of overt and direct control
by the state. The press acquiesces for instrumental reasons when it agrees to
collaborate for reasons unrelated to the arrangements and outcomes associated
with collaboration. In this case, journalists benefit from a collaborative role but
in ways extrinsic to the means and ends of collaboration.

Collaboration through acceptance is the only type that deals specifically and
exclusively with the merits of a collaborative role for journalism. When journalists take into account *what they know* about *the particular circumstances of
collaboration* and judge a collaborative role to be "correct" or "proper," they
enter into a *practical* agreement to cooperate. They in effect agree that, given
what they know about the means and ends of a collaborative relationship with
the state, it is right to collaborate. When, however, journalists take into account

all that needs to be known about the *particular arrangements and outcomes of collaboration,* including an assessment of the consequences of cooperation for the larger community, and judge a collaborative role to be "correct" or "proper," they enter into a *fully normative* agreement to collaborate. They in effect agree that, given what they know about the means and ends of a cooperative relationship with the state *and the conceivable consequences of these means and ends for everyone affected by them,* it is right to collaborate.

A truly normative agreement represents a regulative ideal, an aspirational standard, what Held describes as a "hypothetically projected agreement" (1995, 162). It posits an idealized set of circumstances in which everyone affected by a collaborative role for the media consents to it. If, realistically, journalists cannot consult the community every time they consider a collaborative role, the demands of a normative agreement require that journalists prepare, intellectually and temperamentally, for an open and public discussion of the merits of their decision. While the ideal of a broad consensus, rooted in public debate, applies to any media role, it is especially important in the case of a collaborative role, insofar as collaboration contravenes the generally accepted separation of the press from the state.

The State and Development Journalism

The term "development journalism" denotes certain media practices and arrangements presumably appropriate for "transitional" nations whose political, economic, and cultural institutions lack the maturity that a truly free press arguably requires. For nearly three decades the term applied to nations of the so-called Third World, a Cold War and now obsolete term for countries outside the core of industrialized nations of North America, western Europe, Japan, Australia, and New Zealand (First World) and not aligned with the Soviet Union and its allies (Second World). With reference today to "underdeveloped, "developing," or, more positively, "advancing" nations, the idea of development journalism retains its focus on a media system that works, typically but not exclusively, with the state to develop and strengthen existing institutions. Development journalism calls on the media to stand alongside, rather than apart from, other institutions in society; together, these institutions pursue the benefits of modernization for themselves and for the nation as a whole. Whereas conflict, in different ways and for different reasons, dominated what Altschull describes broadly as the "press philosophies of the market and socialist systems," the "operative word in the ideology of the advancing press system was cooperation" (1984, 154–55).

Collaboration in the tradition of development journalism usually involves a partnership with the state, though not always a formal one, a relationship premised on a commitment by the press to play a positive role in the processes of development. From this perspective, responsibility tempers press freedom; journalists can question, even challenge, the state, but not to the point where they undermine a government's basic plans for progress and prosperity. As a prominent local journalist explained at a conference in Ibadan, Nigeria, in 1980,

> So long as the journalist is aware of his responsibility towards the community— principally that of helping development—so long as he realizes that his freedom has bearing on what is good for society and as such is not freedom without limits, the tradition of mistrust will be dissolved, and government and journalism will become twin agents of socioeconomic progress. (quoted in Altschull 1984, 159)

The concept of development journalism originated in the 1960s as "independent journalism that provided constructive criticism of government and its agencies, informed readers how the development process was affecting them, and highlighted local self-help projects," as Shah (1996, 143) recounts the history of the term. However, it too often devolved into a "rationale to take control of mass media to promote state policies, often as a part of larger campaigns of repression." In light of this history, newer versions of development journalism generally steer clear of claims to support a state–press partnership and instead highlight the importance of a press that promotes and strengthens citizen involvement in programs of social change. Among others, Shah (1996) articulates an alternative approach to the question of modernization, in his case a "model of journalism and national development" that accentuates an emancipatory role for the press.

Shah's model of emancipatory journalism establishes a "position from which to consider a role for journalists as participants in a process of progressive social change" (1996, 144). It focuses "on specific and locally defined views of identity and community that recognize differences among and within marginalized groups" (146). By emphasizing roles for alternative media that "exist alongside and produce content different from the mainstream media" (162, n. 7), Shah posits a model that is arguably "more complete and more complex" than earlier versions of development journalism. It is more complete, Shah contends, because it "provides a theoretical link between citizen access to mass media and social change and because it articulates a specific mechanism by which journalists can participate in social change." And it is more complex insofar as it "incorporates principles of diversity and fluidity in the process of building cultural identities and communities and because it challenges journalistic practice by abandoning the idea of objectivity" (146).

Although it is an example of the "better and more positive version" of development journalism that McQuail (2000, 155) advocates, Shah's conception of emancipatory journalism—similar in many ways to the claims made for the media under the facilitative and radical roles (see chapters 7 and 8)—fails to address the power of the state and the state's interest in maintaining certain roles for the mainstream media. It also fails to question the extent to which dominant media might overshadow alternative media in ways that render the latter ineffectual. Like others who appreciate the need for a multiplicity of media—a "media tier" that serves "differentiated audiences," as Curran (2000, 140) puts it—Shah makes the case for a more open and more democratic form of journalism. But key questions remain unanswered, even unasked: What is the nature of the role of an ostensibly independent press that limits itself, at least in certain areas, to constructive criticism of the state? What does it mean for an independent press to operate by the original definition of development journalism, a role that honors the mutual interests of the media and the state in strengthening and perhaps refining, but certainly not undermining, a national consensus? Specifically, Shah's model fails in its application to countries like Singapore, where the state turns to the media for assistance in a nation-building agenda.

The Politics of Consensus: The Case of Singapore

A multicultural society ensconced in a modern city-state, Singapore embraces what can be fairly termed an "authoritarian democracy," a political system of elites that honors the value of free and open markets while maintaining tight control over the mainstream press and other venues for public expression. One of the so-called newly industrialized countries and thus an interesting case study of the scope and duration of a development model of journalism, Singapore insists that it cannot withstand the vagaries of an unrestrained press. With an interventionist state that leaves little room for the development of civil society (Ang 2002, 80), Singapore's approach to progress and reform rests on what it repeatedly describes as consensus politics—a consensus defined by the state and sustained through the state's control of the means of public communication. That is, unlike societies that organize themselves as a "civil association," with emphasis on rules, processes, and procedures, Singapore exists principally as an "enterprise association," an organizing principle that emphasizes "a society-wide adherence to a shared undertaking" (George 2002b, 174). Accordingly, Singapore judges the value and success of its political, cultural, social, and economic institutions, including the press, by their contribution to what the state has defined, though not always in so many words, as Singapore's twin goals: harmony and prosperity.

The leaders of Singapore's ruling People's Action Party have been remarkably candid about what they expect from journalists, expectations that set forth in clear if not always compelling terms the need for an enduring partnership between the state and the media. Lee Kuan Yew, who as prime minister led Singapore from its independence from British rule in 1965 until his retirement in 1990, developed an early aversion to a press that operates with little or no regard for the interests of the state. Suspicious of claims of freedom of the press, especially when they turned out to be little more than a defense of the "freedom of its owners to advance their personal and class interests" (Lee 2000, 213), Lee and his People's Action Party colleagues forged a plan for "managing the media," to cite the revealing title of one of the chapters in Lee's (2000, 212–25) memoirs. The plan was to instill among journalists a sense of responsibility for the success of Singapore and a genuine commitment to the prosperity of Singaporeans.

In a speech to the International Press Institute in Helsinki in 1971, a few years before the passage of legislation that would radically alter the ownership patterns of Singapore's newspapers,[1] Lee reviewed the needs of a "new and young country like Singapore" and outlined what he regarded as a proper role for the media and other agencies of public communication: "to reinforce, not undermine, the cultural values and social attitudes being inculcated in our schools and universities" (2000, 217). Focusing on the importance of moving Singapore beyond its colonial past and into a future of higher "standards of living for our people," Lee pointed to the requisite "knowledge, skills and disciplines of advanced countries" and the "mood" mass media can create "in which people become keen to acquire" them (217). Unwilling to subject Singapore to the unpredictable ire of a fully free press, Lee concluded his remarks to the assembly of journalists with an unequivocal rejection of the model of journalistic autonomy that American journalists embrace: "Freedom of the press, freedom of the news media, must be subordinated to the overriding needs of Singapore, and to the primacy of purpose of an elected government" (218).

By rejecting Western and especially American models of journalism, Singapore establishes for itself a distinctive, though hardly unique, view of the relationship between the press and the state. Given its enthusiasm for a strong, centralized state—one that seeks to create and sustain a national consensus on issues of public importance—Singapore's ruling elite will not allow the media, as Lee put it, "to assume a role in Singapore that the American media play in America, that is, that of invigilator, adversary and inquisitor of the administration" (2000, 223).

In Singapore, but seldom elsewhere, the standard textbook account of Singapore's media highlights the dangers of an unrestrained press and celebrates the power of a press that helps "in nation-building—creating one nation, one people, out of different races, worshipping different gods—by informing and educating Singaporeans of national policies and issues, and inculcating good values in the people" (Tan and Soh 1994, 52–53). Expressly tied to elements of social responsibility theory and media development theory, the received view of the press in Singapore begins with a critique of a libertarian press that challenges or ridicules the prevailing social, moral, and political order and ends with an appreciation for the special contribution the press can make in promoting harmony, solidarity, and tolerance. Citing racial discord fueled by press accounts of it, the government of Singapore expects journalists to exhibit the sensitivity to differences that a culturally plural society requires.[2] And citing the widespread cynicism and disaffection associated with a "watchdog" press that constantly questions the wisdom of a government's plans and policies, Singapore calls on journalists to temper debate and discussion with respect for authority and deference to the state's interest in guiding citizens into a sustainable consensus on core values and key issues.[3]

In Singapore, the state creates the conditions for the media it wants through various laws that restrict content and limit ownership. The state also controls the distribution of publications and programming coming from outside the country. In part the legacy of a British colonial government that often equated controlling crises with controlling communication about them, but also in part a response by the People's Action Party to what it regards as "the harrowing historical and present-day evidence against a free-wheeling libertarian press" (Tan and Soh 1994, 50), the system of media laws in Singapore narrows the domain of civil society by establishing the state as the final arbiter of the range of acceptable expression. Although every democratic state defines and ultimately constrains the scope of civil discourse, Singapore does so to a degree that raises questions about when claims for the legitimacy of the state invalidate the basic premise of self-governance: the requirement of popular sovereignty.

Whether the Singapore government's treatment of the press facilitates or erodes popular sovereignty depends on whether and when the media can create opportunities for the "open and fair" discussions that democracy requires (see Christiano 1996, 3); and this, in turn, depends on what "open and fair" means. Critics contend that Singapore's media remains so heavily sedated by the state that, to shift metaphors, "its main function today seems to be to gorge itself silly with daily Government pronouncements and then regurgitate them for public consumption" (Chee 2000, 2). Others view the media as sufficiently free to engage in what Prime Minister Goh Chok Tong—in a speech in 1995 celebrating the 150th anniversary of the *Straits Times,* Singapore's largest and oldest English-language daily newspaper—recognized as a legitimate, though perhaps subsidiary, role for the media in Singapore: "accurately reporting wrongdoings" and "providing a forum for readers' complaints and debate on national issues." While critics charge that journalists in Singapore lack the independence of judgment they need in order to advance their own agendas, others point out that there is nothing fundamentally undemocratic or otherwise inappropriate about an agenda that focuses on, to cite the editor of the *Straits Times,* "enhancing Singapore's critical success factors, especially strong families, social harmony, education, thrift and hard work" (Cheong 1995, 130).

Given Singapore's history, location, and politics, and given the racial and ethnic mix of its people, the debate over a collaborative role for its press sooner or later turns to the topic of "Asian values"—a term that invariably promises more than it delivers. At an extreme, the debate refers to a clash of civilizations, as though Asian values represent a worldview wholly at odds with the West and Western conceptions of journalism. More moderate versions, the debate points to differences in emphasis between liberal and communitarian theories of democracy (see chapter 3), such that a larger framework of shared principles that provides a context within which to consider different, even divergent, conceptions of democratic practice and press performance.

Leaving aside the contentious proposition that there in fact exist pan-Asian values that inform an arguably Asian model of democracy, certain values in Singapore and elsewhere in Asia (and beyond) do indeed infuse claims about the press and its commitment to nation-building. Government officials in Singapore, through the laws they pass and in their public pronouncements, stress the importance of a press that distinguishes itself as less confrontational, less inflammatory, less sensational, and less driven by conflict than the press in the West; they assign to the press a responsibility to "forge consensus and . . . not fray the social fabric" (Goh 1995, 5). Journalists, too, define their responsibilities with attention to "maintaining a close press–state relationship" in which the media are "prosocial and willingly allied with government for the greater good of nation building" (Massey and Chang 2002, 990). The emphasis on the virtues of respect and obedience shows up even in the Code of Professional Conduct of the Singapore National Union of Journalists: "Every member shall keep in mind the dangers in the laws of libel, contempt of court and copyright" (quoted in Ang 2002, 89).

That the Committee to Protect Journalists finds that in Singapore "journalists have been taught to think of themselves not as critics but as partners of the state in 'nation-building'" (quoted in George 2002a, 7) does not by itself render the lesson unworthy. Likewise, that the state in Singapore teaches this lesson does not by itself render the lesson worthwhile. Just as we do not want to "conflate authoritarian leaders' ideas about the press with the values of journalists and citizens" (6), we do not want to reject these ideas only because authoritarian leaders advance them. A collaborative role for the press in Singapore, or elsewhere, meets the test of legitimacy when the relationship between the state and the press qualifies as a true partnership, an arrangement based on a shared commitment to mutually agreeable means and ends—and an arrangement, moreover, to which the larger community consents. The stringency of this test underscores the importance of distinguishing between the press complying with or acquiescing to a collaborative role and the media (and others) freely accepting the claims and conditions of collaboration.

Little in the history of Singapore's state-press relations offers evidence of the existence of the conditions for a normative agreement on the need for— or even desirability of—a collaborative press role of the kind the state wants. Rather, the state in Singapore engages in strategic and subtle forms of coercion that in effect steer the media toward compliance and acquiescence. Cherian George calls this "calibrated coercion," a form of pressure designed to achieve "maximum effectiveness at minimal cost" (2005, 11). Careful to preserve the credibility of the media, which makes them more useful and persuasive collaborators, the ruling People's Action Party seldom resorts to the repressive tools it has at its disposal—from the detention of journalists to the revocation of a publication's license—and instead relies on the widespread knowledge that these tools have been used in the past and could be used again. "Calibrated coercion," observes George—a former *Straits Times* journalist who now teaches at Singapore's Nanyang Technological University and whose own work, both journalistic and academic, illustrates the government's tolerance of criticism and dissent—"provides journalists with periodic reminders of just who is boss, but also enough leeway to persuade enough of them that there is still a place in Singapore for the professional practice of journalism, and that the space is expanding" (15). Through fear and intimidation, then, and by structuring the media in a way that ensures a regime of compliant publishers, the state orchestrates obedience from media that seldom experience the state's direct and overt interference. The government of Singapore, George points out, "has achieved what possibly no other authoritarian state has done: effective, near-watertight suppression of the press without either nationalizing ownership of the media or brutalizing journalists" (14).

The Dilemma of Censorship: The Case of Israel

Prevailing conceptions of censorship rest, understandably, on a restrictive view of power. Censorship involves coercion, typically coercion by the state, which invariably restricts expression and impedes democratic participation. But as anthropologists and other social theorists point out, censorship also implies a productive view of power. In this expanded and somewhat paradoxical view of censorship, power is conceived as "formative" and "constitutive," to use Judith Butler's (1998) terms. As such, power in part forms the identity of the speaker and in part constitutes the legitimate boundaries of expression. Censorship denies freedom, of course, but also secures it, which is to say that censorship accounts for both the reduction *and* production of power. Thus by "refocusing the issue of censorship and self-censorship," as Alvin Gouldner suggests, on shifting domains of freedom and the privileges of power they confer, the study of censorship becomes in effect the study of political participation: "The fundamental intentions of all political movements today can be appraised, and can be archeologically unearthed, by revealing the theory and practice of censorship with which they operate, tacitly or overtly, whether these be movements of the status quo or those opposed to them" (1976, 159). And because mass media play such a crucial role in so many of these movements, Gouldner finds that "all kinds of freedom today hinge on issues of media censorship" (160).

The nexus between media censorship and political freedom highlights the difficult position journalists find themselves in when censorship, or the prospects for it, expands the media's power but at the same time diminishes their autonomy; it explains, moreover, how journalists can in principle deplore censorship while in practice they benefit from it. Specifically, journalists face this dilemma—the dilemma of expanding their power at the expense of their autonomy—as they consider opportunities to work with the state in developing answers to questions of censorship. While journalists ordinarily believe, usually with good reason, that with autonomy comes power, in fact power trumps autonomy whenever journalists agree to work with state officials on the development of policies concerning what the public can know and how and when it can know it.

Journalists accept the productive power of censorship, and arguably relinquish at least some of the independence of judgment they might otherwise enjoy, whenever the details of national security are shared in confidence with the media but withheld from the general public, a situation that in effect compels journalists to think in more circumspect ways about what they can and should publish. This happens most often during times of war, when the line between circumspection and self-censorship blurs. On these occasions, the state appeals to journalists as a special class of citizen with a special stake in the state's success; under the guise of safety and security, agents of the state and agents of the media work together to keep the public in the dark about certain past, planned, or ongoing activities. In this context, censorship, at once both an expressive and repressive force in society, needs to be understood symbolically as well as legally; it needs to be viewed as a phenomenon involving rites as well as rights. In obvious ways censorship denies the press certain rights, typically by restricting what journalists can publish. But in other ways, which the media seldom acknowledge, censorship empowers journalists by extending to them opportunities and privileges that would not otherwise exist. Thus the requirements of censorship, a set of proscriptions aimed at controlling the form and content of the day's news, work in contradistinction to the rituals of censorship, which position journalists—some journalists at least—as privileged participants in discussions and decisions from which others are excluded.

The rituals of censorship flourish during times of total war, when war transforms a national economy into a war economy and civilian morale matters as much as troop morale (Hallin 1997, 209). When war expands or continues to the point where it takes over a nation's self-image—when, that is, war defines much more than a nation's plans and policies and begins to impinge on everyday life at home—the state and the media often work together to sustain a consensus, which in turn feeds a national identity, which in turn rationalizes the hardships of war. Under these circumstances, war brings about some of the best known and least contested examples of a collaborative role for the media. And nowhere is that role more in evidence than in Israel, where journalists and state officials have worked together for decades on matters of national security.

War in general, but especially war in a small country like Israel, invites involvement from everyone, old and young alike, regardless of their position in society, and journalists are no exception. It would be difficult to overstate the pervasive presence of the military in Israeli society, particularly the Israeli Defense Force (IDF). The IDF provides paramilitary training in high schools; operates vocational schools; assists in the education of soldiers from disadvantaged homes; publishes a popular weekly magazine (Ben Meir 1995, 6); and runs one of Israel's most successful radio stations, which produces a highly regarded news operation. Just about every Israeli shares a direct and everyday connection to the IDF, either through service in the military, active or reserve, or through a family member's service. With a conscription policy that cuts across almost every marker of status in society, including gender, the IDF stands out as one of Israel's most egalitarian institutions.

War in Israel, like war elsewhere, can be understood culturally in terms of what Hallin and Gitlin describe as "an enormously appealing symbolic terrain" (1993, 412); it can serve as "an arena of individual and national self-expression that generates far more emotional involvement than ordinary political events." Under these conditions, the practice of journalism can transform dispassionate and essentially secular reports of strategic gains and battlefield losses into sacred accounts of unity and prowess. With a reverence and deference that journalists ordinarily dismiss as "boosterism," war coverage can feed a public consciousness hungry for stories of might and right, stories where no one doubts the difference between good and evil, justice and injustice, innocence and guilt, heroes and villains. Policies may be disputed, leaders criticized, and issues debated, but the act of war itself almost always becomes an opportunity to honor "us" and vilify "them."

The constancy of war in Israel is palpably real, but it is also a state of mind, an attitude, a general orientation to everyday life. War involves politicians and policies, soldiers and strategies; but it also involves sympathy and solidarity, passion and patriotism. War requires planning and purpose, decisions and determination; it is a technical feat, a political achievement, a military accomplishment. But war also vivifies values, sustains loyalties, and builds consensus. As much as anything else, war can be an affirmation of identity and a celebration of community. For journalists, war can create a hierarchy of roles and responsibilities. As one prominent Israeli editor put it in the early 1980s, "I am first of all an Israeli, then an officer in the reserves, and only after that a journalist and an editor" (quoted in Peri 2004, 86). Just as the Office of Censorship in the United States during World War II, directed by a journalist, depended on the voluntary cooperation of the press (Hallin 1995; Washburn 1990), military censorship in Israel exists as an appeal to shared interests and a strategy designed to soften the distinction between the goals of the state and the responsibilities of the press. As Hallin reminds us, wartime relations between the state and civil society involve "cooperation, co-optation and blurring of the lines, in which state functions were often taken on by institutions like the press, and vice versa" (6).

The system of censorship in Israel began, as did that in Singapore, with the remnants of British colonial law. The British Mandate, which ruled Palestine in the thirty years preceding Israel's independence in 1948, left a legacy of suppression that Israel to this day continues to use for its own purposes. Laws dating to the early 1930s granted British authorities broad powers of censorship aimed at controlling both the domestic and foreign press. These laws were incorporated verbatim into Israeli law and thereby established the legal framework for censorship in Israel today. Initial support for the press censorship in Israel can be explained in terms of a nation that was immediately at war with its neighbors—an official state of war that continues to this day—and journalists who were accustomed to censorship, including their own traditions of self-censorship, were pleased to see the laws of censorship shift from British to Israeli authorities (Lahav 1985; 1993; Limor and Nossek 1995, 5). But initial support for press censorship, including a unanimous vote of consent from editors of Israel's daily newspapers, quickly waned as it became evident that censorship was being defined and implemented in ways that offended journalists. Following months of negotiations—and the closing of several newspapers by military authorities—editors, government officials, and representatives of the military arrived at a written agreement that empowered journalists in unprecedented ways.

Under the agreement, promulgated in 1949 and subsequently revised and amended, a committee of daily newspaper editors—a decidedly "exclusive club," as Caspi and Limor (1999, 27) describe the committee's composition—and the chief military censor negotiate the exact terms of censorship; these terms applied to all media, including media whose executives were not a party to the agreement. Technically, the military censor retains the unilateral right to censor material, but in practice the censor and editors negotiate the content of sensitive stories. Censorship, therefore, continues as "largely the result of a

joint and consensual initiative by the political and communications establish-
ments to restrict the free flow of information under justifiable circumstances"
(214). And part of what makes this "joint and consensual initiative" possible is
the generally "convivial relationship" between Israel's political and media elite,
who "constantly rub shoulders at social events and fraternize at more intimate
gatherings on weekends" (Limor and Nossek 1995, 294).

Journalists do not, then, frame censorship in terms of government versus
journalism but rather as Israelis in different roles whose responsibilities converge
on a common commitment to the security of their country. In the context of
the confrontations and compromises that animate the relationship between the
military and the media, journalists view the military censor as less an adversary
than a partner. Theirs is "not a marriage of love, but one of convenience," as two
Israeli media scholars recently put it: "Marriages of this type usually last for decades, mainly because all the alternatives available to the couple are worse than
remaining together" (Nossek and Limor 2001, 31). Although in principle Israeli
journalists deplore censorship, as a practical matter they condone it. Thus, rites
triumph over rights under the conditions of Israeli censorship, which is to say
that the *practice* of censorship, in contradistinction to the *laws* of censorship,
accommodates newspaper editors—even empowers them—in ways that make
censorship tolerable to the mainstream media.

Understood as a dynamic and fluid process, the mechanisms for military
censorship in Israel provide greater flexibility and more room for negotiation
than the law, read literally, allows. Moreover, the process of censorship serves as
a useful reminder, as journalists themselves acknowledge (Glasser and Liebes
1996), of the responsibilities of the media during times of war; it extends to
journalists a ready and regular forum for discussing the status of Israel's safety
and the role of journalists in securing it. This perhaps explains why so many
Israeli journalists prefer the status quo, even arguing against legislative reform.
New laws and new interpretations by the courts might in principle benefit the
media, but many in journalism prefer the decades of tradition associated with
the existing legal framework, a tradition that includes quiet and creative ways
to circumvent the letter of the law (Limor and Nossek 1995, 284; Nossek and
Limor 2001, 29).

But support for censorship, and with it support for a collaborative role for
the media, is being challenged on several fronts. First, a gap exists between the
"old guard" of Israeli journalism—who grew up as Israel grew up and whose
newspapers benefited directly, but discretely, from the prerequisites and pre-
rogatives associated with the practice of censorship— and newer generations
of journalists who are less inclined to forfeit their independence and professional obligations in exchange for the promise of privileged access to military
secrets and other insider information. Research suggests that older journalists

are more "willing to submerge basic professional values to consideration of national morale, national image and a sweeping definition of national inter-est"; united in their support for the values of press freedom and autonomy, age makes a difference in terms of the "general values . . . most important to them as a guiding principle in their lives." Older journalists favor "collective values such as patriotism, national security and peace," while younger journalists favor "individual values such as happiness and self-fulfillment" (Shamir 1988, 594).

Second, as the computerization of communication creates new venues for domestic journalism, increases access to non-Israeli sources of journalism, and generally weakens the hegemony of the mainstream media, the institutions that support and orchestrate the practice of censorship, like the editors' committee, find it increasingly difficult to sustain an enforceable system of censorship.

Finally, if various peace initiatives in the Middle East end up strengthening Israel's sense of security, the grounds for censorship—and thus the conditions for collaboration—might dissipate entirely. Even in the absence of peace in the Middle East, however, there remain questions about the prudence of a collabo-rate role for the media that depends more on winks and nods than on the rule of law and therefore informally and unofficially privileges some journalists and not others.

Among others, Pnina Lahav (1985; 1993), who offers a formidable critique of the failure of Israel's formal system of law to adequately protect a free and independent press, laments a society in which suppression of communication persists "on a very significant scale" (1993, 178). Although Lahav recognizes the inevitable line any democratic nation draws between "ordinary times and national security crises" (179), she worries about the permanency of Israel's situation—a "never-ending chain of national security crises" (180), as she puts it—and the permanence of the measures used to deal with it. When other de-mocracies in the West—which Lahav regards as the appropriate comparison, given Israel's political aspirations—deal with national security practices, their responses "are temporary and are recognized as undemocratic, at least in hind-sight" (180). Although many Americans now worry about what a protracted "war on terrorism" portends for a permanent erosion of civil liberties, so far Israel distinguishes itself as the only Western democracy to embrace decades of illiberal press controls.

The Media and Public Safety: The Case of the United States

In mostly small and insignificant ways, the media and the state often work to-gether on matters of public safety. Little or no controversy surrounds requests from the state to publish the details of a crime (a description of a suspect, for example), especially when that information might enable citizens to assist local authorities in making a timely arrest. And hardly anyone objects when news-rooms, at the request of law enforcement officials, agree to withhold information that might jeopardize the investigation of suspected criminal activity, such as plans for an undercover operation. But considerable controversy erupted in the mid-1990s when the *New York Times* and the *Washington Post,* two of the most prestigious newspapers in the United States, accepted a recommendation from the U. S. attorney general and the FBI to publish the thirty-five-thousand-word "manifesto" of a domestic terrorist whose bombing spree had spanned seventeen years (for details, see Chase 2003).

The terrorist, popularly known as the Unabomber (from a Department of Justice acronym, UNABOM, which referred to the university and airline officials who were his initial targets) had mailed sixteen bombs, beginning in 1978, that killed three and injured another twenty-three. Despite a massive manhunt that involved an FBI task force with scores of agents assigned to it, a million-dollar reward for information leading to his capture, and the first "wanted" poster to appear in cyberspace, little was known about—and very little was heard from—the usually taciturn Unabomber. That changed in late April 1995 when his sixteenth bomb killed the president of the California Forestry Association in Sacramento, California.

On the same day, the *New York Times* received and later published, though only after the FBI had cleared and edited it, a letter in which the Unabomber offered to stop making and mailing bombs if arrangements could be made to publish in a "widely read, nationally distributed periodical" a lengthy manuscript, still in preparation. Publicly, the *Times* responded cautiously and without a com-mitment to any course of action: "While the pages of *The Times* can't be held hostage by those who threaten violence," said publisher Arthur Sulzberger Jr., "we're ready to receive the manuscript described in the letter. We'll take a care-ful look at it and make a journalistic decision about whether to publish it in our pages" (Dorgan 1995). Notwithstanding critics who viewed any cooperation with the Department of Justice as inappropriate and contrary to the traditions of an independent press, many in the journalism establishment understood and sup-ported the *Times*'s position. Even uninvited and unlikely publishers, for example the *San Francisco Chronicle,* offered to consider taking "extraordinary measures to ensure public safety." Willing to ponder his own possible predicament, the *Chronicle*'s executive editor announced that his newspaper, too, would "give serious consideration to publishing such a document" (Glasser 1995, A19).

Being "ready to receive the manuscript" and being prepared to "make a jour-nalistic decision about whether to publish it" were apparently enough encour-agement for the Unabomber, who within a couple of months completed and submitted his work. Meanwhile, as the FBI distributed his essay privately, hoping that others might find in it some useful clues, the *Times* continued to "study our

options." A couple of months later, after close consultation with law enforcement officials, the details of which have never been disclosed, the *Times* and the
Washington Post decided to go ahead with plans to jointly publish the tract.

At a length and in a style of writing that newspapers normally shun, the sixty-
two-page, single-spaced essay on the evils of modern technology—a "closely
reasoned scholarly tract," as the *Times* described it—filled an eight-page insert
that appeared in the *Washington Post* on September 19, 1995. The publishers of
the *Washington Post* and the *Times*, who had agreed to split the insert's cost,
estimated at a dollar a word, issued a joint statement that cited "public safety
reasons" as the justification for acceding to the terrorist's demands. This was no
rush to judgment, the publishers reminded their readers, for they had known for
three months about the Unabomber's plans to complete a manuscript and his
demand that it be widely disseminated: "From the beginning, the two newspapers have consulted closely on the issue of whether to publish under the threat
of violence. We have consulted law enforcement officials. Both the Attorney
General and the director of the Federal Bureau of Investigation have now recommended that we print this document for public safety reasons, and we have
agreed to do so." Separately, Sulzberger explained that "it's awfully hard to put
too much faith in the words of someone with the record of violence that the
Unabomber has . . . (but) you print and he doesn't kill anybody else, that's a
pretty good deal. You print and he continues to kill people, what have you lost?
The cost of newsprint?" (Hodges 1995, 248–49).

Of course, more was at stake than the cost of newsprint, as any number of
critics pointed out. They took aim at what they regarded as, in the words of one
defender of an autonomous press, "a dangerous erosion of the line between the
media and government, a line that should be fixed and immutable": Journalists
can and do report on threats to public safety, they can even provide commentary
and advice, but "news organizations are not, and should never be, perceived to
be arms of the government" (Kirtley 1995, 249–50). Others, however, questioned
the "sacred line" that presumably separates the media from the state. The media
on "many occasions" consult with government—on kidnapping, hostage takings,
national security. Journalists' "so-called adversarial posture toward government
does not require them to subscribe to the belief . . . that government is to be
regarded as an enemy or hostile power" (Harwood 1995, 252).

Although Sulzberger assured his newsroom that the Unabomber "case was
unique and not likely to become a journalistic precedent" (Hodges 1995, 249),
assurances of this kind do little to deter the perception of a de facto policy
having been established to which editors and publishers in the future can turn
when faced with similar circumstances. Indeed, in their months of discussions,
internally and with law enforcement officials, had any of the key managers at
the *New York Times* or the *Washington Post* recalled, or been asked to recall,

with or without referring to it as a "precedent," the 1976 decision by these two newspapers to publish, along with three other newspapers, a two-column statement by a group calling itself Fighters for a Free Croatia that had killed a police officer and hijacked an airplane with ninety-two passengers aboard? And would it matter to the *Times* or the *Post* that members of the group freed their hostages and surrendered once their statement appeared in print?

Publication of the Unabomber's manuscript led directly to the arrest and later the conviction of Theodore Kaczynski, when his brother noticed similarities between what he read in the press and writings he had found a few months earlier while cleaning out the family home. But unless the *Times* and the *Post* resort to an ex post facto, ends-justifies-the-means argument, their reluctance to talk openly and candidly about the grounds for their decision—the reasons for their choices—has left many questions unanswered:

- Why and when did the *Times* shift from a promise to make a "journalistic decision" about the publication of the Unabomber's manuscript to a decision based on "public safety reasons"?
- With reference to newsrooms that "regularly receive messages from people threatening dire action unless their demands are met," what did Sulzberger mean when he said the *Times*'s "traditional response will continue to serve us well—we notify law enforcement officials, when appropriate, and print nothing." When and why is it appropriate to notify law enforcement officials? When and why is it appropriate to print nothing? Why was it appropriate for the *Times* to submit to the FBI, unopened, the letter it received from the Unabomber?
- Why did the *Times* and the *Post* publish the Unabomber's manuscript instead of insisting that the government serve as publisher by purchasing space in one or both of the newspapers? In other words, why would the *Times* and the *Post* jeopardize the integrity and independence of their newsrooms when they could have positioned the manuscript as an advertisement sponsored and paid for by the FBI?

The absence of answers to these and other questions makes it difficult to reach any conclusions about the nature of the collaborative role these two newspapers played in the Unabomber case. Until these newspapers—or the Department of Justice and the FBI—disclose the details of this particular collaboration between the media and the state, insufficient evidence exists to judge whether in this instance the publication of a terrorist's manuscript illustrates cooperation through compliance, acquiescence, or acceptance—to return to the framework introduced earlier. That is, given what little is known about the Unabomber case, it is impossible to say whether the two newspapers cooperated passively, reluctantly, or wholeheartedly; it is impossible to judge, therefore, the normative legitimacy of the press's collaborative role.

Conclusion

Defiance and deference can at times coexist, as they did in late 2005 when the *New York Times* revealed that in 2002 President George W. Bush had secretly authorized the National Security Agency to engage in domestic spying, without court-approved warrants, by eavesdropping on American citizens and other residents whose international phone calls and emails might disclose threats to the United States. The *Times* challenged the state by exposing a "major shift in American intelligence-gathering practices" and highlighting concerns about the "operation's legality." But in the continuation of the front-page story on page 22, the *Times* acknowledged that it had collaborated with the state by withholding the story for a year and omitting details that might aid terrorists:

> The White House asked *The New York Times* not to publish this article, arguing that it could jeopardize continuing investigations and alert would-be terrorists that they might be under scrutiny. After meeting with senior administration officials to hear their concerns, the newspaper delayed publication for a year to conduct additional reporting. Some of the information that administration officials argued could be useful to terrorists has been omitted. (Risen and Lichtblau 2005, A22)

Editor Bill Keller had little to say beyond what appeared in the story, except to point out that his reporters focused on a "secret policy reversal" and an "expansion of authority" that had "prompted debate within the government" (2005). As the story itself explained, until the *Times* detected dissent within the government, the editors deferred to the administration's claim that "existing safeguards are sufficient to protect the privacy and civil liberties of Americans" (Risen and Lichtblau 2005, A22) and agreed not to make public what they knew about the domestic spying program. "It is not our place to pass judgment on the legal or civil liberties questions involved in such a program," Keller said, "but it became clear those questions loomed larger within the government than we had previously understood."

Predictably, readers wanted to know more. Some readers wanted to know why the *Times* had needed to wait until it could document disagreement among government officials before it felt comfortable publishing the story. Did the *Times* hold back a story that might have affected the outcome of the 2004 election? Others wanted to know who or what gave the *Times*—no matter what debate did or did not take place behind closed doors—the authority to publish classified information, and they welcomed a Justice Department investigation into the unlawful disclosure of a top-secret surveillance operation.

As in 1995 when they faced scrutiny of their decision to publish the Unabomber's manifesto, the editors of the *Times* declined every opportunity to answer questions, including questions from the paper's own staff, and relied instead on a couple of prepared statements from Keller. The public editor at the *Times,* Byron Calame, who was hired to ask questions on behalf of curious and concerned readers, reported a "loud silence" in response to the twenty-eight questions he emailed to Keller and to publisher Arthur Sulzberger Jr. "The *New York Times's* explanation of its decision to report, after what it said was a one-year delay, that the National Security Agency is eavesdropping domestically without court-approved warrants was woefully inadequate," he wrote in a column published two weeks after the story broke. "And I have had unusual difficulty getting a better explanation for readers, despite the paper's repeated pledge of greater transparency." Keller's only response to Calame's inquiry was the underdeveloped claim that there "is really no way to have a full discussion of the back story without talking about when and how we knew what we knew, and we can't do that." Calame surmised this response meant that "the sourcing for the eavesdropping article is so intertwined with the decisions about when and what to publish that a full explanation could risk revealing sources" (Calame 2006).

But the "back story" of importance to readers and others concerned about press roles and responsibilities does not require the *Times* to reveal the identity of sources or otherwise renege on promises of secrecy. There may be legitimate reasons for journalists to be less than candid, at least for a period of time, about how they have gathered information and developed a story, but those reasons do not apply to the morally interesting back story: the reasons for the reasons. Sissela Bok (1978, 104–5; 1982, 112–13), who has written widely on matters of public morality, makes just this point when she distinguishes between acts of secrecy and the practice of secrecy. Just as no one should expect physicians to violate patient confidentiality in order to justify patient confidentiality, no one needs to expect the *Times* to talk openly about particular acts of secrecy in order to explain and defend the practice of secrecy. No *need* for secrecy, in other words, prevents the *Times* from discussing its standards for *allowable* secrecy. Thus, with reference to the principles and policies that apply to, but reveal nothing in particular about, the domestic spying story, Keller and others at the *Times* could have—and should have—addressed any number of questions concerning secrecy in journalism and collaboration with the state:

- With regard to how it deals with state secrets: Under what circumstances, if any, does the rule of law require the *Times* to refuse to accept, with or without plans for publication, what it knows will be an illegally disclosed secret? Under what circumstances, if any, will the *Times* agree to conceal the secret information it retrieves or agrees to receive?
- With regard to the connection between collaboration and consensus: If no one in government regards a secret plan or operation as morally or legally dubious, does the *Times* have any justification for writing about it?

- And with regard to a full disclosure of its relationship with the state: What conditions need to be met before the *Times* will discuss in detail its dealings with state officials?

Articulating and accepting a normatively viable collaborative role for the press requires a more nuanced view of the state and state-press arrangements than most Western views of press freedom permit. So long as journalists insist on casting the state in the role of villain, collaboration with the state will remain a dishonorable and indefensible endeavor. Such disdain for any relationship with government officials is especially prevalent in the United States, which has over the years contributed more than its fair share to the world's literature on why the state needs to steer clear of any entanglements with the press. A rich folklore surrounds other roles for the media, particularly ones that pit the media against the state, but no mythology exists that celebrates cooperation, especially cooperation with the state. This state of mind deprives journalists of the cultural capital they need to develop for themselves—and for the public, an appreciation of the history and importance of state-press partnerships. In addition, it delays discussion of the various forms of collaboration, discussed earlier and outlined in table 2, and the very different grounds for them. Collaboration as a normative ideal, a partnership based on mutually agreeable means and ends, differs in important ways from other forms of collaboration, but these differences end up getting lost in the rhetoric of independence and autonomy.

Like any of the media roles we discuss in this book, a collaborative one needs to be understood in the context of its application. Roles apply in particular instances and at particular times. On any given day, most news media play multiple roles. Even in the context of a single project or story, the media can shift postures and play more than one role, depending on what practitioners want to achieve and how they want to achieve it. No role precludes another.

When the media refuse to discuss, openly and candidly, their criteria for collaboration, it invites the perception of collusion. This is why collaboration as a normative agreement, the most morally appealing form of collaboration, demands not only transparency but a deliberative process through which journalists and nonjournalists alike can assess the merits of a collaborative role for the media. In short, the legitimacy of such a role depends on publicity, which, Bok reminds us, requires more than mere openness regarding actual practices: "the arguments for and against these practices must themselves be submitted to debate" (1982, 113).

Notes

1. Legislation passed in 1977 virtually eliminated a privately owned press by prohibiting anyone from owning more than 3 percent of the ordinary shares of a newspaper, and by creating a special category of management shares—"golden" shares—that pay

the same dividends as regular shares but have two hundred times the voting power. The government approves the distribution of management shares and thus indirectly controls the fate of Singapore's newspapers (Ang 2002, 81–82; Lee 2000, 218; Soon and Soh 1994, 37–38).

2. The most frequently cited example of inflammatory journalism is the coverage of the decision to remove a young girl, Maria Hertogh, from her Muslim foster mother and place her with her Dutch Christian parents. Before departing for Holland, Maria stayed at a Roman Catholic convent, where journalists took photographs of her crying beside a nun and praying before a statue of the Virgin Mary. Outraged Muslims took to the streets, attacking Europeans and Eurasians, in what turned out to be some of the worst rioting in Singapore's history.

3. Officials in Singapore enjoy citing studies that show that "three times as many Singaporeans have a great deal of confidence in our press as Americans have in theirs, and three times as many Americans as Singaporeans view their domestic press with little confidence" (Goh 1995, 3). They also enjoy citing the Philippines as an example of the freest press in Southeast Asia and one of the worst records of modernization and economic progress (Tan and Soh 1994, 46).

Prospects

10

Media Roles under Challenge

We have outlined the underlying normative principles by which the media's contribution to the democratic political process has typically been judged. We have also tried to describe the various journalistic roles that the media themselves choose to play in society, in varying degrees and with varying consequences. Although the so-called free media choose their own actions in these matters, their freedom is circumscribed. Many constraints and inducements affect them—social, political, and financial. The more extensive and potentially influential the media are, the more likely is pressure to conform to the wishes of others, despite nominal or last-resort independence. The media are too locked in to the affairs of the wider society to ignore the pressing expectations they are exposed to, quite apart from the requirements of their own audiences. On the other hand, even the freest media are bound by their internal values and thus follow a certain normative line. Therefore, it is a libertarian illusion to assume that some media are free while others are unfree; they are all extensions of social forces of some kind. Accordingly, media freedom should not be seen as an isolated concept but as inseparable from its counterpart: responsibility, whether attributed or self-chosen.

Contemporary Critiques of Media Performance

Our story has spanned a period during which much has changed and continues to do so. A central aspect of change has been what was widely understood fifty years ago as the press becoming the contemporary mass media or news media, with television still playing a central role but increasingly challenged by new media forms. This reflects not only the transformation of dominant technologies, from printing to electronics, but also increased uncertainty about the very identity of the press that gained its status in struggles for democracy over the last two hundred or more years. Forged in the primarily industrial world through the processes of democratization, liberalization, and social reform, the institution's central character has come into question. The press is caught between conflicting demands that it provide both more diversion and entertainment and more specific, detailed, and technical information, quite apart from the demands of the market for profit and from pressure groups' efforts to shape the news. One feature of the older press that remains largely unchanged is its centrality for political life. For this reason, we concentrate initially on the links between media and democratic politics, before considering wider issues.

Increasing expressions of gloom have been heard about the rather poor condition of democracy in many countries, especially in North America and Western Europe but also in Asia and elsewhere (Bennett 2003; Bogart 1995; Entman 1989; Fallows 1995; Patterson 1994). The manifestation of problems has been seen in low or declining voter turnout in elections, lack of interest and participation, and increased apathy and disenchantment about politics in general among citizens. There is a widespread impression that the quality of civic life and citizenship is on the decline. Along with minimal turnout and interest, low or falling average levels of political knowledge are reported. There is some evidence of declining trust in politicians and in established political institutions in several major democracies.

Contributing to the alleged malaise of democratic politics has been the behavior of politicians, especially in the form of so-called modern or simply American campaigning methods (see Sussman and Galizio 2003; Swanson and Mancini 1996). Essentially the professionalization of political campaigns, these methods involve employing experts and the extensive application of commercial advertising and marketing strategies as campaigning practices. The newer methods of campaigning also require the tracking, controlling, and flattering of opinion. None of these methods is entirely new, but they have been adopted more widely and without question, without attention to the possible side effects. One such serious effect is increased cynicism and distrust on the part of the electorate, who are treated as targets for selling some candidate or policy or spectators to be diverted by spectacle, rather than as thinking and involved citizens.

More recently, world events have added a new dimension to the difficulties facing the news media in carrying out their democratic role, especially in a number of countries affected. Governments' fixation on the dangers of terrorism in the wake of the terrorist attacks of September 11, 2001, has encouraged the view that the news media can and should be co-opted into the fight or defense against terrorism. This trend has been accentuated by the military actions in Afghanistan and Iraq, which have tended to make media cooperation with government agencies an issue of patriotism, often with approval from public opinion. The consequences have been a narrowing of the interpretive frames of key events and a diminished range of sources of news, and some real reductions in freedom of information and protections for journalists. The independence of journalism from centers of power has to some extent been compromised.

The "decline of democracy" thesis has also been rather closely connected with a long-running and now accelerating critique of the media, as if the media were primarily responsible for the public's apparent loss of interest and trust in established institutions. Blumler and Gurevitch, for instance, have summed up the argument in their *Crisis of Public Communication* (1995; see also Blumler and Kavanagh 1999). The concept of "video-malaise" was floated in Germany as a consequence of the arrival of commercial television (Schulz 1998), with television entertainment being blamed for diverting citizens from their civic duties. The main points of the critique and the perceived connection between low media performance and political decline include:

- Commercial pressures and incentives are lowering standards of journalism all around and especially drawing resources and attention away from unprofitable types of news, a category that typically includes a strong component of political background information as well as international news. Such journalism does not usually attract large audiences but is widely seen as essential to political life.
- The result is to devalue political content, by giving it less attention or treating it less seriously and concentrating on human interest, scandal, and sensation. The general trend has typically been called "tabloidization," referring to the stereotype of this news format as populist, superficial, and sensational.
- Political news coverage tends to frame politics in terms of contests, games, or personal conflicts, neglecting the substance of debate and the content of issues. This horse-race or "strategic" coverage leads to ignorance and cynicism (Cappella and Jamieson 1997).
- Deregulation and, in Europe, the decline of public service broadcasting have weakened the media that are dedicated to maintaining broad coverage of public and political issues relevant to the whole society. The resulting deficiency has not been made up by the flood of new, more commercial channels.
- A somewhat dated argument is still heard that television in particular is both a visual medium that conveys little hard information and a domestic and privatizing medium that encourages passivity and individual isolation rather than public participation (Putnam 2000).
- In general, the media are more and more devoted to promoting individual consumerism and increasingly neglect larger social concerns.

It is noticeable that in the long tradition of critical attention to the mass media, the ground of attack has shifted, and there is much less emphasis on the media's bias, hidden ideology, or hegemonic influence. The media are viewed now as rather absent of political or social commitment (although still open to co-option by official sources) and thus leading to citizen disengagement rather than acting as deliberate agents of manipulation or control.

Alternative Perspectives on Changing Media and Politics

The plausible argument logically linking two apparently secular trends (decline of politics and decline of media quality) is less convincing when looked at closely, and neither trend is firmly established (see Norris 2001 for an entirely different view). In the case of politics, the empirical evidence of citizen detachment varies from place to place, and the supposed decline of democracy is rarely given a time-scale or indication of pace. The appropriate standard for news in a healthy democracy is rarely specified. We can observe both a rise and fall in the quality of overall media performance and cannot rule out the possibility that new situations may have a politically energizing effect, quite apart from the unexploited potential of new media.

Even if traditional organized party politics is declining in popular favor or failing to engage it, other parallel developments tell a different story. An expansion of extrainstitutional politics is evident, as well as an emergence of new social movements associated with single issues or large causes like the environment, feminism, antiwar, and antiglobalization movements, or mobilization against immigration. The new movements may not all be in tune with traditional democratic principles of reason and justice, but they nevertheless indicate active political involvement. Observers have noted an increasing privatization and individuation of politics, with attention to issues of consumerism and lifestyle. People are mobilizing around questions that seem to have more direct bearing on their lives. These trends pose new challenges for political institutions (see Dahlgren and Gurevitch 2005).

Lance Bennett (2003) suggests that the negative assessment of trends in political engagement may stem from a commitment to an older tradition of modernist thinking. According to postmodern perceptions, new forms of public identity and civic life are emerging. These newer forms of civic engagement are more closely linked to personal lifestyles. The popularizing trend of contemporary mass media can be seen as reflecting the "new politics" and also a decline in the traditional male domination of the journalistic world. The press has in some respects become more gender inclusive as it seeks to redefine its traditional role, and women are occupying a larger share of the professional pool.

The criticisms of the mainstream news media noted above cannot all be dismissed. But complaints of lower standards do not usually go far below the surface and are rooted in rather unbending norms of a serious journalism more suited to the needs of the political elite than the mass electorate. New styles and formats for presenting reality may attract the denigratory labels "infotainment" and "tabloidization," without serious attempts to differentiate among many different cases and subgenres or to weigh the benefits of engaging audiences against the seeming lack of substance or sophistication. Popular journalism and infotainment may be necessary conditions for effectively involving nonelites. Political communication should include a place for the personal and emotional concerns of the private sphere.

The critique of news media declining in their political role tends to be directed at the traditional flagships of journalistic authority, especially the prestigious national press and certain periodicals, and the main public service or network news channels that typically serve the political elite. Critics make little attempt to take account of the total volume and diversity of sources of political information now available. It is possible that the critique reflects more of what Manheim (2007) calls the mythology rather than the reality of journalism. There is evidently considerable room for alternative norms of adequacy, and it is clear that the quality of democracy depends on the contribution of several different partners besides the media—citizens, businesses, politicians, and governmental actors generally.

With these remarks about what is essentially a change in the cultures of society and media, we are challenging the traditional normative standards for journalism that usually embody some version of what Zaller (2003; and see chapter 5 here) has called the "full news standard." By the same token, we call into question the expectations that legitimate the news media roles we have outlined. Why should the press have obligations to report systematically on events and circumstances as selected by political institutions, when there is no objective measure of what is more or less significant? Why should reporters cooperate with authorities or serve community purposes beyond what is necessary or in their self-interest? Why should it be their task to uncover or criticize abuse? There is no longer any authoritative answer to such questions and no basis for a coherent response that is in tune with the current trends underway.

The Wider Critique

The contemporary critical attention to the role of the news media in the democratic political process comes on the tail of a wider debate about media quality that has accompanied the development of the modern media and has not yet been resolved or superseded. The many failings of the media in relation to democracy have underlying causes that are hardly new. These include the ever-increasing scale of media operations, their global ownership and control, higher degrees of concentration and cross-ownership, and the pressures resulting from the commercialization of journalistic objectives. Each trend reduces the likelihood that any media organization will meet its potential obligations to society, which are in any case increasingly denied or disregarded as irrelevant and unprofitable. Between them, contemporary tendencies work toward a concentration of communicative power in a few hands nationally and globally. They place the goals of profit before other purposes and subordinate standards of professionalism to the same criteria.

The consequences are highly selective information and systematically biased opinion. The media's concentration opens them to greater penetration by sources with economic or political power. Business connections with other economic branches are strengthened, reducing still further the media's independence. Accountability to shareholders and owners takes precedence over professional accountability and public responsibility. As the new media develop and become popular, they are drawn into the same nexus of control and priorities. Although there are undoubtedly many more voices and channels broadcasting views and news than before, their direct reach is generally limited and highly fragmented. Many commentators have drawn attention to the increasing possibility of the communications media, especially in their digital electronic forms, providing the means of centralized surveillance of nearly everyone on behalf of agencies ostensibly set up to protect society from its enemies. Our acts of communication, like our acts of consumption, are likely to be monitored or logged in computer records, as well as by concealed cameras in public places. As our possibilities for communicating and receiving communication have increased, so have the possibilities for others to know how we use our freedom in this respect.

None of this is particularly new as critique, but it is made more serious in its consequences by the centrality of large-scale media in an "information society" in which the control and flow of public knowledge is a key resource. The concern is also accentuated by the almost total neglect of initiatives for reform on behalf of the public interest, whether by governments or by media institutions themselves. In the Western world, there is little serious challenge to the view that the media are primarily a business and that the freedom of the media is the freedom to trade. Media regulation and policy are now largely devoted to promoting the technological and commercial development of media business opportunities, treating the opening of yet more hardware and software markets as an end in itself. Measures to limit these trends described are widely regarded as interference with the sacred principles of free markets. Instead politicians use the media for their own purposes—partisan, propagandist, and manipulative, often more disinformational than informational—seeking to avoid rather than welcome open-ended public debate in such forums that still exist for this purpose.

Changes Affecting the Old Media

The traditional media are themselves undergoing significant changes. Some of these changes reflect innovations in communication technology. The operating environments of older media are being changed by the arrival of genuinely new media, such as the Internet and mobile communication, and by the new market conditions that are resulting. The newspaper press has been the main traditional channel of political communication in the past, whether by voluntarily adopting a partisan political role or by giving priority to its role as a neutral carrier of views and information to the wider public. After a long period of maturity and relative stability, the press is being obliged to adapt to new circumstances. This shows up in several ways, including the continued trend toward concentration of ownership and a frantic search for new audiences and new formulas and forms. In many countries, too many publications are competing for an advertising and reader market that is stable or falling. Newspapers fear, with some justification, a declining and aging audience and intensifying competition from other more attractive media.

They also fear the loss of certain profitable forms of advertising, such as for jobs, travel, houses, and other personal goods and services, to the Internet. One form of adaptation is for large newspaper firms to enter into the new media as owners or content providers, thus hedging investment bets by making the new media into extensions of the old (see Boczkowski 2002; van der Wurff 2005). Computers and digitalization have connected the print media much more closely with other media platforms, making them less distinctive and in some respects less independent. Fortunati (2005) has described a process of the Internet's "mediatization," as the mass media extend into the new forms of distribution, coupled with an "Internetization" of the mass media, as they adapt to new challenges and a new operating environment. It is not yet clear that newspapers have changed very significantly or that the Internet has established itself as a major alternative news supplier (see below). In this process of convergence—which is also one of new media emergence—there is a possibility that the journalism profession is being weakened by the loss of their professional monopoly as gatekeepers of the public flow of information and their exclusive claim to be the chief information professionals.

The process of adaptation to a changed media situation and new social trends is making the traditional newspaper into more of an entertainment-oriented and visually attractive medium, appealing to popular taste, to young readers, and to what it perceives as of interest to women. All this is enough on its own to explain the widely observed phenomenon of tabloidization. Whatever the explanation, the newspaper can no longer be relied on to provide the traditional automatic service to the democratic political process, either because it cannot or because it no longer sees this as a profitable path. There is very little obligation or incentive to constrain the press to meet such unwritten social obligations, aside from the pressures to be patriotic when national security is at stake.

Television has been undergoing similar changes, a trend especially notice-able in Europe, after decades of democratic political control and subjection to assigned social and political roles. Television has also lost some of its actual or perceived influence as the single most authenticated and widely consulted source of information about politics for most ordinary citizens. The newer technolo-gies of distribution by cable and satellite that sparked a process of deregulation and competitive expansion in the 1980s, accompanied by a relative decline of public service broadcasting, have resulted in the change in television's position. In many countries, several, even many, commercial television channels have arrived, competing for the same general television audience. In addition, a few special interest channels have entered the scene, some of them transnational, although there is little new provision specifically dedicated to politics.

What we call television is also changing because of new means of delivery and digitalization that accelerate the process of channel proliferation and possibly diversification. While technology is an obvious cause, there are certainly other contributory factors to be found in the social and cultural trends of our time. An important aspect of change has been the gradual decline or even disappear-ance of the mass audience, typical of the 1970s and 1980s, when over-the-air television could no longer deliver a majority of the population for its popular transmissions or even for the regular main evening news bulletin (Webster and Phelan 1997). This fragmentation of total viewing across multiple channels has been accompanied by planned segmentation designed to match these chan-nels with income and lifestyle segments of the consumer market. Arguably, the political role of television has been downgraded, in relative terms at least, especially in circumstances where it cannot be used for political advertising as in most of Europe.

Despite the continuation of certain regulatory controls and pressures to se-cure an adequate and diverse supply of news and information—controls that are gradually weakening in their effect—television has generally become even more entertainment-oriented and populist in its program policies than it used to be. Television now finds it hard to effectively deliver on its voluntary or invol-untary commitments to serve the political process with information and access for politics at time slots that will reach large audiences. Political information in its traditional forms is becoming more marginalized, and the service con-sciously rendered to democracy is being given a lower priority than success in the market place.

Despite the radically increased range of transmission of television and the existence of some international channels, little has come of the large expectations of a global public for news and information. Many of the same barriers that apply to the printed press also apply to television when it comes to news and political opinion. There is no global democratic system to support demand.

The Potential of New Media

The perception that what are now called "new media" can be an aid to democracy dates back to the late 1960s, when the potential of the emerging electronic communication technology to subvert the dominant forces of society was first recognized. The inspiration was mainly derived from radical and libertarian movements of the 1960s but was coupled also with ideas about the grass roots, community, and democracy (Enzensberger 1970). There was a flowering of an underground press in these years (especially in the U.S.), and micromedia were making their appearance in developing countries and countries enduring dictatorial rule (Downing 2001). There was much praise for the achievements of the samizdat press in the Soviet Union. The relevant "technologies of liberation" included local radio, community television by cable, transistor radios, cassette recorders, mobile printing presses, Xerox machines, and personal or low-tech television cameras. Only later, during the early 1980s, did the relevant technologies come to include computer-based communication possibilities and even the telephone. The emerging new media, in their political dimension, were seen as connected with alternative and counterculture politics rather than with mainstream democracy.

The more recent (post-1990) phase of new media thinking has emphasized the potential for the media to revive mainstream democratic national or society-wide politics. Theorizing has tended to be somewhat technocentric, in contrast to earlier, more society-derived theory. Even so, this division remains, with one school of thought extrapolating benefits to politics as an effect of technology and another looking to technology to facilitate the democratic process, especially by way of wider and deeper involvement. As time has gone by, experience and research evidence have combined to dim technocratic hopes and reinstate the social-political perspective.

A number of possible benefits to the normal democratic political processes have been identified by several authors (e.g., Axford and Huggins 2001; Bentivegna 2002; Dahlgren 2005; Hacker and van Dijk 2000; Norris 2001). These benefits include more direct democracy by electronic polling; improved access for citizens to party leaders and candidates, with more interaction between them; greater capacity to mobilize and organize support and action. In addition, the new electronic media remove some barriers to publication and reduce the power of the mass media as gatekeepers. In general, we can expect a greater volume and diversity of politically relevant information to circulate.

Scattered evidence in support of some of these benefits has been found, although no real estimate can be made of any significant difference in political enlightenment or involvement in the political process. The findings now emerging from research into the use of the new media in politics generally sound a warning against high expectations of fundamental change in the overall situation. The reasons lie variously in the relative youth of the Internet and the resistance of existing institutions. In addition are some obstinate facts of social behavior, media structure, and media use habits that include the following:

- Access to the media, including new media, whether as sender or receiver remains very unequal and socially stratified. There are still many barriers to the easy use of new media.
- The salience of politics to new media users remains on the whole low, compared to the many competitors for attention that are better advertised and promoted. Making more political content readily available does not necessarily gain a wider audience.
- The new media offer many specialist opportunities to politicians and already active citizens, without enlarging the general appeal of politics. Those who are excluded or alienated by politics are no more easily reached than by traditional means.
- The new virtual communities made possible by the Internet are not reliable, trustworthy, or stable as social networks, often lacking the social cement and common interests of "real" groups.
- Already, multimedia businesses or governments are extending control over the gateways and uses of the Internet, neutralizing much of the hoped-for liberating potential.
- Established political parties and authorities are not strongly motivated to explore the truly new potential of the new media, except where it serves their own organizational purposes. There has been a tendency to use new media in old ways. Politics itself has generally become more institutionalized and closely managed from the center or top.

The arrival of new, online media has given rise to a number of new issues and new uncertainties about the proper conduct of those who seek to use them for communication in the public domain. Partly because of the essentially unregulated character of the Internet, as yet there are no or few ethical rules and guidelines to apply in cyberspace (but see Hamelink 2000). In the absence of any new legal framework, the existing laws concerning public communication also apply to the Internet, especially where harm to others or the state or property rights might be involved. Similarly, where the Internet is used for typical old media activities such as news journalism, we can expect the same professional norms and ethics to apply and for the same reasons. These reasons include the need to meet the criteria of quality and, in the case of news, to establish relations of trust and credibility. Where market relationships are involved in Internet communication, there are also ethical guidelines for practice that cannot be evaded. Even so, there are quite a few gray areas where existing rules do not fit or do not really exist. The freedom claimed for the new online media is at the core of many difficulties. Ultimately freedom involves a denial of all accountability and a challenge to all constraints and obligations of morality, law, public opinion, and the public interest. This position can be and is being contested, especially on behalf of state security and law enforcement, though it can receive some support from the character of Internet technology itself.

Certainly, there is no sure ground for expecting only or even predominantly beneficial uses regarding the political process. The flow of political communication in cyberspace can be just as biased, manipulative, propagandist, disinformational, distorted, manipulative, cynical, and xenophobic as in the conventional channels of present-day mass media. Paradoxically, the very openness and lack of institutional control over the new media may negate the potential benefits. But this is not so paradoxical if one considers the history of the previous democratic channels of public communication: the press and broadcasting.

Indeed, one may ask whether the public and open nature of political life is better served by old than by new media. The former are currently more inclusive, and give visibility, structure, and consistency to currents of opinion and social action. Direct, tangible contact as well as institutional continuity are still needed, at least for the conduct of "old politics." Trust and loyalty between participants in political life require transparency and continuity if they are to develop, and new media tend to operate without transparency and in fleeting forms. However, this assessment does not take adequate account of the increasing sclerosis of politics and the various ills outlined earlier in this chapter. What remains untested is whether there is any new form of democratic politics that might develop intimate connections with the new technology. Such new forms have already been imagined, and proposed but it is hard to see how they could be generally adopted, and if not, they would not be democratic. No verdict is possible at this moment (see Bonham 2004).

In fact, no single outcome to the transformation of political communication is likely as a result of the new media. Lincoln Dahlberg (2001), for instance, has described three different visions or rhetorics concerning the impact of the Internet on democratic processes. The terms he uses echo differences in democratic theory that we have described earlier in this book (see chapter 4). He identifies, first, a rhetoric of "liberal individualism," according to which the new media free rational citizens from the constraints of party and ideology. Citizens can make their own choices in a large market of ideas and policies. Democratic processes such as voting can be carried out by way of the Internet. The tendency is likely to be toward majoritarian and plebiscitary decision making, but operating according to market rules, with possibilities for diversity. The second rhetoric is that of communitarianism that celebrates the local, the social or cultural group, and the community. Networks are based on such categories rather than being commercial, governmental, or society-wide. Different ends and ways of doing things are likely to be promoted. Third, there is the rhetoric of deliberation, with the new media providing the basis for a virtual public sphere (Barber 1984) and with much greater emphasis on and possibility for extensive dialogue and debate. There is no reason to suppose that any one of these models will triumph. However, it is reasonable to expect, given the Internet's current direction, that liberal individualism will still be dominant and market relations will continue to influence political relations.

This variety of visions for the mediation of politics by the Internet reflects the diversity of what makes up the Internet and its many uses in different aspects of democratic political processes. Dahlgren has identified five distinct ways the Internet intervenes in the conduct of politics or affects its course. He describes these "different sectors of Net-based Public Spheres" as follows:

1. Versions of *e-government,* usually with a top-down character, where government representatives interact with citizens and where information about government administration and services is made available.
2. The *advocacy/activist* domain where discussion is framed by organizations with generally shared perspectives, values and goals—and geared for forms of political intervention.
3. The vast array of diverse *civic forums* where views are exchanged among citizens and deliberation can take place.
4. The prepolitical or *parapolitical* domain, which airs social and cultural topics having to do with common interests and/or collective identities.
5. The *journalism domain* which includes everything from major news organizations that have gone online to Net-based news organizations (usually without much or any original reporting) such as Yahoo! News, alternative news organizations such as Indymedia and Mediachannel, as well as one-person weblog sites. (2005, 153)

This classification reminds us that effects from the new media can flow in quite different streams, each with somewhat different consequences for, and various interactions with, established forms of political communication. It is clear from Dahlgren's list that the formulation of media roles cannot simply be transferred from the traditional press to new branches of the media. There are too many substantial differences of form, content, and purpose. The roles we have identified are still generally relevant to the enlarged journalism domain, but there are also new roles emerging, especially those relating to active participation, empowerment, and dialogue.

Lessons for and from Press Theory

The various media changes we have mentioned do appear to undermine the conventional basis of a unified democratic media institution—one that would be universally available and responsive to the citizens of a given national society, according to some more or less commonly accepted principles of operation and norms for conduct. Of significance is the diversification and individuation of media use and the escape of increasing sections of the public from exposure to a more or less common diet of political information and ideas. The new diversity is to be valued, but the loss of a shared public space must also be regretted.

As we noted at the outset of this book, the older institution of the press— essentially news and journalism—gradually acquired a set of customary rights and obligations, and even an element of de facto monopoly over the production and flow of information in the public sphere. It rested on a foundation of law and custom, with strong professional underpinnings. As a result of media industry changes, what was once understood as the press is simply one component of larger media industries—often multimedia conglomerates. Typically there is no clear organizational separation for the press, and it is subject to the same logics and pressures as other components of the media industry. The result of other changes that are mainly technological is to bring the press's identity and autonomy into question and introduce numerous ill-defined informational activities into its domain. The outcome is untidy and sometimes disturbing, but this is not in itself necessarily undemocratic. Perhaps even the reverse is true, since it also has the effect of weakening the grip of monopoly control of news, as well as control by professional newspeople. More is involved than a territorial dispute and control over the rules of the game. There is a new uncertainty about, and a fragmentation of, press roles as we have come to understand them.

Our account of different traditions of normative thinking about public communication has portrayed an expanding and diversifying set of ideas about the accounts of reality that lie at the core of journalistic practice. Our account also makes clear that, as observed in *Four Theories,* prescriptive theory always reflects the nature of the society and of the times. Our story begins with aspirations of reaching a high standard of truth, in its fullest and deepest sense. These were modified as libertarian, and then democratic, claims arose of an inalienable individual right to seek and determine a personal truth. In the last century, when journalism acquired its modern institutional form, embedded in media organizations with essential functions for the economy and government of industrial states, a kind of compromise was reached between absolutist truth claims and disorderly individual liberty. This compromise was encapsulated in rules for professional journalism that were mainly self-policed by the industry and journalists themselves, with variations according to national contexts. The compromise was also shaped and sometimes guided on behalf of the society or state by guarantees of protection and some elements of regulation or control. A concept of public interest in the conduct of news media, for good or ill, gradually emerged, though in disparate forms. Service to the democratic political process was one of the principal legitimations for trying to protect a public interest, although there were other reasons.

The global post–World War II restoration of media systems in countries that had been occupied or defeated effectively linked a certain procedural model of democracy—largely based on the Anglo-Saxon example—with a particular model of good journalism. This settlement of the issues was not all that settled, although it has survived as a central reference point. To a certain extent, the account we have given of journalistic roles is largely in conformity with this model, although the edifice of journalistic-democratic symbiosis is less solid and enduring than it may seem. Some of the challenges to the model were relatively easy to dismiss, especially the unconvincing theory of an objective historical truth that Communist regimes deployed to justify the conflation of news with propaganda. Other objections, however, carried more weight. From the perspective of the developing world that was being encouraged to aspire to Western democracy, Western journalistic practice looked distinctly unimpressive when tested against its own truth claims. The omissions from and ethnocentricity of what passed for accounts of what was happening in the world were just too glaring.

From within Western democracies also came no shortage of criticism of the failings of supposedly objective news, whose narratives were systematically shaped by selective frames and implicit national or political ideologies. Journalistic reform movements emerged, beginning with the advocacy of a new journalism that would be personal, engaged, and subjective. Later they included programs for civic or public journalism that would serve the local community and foreground the interests of the audience. In our account of normative theory in chapter 3 we emphasized the rise of aspirations toward more participatory and activist forms of journalism that would promote positive goals as well as useful criticism, geared to the needs of groups or communities. These normative aspirations were sustained in part by new technologies of production and transmission that have continued their advance since the early days of cable. The challenges from these quarters were sometimes linked to a fundamental critique of industrial capitalist society and involved a rejection of the alleged centralism, elitism, and hegemonic tendency of metropolitan and international mainstream journalism.

The ground was thus well prepared theoretically for the arrival and adoption of the Internet and the World Wide Web as the medium par excellence for enriching citizenship and civic engagement. Communication could become more democratic by several clear criteria, with seemingly unlimited space and access for expression, information, dialogue, and the propagation of new ideas and movements. However, it is not clear that the changes that are under way, or are considered possible, are based on any new journalistic norms. This is not surprising, given the lack of any directing hand or clear form of governance or even self-governance. The Internet has no obvious central purpose or definition as a medium within the spectrum of what is familiar. It simply develops in directions toward which its providers and users are inclined, driven by innovation and market opportunities. With increasing success, commercial pressures have also increased. Despite the lack of coherence and direction, a few principles affecting journalistic practice that the Internet has encouraged are to a limited extent an alternative to the mainstream model. They are also disparate and sometimes contradictory. They include: a highly relativistic notion of truth as expressed opinion loosely associated with a universe of certified facts uncovered by search engines; a principle of equality that equates all sources and views and recognizes no hierarchy among them; a high value placed on intimacy, subjectivity, and personal interaction; and considerable liberty of individual expression.

As is reflected in the typology of Internet-mediated content we have outlined, it is no longer feasible to propose the same prescriptive guidelines for all forms of journalism. This was always a rather doubtful project, by turn quixotic and imperialistic, designed to protect and advance journalism's mainstream institutional forms, often with the good intention of securing the news product's minimum quality. This is no longer realistic because of the increasingly successful incursions into the flow of information by other variants. It is also no longer in keeping with the media's changing structure. The main mass media of the latter twentieth century were mass newspapers or general television channels, both centered on the provision of hard news and deriving their identity in this way. The mass newspaper has been in a slow but steady decline for some time, although what looks like decline by a criterion of mass impact is partly a matter of transformation into a different kind of medium, in which breaking headline news is no longer the key feature. The typical television channel is no longer strongly anchored in a journalistic role, compared to its counterpart of twenty-five or more years ago, and its varied functions are now often dispersed.

Our own prescriptive approach to normative theory for the media should not unthinkingly adopt the values and standards of an earlier phase of press history, especially that which followed the *Four Theories* and midcentury modernity generally. This does not mean adopting a relativistic populism, but being sensitive to the diversity of expression and multiplicity of values in contemporary political realities. We should not treat the emerging new media, the Internet in particular, as a mass medium like press and broadcasting that plays much the same role, although it does share some of the same tasks and can accommodate mass media functions along with many others. We need to indicate the ways in which the norms of democratic communication have implications for the Internet, for example, in matters of ethics, accountability, responsibility, and legitimate claims from the public.

In terms of normative theory itself, one of the significant issues at present is the changing conception of the public sphere. Normative theory has always been concerned with the ways freedom and equality can be reconciled with the effectiveness of collective decision making. Overall the main concern is with preventing autocrats and oligarchs from taking advantage of relative freedom and fluidity to dominate the space of public decisions. The trend in late modernity is toward an increasing concentration of socio-political-economic power at the level of the nation-state. The ordinary person becomes little more than a helpless spectator. The great social movements that have struggled with the concentrations of power at the national and transnational levels have largely been absorbed by the dominant political-economic logic. The appeal to the social responsibility of socioeconomic power blocs and to the values of professionalism has had limited success, especially in postcolonial societies built on a base of imperial exploitation. What is occurring is a redefinition of the concept of the public sphere from the nation or city to small, transient, nonprofessional "collective happenings." In the face of the large-scale strategies, people seize on those spaces of less intensive control to establish a new worldview and a new set of norms. Since most of the essentialist concepts of rights, legal defenses, religious idealism, and movement ideologies have been incorporated by the dominant political-economic concentrations of power, spontaneous small-scale confrontations appeal more to the constructions of meaning that are based on a personal sense of identity. Learning to deal with a multiplicity of cultural identities through dialogue to understand better one's own identity becomes a primary objective.

Normative theory continues to deal with the structuring of public communication in a way that enables people to participate in decision making. The theory presents reasoned explanations of why a public sphere should be structured in a particular way. If the task in liberal democracies during the nineteenth and early twentieth centuries was to put national service structures into place to support personal moral responsibilities, today the public endeavor is to protect personal life space from domination by the same national service structures because they are now part of the dominant systems of power. If normative theory once dealt more exclusively with political economic systems, increasingly it is expressed in all areas that confront constraints on human existence.

The relevant issues for a normative theory of the media can be discussed at a number of other levels, as indicated for instance in figure 1 (see chapter 1). In particular, we can differentiate the level of a public philosophy for social communication with a universal reference from that of principles for national or international communication systems that indicate broad responsibilities of the media in society, and from that of professional actors in a given terrain of media work. In our own treatment of the larger issue, we have generally opted for a philosophy of public communication that sees the mass media as having an essential part to play in larger social and cultural processes. We accept as legitimate the claim, at the level of a media system at least, that the news media have particular responsibilities to make public the concerns of society, as embodied in a variety of voices, ranging from those of individuals and social groups to governments. This does not mean that any particular media organization can properly be compelled to do what it does not choose to do, but it points the way for responsible actions that aim to achieve public goals consistent with both professional and business norms. At the level of media organization and professional practice, we identified four primary roles that lie at the heart of the necessary public tasks of the media in society, as we see them. Although much has changed and is changing in the activities and operating environment of the media, the essence of these roles endures. The essence of each provides a useful focus for assessing the impact of change and useful guidance in pursuing the larger normative goals we have identified.

Challenges Reviewed

A brief review of the contemporary challenges and opportunities arising in the pursuit of the four roles is in order. The monitorial role of journalism remains at the core of the task of informing the public and is not essentially changed by new circumstances. If anything, there is a greater need for information over a wider range of topics from more sectors of society, with more exacting criteria of informational value. The new online media have already made a quantitative contribution to the performance of this role by opening up much greater media capacity and a qualitative contribution by increasing the diversity of what is available and by expanding the interactive search capacity of information seekers. These media have reduced the de facto monopoly of the dominant media over the gatekeeping process, although these dominant media have also entered the field of online news provision and still dominate most of the news discovery that takes place. They have also become to some extent informal and unsystematic gatekeepers for alternative news sources, directing attention to websites and treating the Internet as a source, albeit a somewhat unreliable one.

On the deficit side, dominant sources and suppliers of information (especially governments but also various industry groups, professions, and lobbies) have mounted an accelerated, and perhaps more effective, effort to manage the monitorial process to their own advantage than had been possible in the past. Economic and organizational factors often lead the news media to accede to such well-organized pressures. The alternative route to monitoring by way of alternative media or the Internet tends to be marginalized or restricted by the lack of resources and uncertainties about credibility, among other things. The gains made in media monitoring by additions to the media spectrum have to be balanced against the generally declining reach of traditional news media. More to the point of this discussion, however, are doubts about the quality of the new or alternative news sources. Despite many limitations in the quality of traditional news reporting and actual failures of performance, the truth claims that were made were usually open to challenge or confirmation according to some clear standards.

The facilitative role of journalism, in our account, has been associated largely with the encouragement of deliberative democracy at the grassroots level and with encouraging debate and circulation of ideas and information in the public arena. Almost certainly new media forms have reinvigorated the performance of this role, across the whole spectrum of public communication. However, as noted, there are alternative possibilities for the further development of the Internet, and it is not clear how much it will contribute in the longer term. Almost certainly, however, we should conclude that the facilitative role cannot be performed only by the new media. These media will only contribute to deliberation when they are interrelated with channels that both reach a larger public simultaneously and have also earned credibility by their independence and commitment to truth over a period of time.

The status of journalism's radical role can be assessed against much the same background and with many of the same conclusions. Independent criticism and comment matter more than ever on a wider range of issues that are becoming more complex to assess with any certainty, for instance in relation to the environment, biomedicine, and many social problems. The alleged "retreat from ideology," especially any belief system that challenges the social or economic order, has made it harder to mount a coordinated and coherent radical critique of the status quo on a broad front. The established mass media do not see a great deal of profit in criticism that goes beyond partisan position-taking and the perennial attraction of scandals and conflicts. The Internet and other personalized media are not really a substitute for significant representation of critical viewpoints in the media spectrum. The personal media are unsuitable because of their maverick character and inherent unreliability, not to mention their relative lack of reach to any large audience or political constituency. The result is, rather than a deepening critique, a fragmented and personalized pattern of critical ideas in circulation. The multiplication of media channels and segmentation of markets has supported the existence of what might be called critical subcultures, but this situation does not guarantee sustained and coherent critique. As always, however, major events, such as the invasion of Iraq and its consequences, do force certain issues onto the attention of a wider public and generate a society-wide debate.

The collaborative role of journalism remains very much in evidence, especially at times of crisis or disaster and with respect to the routine needs of political, social, and cultural institutions. Cooperation on many matters is supported by public opinion and thus by the publics of different media. It is often freely chosen by the media themselves, despite the ambivalence attached to the notion of a press that puts an overriding purpose for some particular information ahead of simply pursuing truth or serving the information needs of an audience. In the traditional notion of a free press, purpose is left to the original sources of news. Judgment and need are the domain of the receiver, and the media play a neutral role as messenger. The problems associated with this norm of collaboration are much the same as they ever were. They stem especially from the unequal relations of power between those typically seeking cooperation—state and military authority, government officials, powerful lobby groups—and the media and alternative voices seeking cooperation on issues whose coverage is not well funded or universally popular. In this equation, the audience is also subordinate, lacking the basis of information needed for questioning the message. The new media have neither added to nor taken much away from the practice of collaboration, either in terms of amount or value. Although the Internet has typically been identified with alternative voices and diversity, the medium is also very much at the service of propagandists. In fact, there is rather less constraint against illegitimate forms of collaboration than is to be found in mainstream media.

The main trends of contemporary society and industry are weighted toward stronger and less legitimate claims for collaboration that the media, for reasons of commercial self-interest, are less likely to resist than in the past. The demands made either explicitly or implicitly, whether by government or public opinion, commercial pressure or organizational necessity, to collaborate in the amorphous and unending war on terror are a primary cause of this role's distortion. The most visible recent manifestations of collaboration have been the subordination of journalism to military and political control, by way of correspondents being embedded in the armed forces. This has led to systematic distortion or omission of information about the course and consequences of warfare, compounding a failure to inquire deeply into warfare's causes in the first place (Kamilopour and Snow 2004; Sylvester and Huffman 2005). Each country has its own way of practicing and justifying collaboration in the name of security or patriotism, but the general outcome is to enfeeble any claim to monitoring reality on behalf of democratic process. Commercial pressures can also lead to collaboration in the form of self-censorship—as in the cases of both Rupert Murdoch's satellite television and Google's Internet services in relation to China—for reasons of expedience, given the enormous financial stakes. The nature of the pressures at work makes it unlikely that new media will aid significantly in reaching the acceptable level of transparency that we have advocated (in chapter 9) for this role.

Conclusion

The quality of performance and of systems varies a good deal from place to place, despite superficially shared notions of the media's role in society. No general assessment is possible, since the roles we have highlighted have diverse forms and sometimes contradict each other. On many occasions, the traditional journalistic obligations we have outlined are still fulfilled conscientiously and well despite some reasons for pessimism that have been mentioned. But our tone has been more pessimistic than optimistic.

We recognize that the conditions the media operate in are becoming more and more restrictive and oppressive. This is especially true when it comes to the crucial issue of having a financially profitable media system that is both committed to public enlightenment and sufficiently independent and capable of holding agencies of power in society to account—economic, political, and military. Those at the heart of power do not have to answer to the media, and the media are usually reluctant to press the issue for fear of consequences or because they have close ties to the established order. Where some media appear to have an independent capacity to challenge the powerful, often too much is at risk and too many interconnections exist with outside interests to make challenges even likely. Where the media are vigilant and critical as well as independent, they are also likely to be marginal in the landscape of the big media, unknown to the potential public and easy for the powerful to ignore. It is unrealistic to expect media to operate as an effective and equal fourth estate unless this role is also strongly supported by others operating in the public sphere—democratic politicians, to say the least.

This view does not invalidate the many efforts that are possible to increase the autonomy and principled conduct of media professionals. But we suggest that it is time to take a wider view of the developing range of possibilities for public communication and of what is still referred to as the "new media." In considering the requirements of democracy and civil society, too much atten-tion has probably been paid to the established, traditional media—a tendency of this book as well. The core of the traditional press, with its public and political tasks, is diminishing in significance, with smaller audiences and subordination to more profitable activities and less independence of voice. We may have to recognize that it is no longer adequate as the keeper of society's conscience, if it ever has been. There are no adequate institutional means available to the media for fulfilling this role, and both the moral claim and the political obligation to do so have been weakened.

New burning model is what is needed !!!

We need, in any case, to widen our theorizing to encompass those activities that might have a better claim to fulfill this role, even if their means seem weaker. This means, first, paying more attention to the many means of public communication, often small media and other forms of communication that do not seek or claim any mass range or influence but at least escape the deadening grip of management for profit only. We refer not simply or even primarily to Internet-based communication sources, which are still subject to many limiting factors and are not yet guaranteed the freedom originally claimed for the Internet. We mean all forms of communication for social, cultural, and political purposes that are coming to occupy more of society's available communication space than before, leading us to such concepts as "mediascape" (Appadurai) and "media ecology" (Postman). These forms include the many technologies available for personal use, such as photography, recording, computers, mobile phones, as well as art and performance of all kinds, and demonstrations and staged events. In these alternative areas, we need to look for and apply guiding communication norms and values for the twenty-first century.

Second, and at the same time, our theorizing should pay more attention to the many extramedia activities of research, monitoring, reflection, and means of accountability that subject the media themselves to scrutiny, both according to diverse perspectives and in a transparent manner. Many such forms of activity exist in contemporary civil society, amounting to what could be (and has been) termed a "fifth estate" (Ramonet 2003)—to which this book can be considered one small contribution.

Our quest began with an account of *Four Theories of the Press* as a significant benchmark in a much longer history of reflection and theorizing about the proper conduct of journalism in contemporary democracies. Today's society has no reason to go back to that moment to rediscover lost tablets that would provide ethical guidelines for the present. The ensuing decades of experience with proliferating forms and endlessly expanding news media, not to mention the lessons of contemporary history, have generated many new and more relevant ideas about how journalism ought to operate in order to fulfill a diversity of political and social purposes. Many of these ideas have been contributed by journalists themselves and have received support from professional associations, as well as from an apparatus of research and scholarship in the academy; in this way, professional journalism and media scholarship together have provided a counterweight to external and industry pressures. In addition, they increasingly recognize the need for and legitimacy of mechanisms of social and personal accountability that can be applied beneficially to the news media.

We cannot adequately understand the restructured media forms that are emerging as a result of the ongoing technological revolution that began in the late twentieth century in terms of the perspectives that informed the work of Siebert and his coauthors, even if many components of their thinking are still relevant when it comes to basic values. There have already been significant changes in the media and the context of their operation, with several consequences, including especially the impossibility of making an exclusive claim to a superior comprehensive vision for the media's role in society. There is no overarching criterion to be chosen above others, such as liberty, public service, participation, even truth itself. There is no longer a single shared tradition for handling these and related issues. Not least, the trend toward globalization has weakened the ties between a national society, its culture and polity, and its media.

Any normative framework for the analysis or guidance of the media that we might erect would have to take into account the great diversity of purposes and perspectives among the many actors in public communication, inevitably involving conflicts and inconsistencies. The fundamental normative issues of communication have not changed all that much, having to do with truth, purpose, effects (good or bad), and accountability. But the available normative codes for tackling them are changing and multiplying, in matters of morality, ethics, law, social theory, and professional practice, to name a few.

Despite the evident limitations of the tradition of press theorizing that we have explored, the enterprise still has value, and not simply a heuristic one. It serves as an accessible and orderly archive of ideas, principles, and examples. It encourages connections and comparisons. Its accumulated contents are a resource for critically assessing problems and policies. Even revisions and rejections are potentially illuminating. Apart from everything else, work in this field is itself an aspect of making the media accountable.

We have not been searching for any new theories of the press, which would in any case be fruitless. But there is still much searching to be done in this territory. In particular, the various roles for journalism we have described and the rules that have arisen for carrying them out exist in rather primitive or simply pragmatic forms connected with daily practice. They lack much subtlety, and this actually reveals a certain robustness, but it also leaves the roles disconnected from wider ethical considerations and too easy to disregard or disrespect.

The next phase of normative inquiry should pay more attention to the connections between the rights and duties of those who produce the news and the wider issues of human rights relating to those who receive the news, are the subject of news, or are affected by news. This means going beyond the principle of free speech and publication as seen from the newsmakers' perspective. In practice, despite the changes affecting the media that have occurred over the last half century, we have not escaped far from the central issue that preoccupied the authors of *Four Theories*.

References

Ackerman, Bruce, and James Fishkin. 2005. *Deliberation Day*. New Haven, CT: Yale University Press.

Agee, Warren K., Phillip H. Ault, and Edwin Emery. 1994. *Introduction to Mass Communication*. 11th ed. New York: Harper Collins.

Allen, David S. 2002. "Jürgen Habermas and the Search for Democratic Principles." In *Moral Engagement in Public Life: Theorists for Contemporary Ethics*, eds. Sharon Bracci and Clifford Christians, 97–122. New York: Peter Lang.

Althusser, Louis. 1984. *Essays on Ideologies*. London: Verso.

Altschull, J. Herbert. 1984. *Agents of Power: The Role of the News Media in Human Affairs*. New York: Longman.

———. 1995. *Agents of Power: The Media and Public Policy*. 2nd ed. New York: Longman.

Anderson, Charles W. 1990. *Pragmatic Liberalism*. Chicago: University of Chicago Press.

———. 2002. *A Deeper Freedom: Liberal Democracy as an Everyday Morality*. Madison: University of Wisconsin Press.

Andsager, Julie L., and M. Mark Miller. 1994. "Willingness of Journalists to Support Freedom of Expression." *Newspaper Research Journal* 5(4): 51–57.

Andsager, Julie L., Robert O. Wyatt, and Ernest Martin. 2004. *Free Expression in Five Democratic Publics*. Cresskill, NJ: Hampton Press.

Ang, Peng Hwa. 2002. "Media Ethics in Singapore: Pushing Self-Regulation in a Tightly Controlled Media Environment." In *Media Ethics in Asia: Addressing the Dilemmas in the Information Age*, ed. Venkat Iyer, 80–89. Singapore: AMIC.

Angus, Ian. 2001. *Emergent Publics: An Essay on Social Movements and Democracy*. Winnipeg: Arbeiter Ring.

Apel, Karl-Otto. 2001. *The Response of Discourse Ethics*. Leuven: Peeters.

Arato, Andrew. 2000. *Civil Society, Constitution and Legitimacy*. Lanham, MD: Rowman and Littlefield.

———. 2005. "Post-election Maxims." *Constellations* 12(2): 182–93.

Arblaster, Anthony. 1994. *Democracy.* 2nd ed. Minneapolis: University of Minnesota Press.

Arendt, Hannah. 1963. *On Revolution.* New York: Viking Press.

Arens, Edmund. 1997. "Discourse Ethics and Its Relevance." In *Communication Ethics and Universal Values,* ed. Clifford Christians and Michael Traber, 46–47. London: Sage.

Atkinson, Derek, and Marc Raboy. 1997. *Public Service Broadcasting: The Challenges of the Twenty-First Century.* Paris: UNESCO.

Atton, Chris. 2002. *Alternative Media.* London: Sage.

———. 2003. Editorial. In "What Is 'Alternative' Journalism?" Special issue. *Journalism* 4(3): 267–72.

———. 2004. *Alternative Internet.* Edinburgh: Edinburgh University Press.

Axford, Barry, and Robert Huggins, eds. 2001. *New Media and Democracy.* London: Sage.

Baker, C. Edwin. 1989. *Human Liberty and Freedom of Speech.* New York: Oxford University Press.

———. 2002. *Media, Markets, and Democracy.* New York: Cambridge University Press.

Barber, Benjamin R. 1984. *Strong Democracy: Participatory Politics for a New Age.* Berkeley: University of California Press.

———. 1996. "Foundationalism and Democracy." In *Democracy and Difference,* ed. Seyla Benhabib, 348–59. Princeton, NJ: Princeton University Press.

———. 1998. *A Passion for Democracy: American Essays.* Princeton, NJ: Princeton University Press.

———. 2007. "Pluralism." *Ethics* 117(4) (July): 747–54.

Barker, Chris. 2000. *Cultural Studies: Theory and Practice.* London: Sage.

Bauman, Zygmunt. 1993. *Postmodern Ethics.* Oxford: Blackwell.

Ben Meir, Yehuda. 1995. *Civil-Military Relations in Israel.* New York: Columbia University Press.

Benhabib, Seyla. 1992. *Situating the Self: Gender, Community and Postmodernism in Contemporary Ethics.* Cambridge: Polity.

———. 2002. *The Claims of Culture: Equality and Diversity in the Global Era.* Princeton, NJ: Princeton University Press.

———. 2006. *Another Cosmopolitanism: Hospitality, Sovereignty, and Democratic Iterations.* New York: Oxford University Press.

Bennett, W. Lance. 1990. "Towards a Theory of Press-State Relations in the U.S." *Journal of Communication* 40(2): 103–25.

———. 2003. "The Burglar Alarm That Just Keeps Ringing: A Response to Zaller." *Political Communication* 20: 131–38.

Bennett, W. Lance, and Robert Entman, eds. 2001. *Mediated Politics: Communication in the Future of Democracy.* Cambridge: Cambridge University Press.

Bensman, Marvin R. 2000. *The Beginning of Broadcast Regulation in the Twentieth Century.* Jefferson, NC: McFarland.

Bentivegna, Sara. 2002. "Politics and the New Media." In *The Handbook of New Media*, ed. Leah Lievrouw and Sonia Livingstone, 50–61. Thousand Oaks, CA and London: Sage.

Berlin, Isaiah. 1969. *Four Essays on Liberty*. London: Oxford University Press.

Berry, David, and John Theobald, eds. 2006. *Radical Mass Media Criticism: A Cultural Genealogy*. Montreal: Black Rose Books.

Bertrand, Claude-Jean. 2003. *An Arsenal for Democracy: Media Accountability Systems*. Mahway, NJ: Lawrence Erlbaum.

Bessette, Joseph M. 1980. "Deliberative Democracy: The Majority Principle in Republican Government." In *How Democratic Is the Constitution?* ed. Robert A. Goldwin and William A. Schambra, 102–16. Washington, DC: American Enterprise Institute.

Best, Steven, and Douglas Kellner. 2001. *The Postmodern Adventure: Science, Technology, and Cultural Studies at the Third Millennium*. New York: Guilford and Routledge.

Blanchard, Margaret. 1977. "The Hutchins Commission, the Press, and the Responsibility Concept." *Journalism Monographs* 49 (May):1–59.

Blasi, Vincent. 1977. "The Checking Value in First Amendment Theory." *American Bar Foundation Research Journal* 2(3): 522–649.

Bledstein, Burton J. 1976. *The Culture of Professionalism*. New York: Norton.

Blum, Roger. 2005. "Bausteine zu einer Theorie der Mediansysteme." *Medienwissenschaft Schweiz* 16(2): 5–11.

Blumler, Jay G., ed. 1992. *Television and the Public Interest*. London: Sage.

Blumler, Jay G., and Michael Gurevitch. 1995. *The Crisis of Public Communication*. London: Routledge.

Blumler, Jay G., and Dennis Kavanagh. 1999. "The Third Age of Political Communication: Influences and Features." *Political Communication* 16(3): 209–30.

Boczkowski, Pablo J. 2002. "The Development and Use of Online Newspapers." In *The Handbook of New Media*, ed. Sonia Livingstone and Leah A. Lievrouw, 270–86. London: Sage.

Bodéus, Richard. 1993. *The Political Dimensions of Aristotle's Ethics*. Translated by Jan Edward Garrett. Albany: State University of New York Press.

Bogart, Leo. 1995. *Commercial Culture: The Media System and the Public Interest*. Chicago: University of Chicago Press.

Bohman, James. 2000. *Public Deliberation: Pluralism, Complexity and Democracy*. Cambridge, MA: MIT Press.

———. 2004. "Expanding Dialogue: The Internet, the Public Sphere and Prospects for Transnational Democracy." In *After Habermas: New Perspectives on the Public Sphere*, ed. Nick Crossley and John M. Roberts, 131–55. Blackwell Sociological Review Monograph Series. Oxford: Blackwell.

———. 2007. *Democracy across Borders: From Demos to Demoi*. Cambridge, MA: MIT Press.

Bohman, James, and William Rehg, eds. 1997. *Deliberative Democracy: Essays on Reason and Politics*. Cambridge, MA: MIT Press.

Bok, Sissela. 1978. *Lying: Moral Choice in Public and Private Life*. New York: Random House.

————. 1982. *Secrets: On the Ethics of Concealment and Revelation*. New York: Random House.

Boler, Megan, ed. 2008. *Digital Media and Democracy: Tactics in Hard Times*. Cambridge, MA: MIT Press.

Bollinger, Lee C. 1991. *Images of a Free Press*. Chicago: University of Chicago Press.

Borden, William. 1995. *Power Plays: A Comparison between Swedish and American Press Policies*. Kungälv, Sweden: Department of Journalism and Mass Communication, Göteborg University.

Botein, Stephen. 1981. "Printers and the American Revolution." In *The Press and the American Revolution*, ed. Bernard Bailyn and John B. Hench, 11–58. Worcester, MA: American Antiquarian Society.

Bracci, Sharon L. 2002. "The Fragile Hope of Seyla Benhabib's Interactive Universalism." In *Moral Engagement in Public Life: Theorists for Contemporary Ethics*, ed. Sharon L. Bracci and Clifford G. Christians, 123–49. New York: Peter Lang.

Brett, Annabel, and James Tully, with Holly Hamilton-Bleakley, eds. 2006. *Rethinking the Foundations of Modern Political Thought*. Cambridge: Cambridge University Press.

Brown, Peter. 1992. *Power and Persuasion in Late Antiquity: Toward a Christian Empire*. Madison: University of Wisconsin Press.

Buber, Martin. 1958. *I and Thou*. 2nd ed. Translated by M. Friedman and R. G. Smith. New York: Scribner's.

Butler, Judith. 1998. "Ruled Out: Vocabularies of the Censor." In *Censorship and Silencing: Practices of Cultural Regulation*, ed. Robert C. Post, 247–59. Los Angeles: Getty Research Institute for the History of Art and the Humanities.

Calame, Byron. 2006. "Behind the Eavesdropping Story, a Loud Silence." *New York Times,* January 1, 2006, sec. 4, p. 8.

Campbell, Richard, and Jimmie Reeves. 1989. "Covering the Homeless: The Joyce Brown Story." *Critical Studies in Mass Communication* 6: 21–42.

Canclini, Néstor García. 1995. *Hybrid Cultures: Strategies for Entering and Leaving Modernity*. Minneapolis: University of Minnesota Press.

Canning, J. P. 1988. "Introduction: Politics, Institutions and Ideas." In *The Cambridge History of Medieval Political Thought*, ed. J. H. Burns, 341–66. Cambridge, UK: Cambridge University Press.

Cappella, Joseph N., and Kathleen Hall Jamieson. 1997. *Spiral of Cynicism: The Press and the Public Good*. New York: Oxford University Press.

Carey, James W. 1975. "A Cultural Approach to Communication." *Communication* 2: 1–22.

————. 1987. "Journalists Just Leave: The Ethics of an Anomalous Profession." In *Ethics and the Media*, ed. Maile-Gene Sagen, 5–19. Iowa City: Iowa Humanities Board.

————. 1996. "Where Journalism Education Went Wrong." In *Journalism Education, the First Amendment Imperative, and the Changing Media Marketplace*. Murfreesboro, TN: College of Mass Communication, 4–10.

————. 1999. "In Defense of Public Journalism." In *The Idea of Public Journalism*, ed. Theodore L. Glasser, 49–66. New York: Guilford.

Carpentier, Nico, and Bart Cammaerts. 2006. "Hegemony, Democracy, Agonism and Journalism: An Interview with Chantal Mouffe." *Journalism Studies* 7(6): 964–75.

Carpentier, Nico, Rico Lie, and Jan Servaes. 2007. "Multitheoretical Approaches to Community Media: Capturing Specificity and Diversity." In *Community Media: International Perspectives,* ed. Linda K. Fuller, 219–35. New York: Palgrave Macmillan.

Cartledge, Paul. 2000. "Greek Political Thought: The Historical Context." In *The Cambridge History of Greek and Roman Political Thought,* ed. Christopher Rowe and Malcolm Schofield, 11–22. Cambridge, UK: Cambridge University Press.

Caspi, Dan, and Yehiel Limor. 1999. *The In/Outsiders: Mass Media in Israel.* Cresskill, NJ: Hampton.

Castells, Manuel. 1996. *The Rise of the Network Society.* Vol. 1, *Information Age: Economy, Society and Culture.* Oxford, UK: Blackwell.

Cavalier, Robert J., ed. 2005. *The Impact of the Internet on Our Moral Lives.* Albany: State University of New York Press.

Chapman, Jane. 2005. *Comparative Media History. An Introduction: 1789 to the Present.* Cambridge, UK: Polity.

Chee, Soon Juan. 2000. "Media in Singapore." Paper presented at conference organized by the Research Institute for Asia and the Pacific and the Centre for Democratic Institutions entitled "The Media and Democracy," University of Sydney, February 24, 2000.

Cheong, Yip Seng. 1995. "Journalism with a Cause." *Straits Times,* February 15, 1995, 130–32.

Christiano, Thomas. 1996. *The Rule of Many: Fundamental Issues in Democratic Theory.* Boulder, CO: Westview Press.

Christians, Clifford. 1977. "Fifty Years of Scholarship in Media Ethics." *Journal of Communication* 27(4): 19–29.

———. 1997. "The Ethics of Being in a Communications Context." In *Communication Ethics and Universal Values,* ed. Clifford Christians and Michael Traber, 3-23. London: Sage.

———. 2004. "*Ubuntu* and Communitarianism in Media Ethics." *Equid Novi* 25(2), 235–56.

Christians, Clifford G., John P. Ferré, and P. Mark Fackler. 1993. *Good News: Social Ethics and the Press.* New York: Oxford University Press.

Christians, Clifford, and Michael Traber, eds. 1997. *Communication Ethics and Universal Values.* Thousand Oaks, CA: Sage.

Cohen, Bernard. 1963. *The Press and Foreign Policy.* Princeton, NJ: Princeton University Press.

Cohen, Jean L., and Andrew Arato. 1992. *Civil Society and Political Theory.* Cambridge: MIT University Press.

Cohen, Joshua. 1993. "Moral Pluralism and Political Consensus." In *The Idea of Democracy,* ed. D. Copp et al. Cambridge, UK: Cambridge University Press.

———. 1997a. "Deliberation and Democratic Legitimacy." In *Deliberative Democracy,* ed. James Bohman and William Rehg, 67–91. Cambridge, MA: MIT Press.

———. 1997b. "Procedure and Substance in Deliberative Democracy." In *Deliberative*

Democracy, ed. James Bohman and William Rehg, 407–37. Cambridge, MA: MIT Press.

———. 2002. "Deliberation and Democratic Legitimacy." In *Democracy*, ed. David Est-lund, 87–106. Oxford, UK: Blackwell.

Cohen, Joshua, and Joel Rogers. 1983. *On Democracy: Toward a Transformation of American Society.* New York: Penguin Books.

Colish, Marcia L. 1990. *The Stoic Tradition from Antiquity to the Early Middle Ages.* Vol 1. *Stoicism in Classical Latin Literature.* Vol 2. *Stoicism in Christian Latin Thought through the Sixth Century.* Leiden: Brill.

Commission on Freedom of the Press. 1947. *A Free and Responsible Press.* Chicago: University of Chicago Press.

Conboy, Martin. 2004. *Journalism: A Critical History.* London: Sage.

Cornell, Drucilla. 1985. "Toward a Modern/Postmodern Reconstruction of Ethics." *University of Pennsylvania Law Review* 133: 291–377.

Couldry, Nick, and James Curran, eds. 2003. *Contesting Media Power: Alternative Media in a Networked World.* Lanham, MD: Rowman and Littlefield.

Crocker, David A. 2000. "Truth Commissions, Transitional Justice, and Civil Society." In *Truth v. Justice: The Morality of Truth Commissions,* ed. Robert I. Rotberg and Dennis Thompson, 99–121. Princeton, NJ: Princeton University Press.

Curran, James. 1991a. "Mass Media and Democracy: A Reappraisal." In *Mass Media and Society,* ed. James Curran and Michael Gurevitch, 82–117. London: Edward Arnold.

———. 1991b. "Rethinking the Media as a Public Sphere." In *Communication and Citizenship: Journalism and the Public Sphere in the New Media Age,* ed. Peter Dahlgren and Colin Sparks, 27–57. Padstow, Cornwall, UK: Routledge.

———. 1996. "Mass Media and Democracy Revisited." In *Mass Media and Society,* 2nd ed., ed. James Curran and Michael Gurevitch, 81–119. London: Edward Arnold.

———. 2000. "Rethinking Media and Democracy." In *Mass Media and Society,* 3rd ed., ed. James Curran and Michael Gurevitch, 120–54. London: Edward Arnold.

———. 2002. *Media and Power.* London and New York: Routledge.

———. 2003. "Global Journalism: A Case Study of the Internet." In *Contesting Media Power: Alternative Media in a Networked World,* ed. N. Couldry and J. Curran, 227–41. Lanham, MD: Rowman and Littlefield.

Curran, James, and Myun-Jia Park, eds. 2000. *De-Westernizing Media Stuidies.* London: Routledge.

Dahl, Robert A. 1967. *Pluralist Democracy in the United States: Conflict and Consent.* Chicago: Rand McNally.

Dahlberg, Lincoln. 2001. "Democracy via Cyberspace." *New Media and Society* 3(2): 157–77.

Dahlgren, Peter. 1995. *Television and the Public Sphere.* London: Sage.

———. 2000. "Media, Citizenship and Civic Culture." In *Mass Media and Society,* 3rd ed., ed. James Curran and Michael Gurevitch, 310–28. London: Edward Arnold.

———. 2005. "The Internet, Public Spheres, and Political Communication: Dispersion and Deliberation." *Political Communication* 22: 147–62.

Dahlgren, Peter, and Michael Gurevitch. 2005. "Political Communication in a Changing World." In *Mass Media and Society,* 4th ed., ed. James Curran and Michael Gurevitch, 375–393. London: A. Hodder Arnold.

Danaher, Geoff, Tony Schirato, and Jen Webb. 2000. *Understanding Foucault.* London: Sage.

Dare, Olatunji. 2000. "The Role of the Print Media in Development and Social Change." In *Development Communication in Action: Building Understanding and Creating Participation,* ed. Andrew Moemeka, 160–78. Lanham, MD: University Press of America.

Davidson, Ivor J. 2001. *Ambrose* De Officiis. Vol. 1. *Introduction, Text and Translation.* Oxford, UK: Oxford University Press.

De Polignac, François. 1995. *Cults, Territory, and the Origins of the Greek City-State.* Translated by Janet Lloyd. Chicago: University of Chicago Press. Originally published as *La naissance de la cité greque* (Editions La Découverte, Paris, 1984).

de Romily, Jacqueline. 1998. *The Great Sophists in Periclean Athens.* Translation by Janet Lloyd. Oxford, UK: Clarendon. Originally published as *Les grandes sophists dans l'Athèns de Périclès* (Paris: Editions de Fallois, 1988).

Denzin, Norman. 1997. *Interpretive Ethnography: Ethnographic Practices for the Twenty-First Century.* Thousand Oaks, CA: Sage.

———. 2003. *Performance Ethnography: Critical Pedagogy and the Politics of Culture.* Thousand Oaks, CA: Sage.

Dervin, Brenda, and Robert Huesca. 1997. "Reaching for the Communication in Participatory Communication: A Meta-theoretical Analysis." *Journal of International Communication* 4(2): 46–74.

De Smaele, Hedwig. 1999. "The Applicability of Western Models on the Russian Media System." *European Journal of Communication* 14(2): 173–90.

Deuze, Marx. 2005. "What Is Journalism? Professional Identity and Ideology of Journalists Reconsidered." *Journalism* 6: 442–62.

Deveaux, Monique. 2000. *Cultural Pluralism and Dilemmas of Justice.* Ithaca, NY: Cornell University Press.

———. 2007. *Gender and Justice in Multicultural Liberal States.* New York: Oxford University Press.

Dicken-Garcia, Hazel. 1989. *Journalistic Standards in Nineteenth-Century America.* Madison: University of Wisconsin Press.

Donohue, G. A., Philip Tichenor, and C. N. Olien. 1995. "A Guard-Dog Perspective on the Role of the Media." *Journal of Communication* 45(2): 115–32.

Dooley, Brendan, and Sabrina Baran, eds. 2001. *The Politics of Information in Early Modern Europe.* London: Routledge.

Dorgan, Michael. 1995. "Unabomber Details Motives in Three Letters." *San Jose Mercury News,* April 26, 1A.

Downing, John. 2001. *Radical Media: Rebellious Communication and Social Movements.* Thousand Oaks, CA: Sage.

———. 2003. "The Independent Media Center Movement and the Anarchist Socialist Tradition." In *Contesting Media Power: Alternative Media in a Networked World,* ed. N. Couldry and J. Curran, 243–57. Lanham, MD: Rowman and Littlefield.

Downs, Anthony. 1957. *An Economic Theory of Democracy*. New York: Harper and Row.

———. 1962. "The Public Interest: Its Meaning in a Democracy." *Social Research* 19(1): 1–36.

Durham, Meenakshi Gigi, and Douglas Kellner, eds. 2001. *Media and Cultural Studies: Key Works*. Malden, MA: Blackwell.

Durkheim, Emile. 1960. *The Division of Labor in Society*. Glencoe, IL: Free Press.

———. 1957–92. *Professional Ethics and Civic Morals*. London: Routledge.

Dworkin, Ronald. 1993. *Life's Dimension: An Argument about Abortion, Euthanasia and Individual Freedom*. New York: Knopf.

Dyer-Witherford, Nick. 1999. *Cyber-Marx: Cycles and Circuits of Struggle in High-Technology Capitalism*. Urbana: University of Illinois Press.

Edwards, Michael. 2004. *Civil Society: Themes for the Twenty-first Century*. Cambridge, UK: Polity.

Einstein, Mara. 2004. *Media Diversity: Economics, Ownership and the FCC*. Mahwah, NJ: Erlbaum.

Elliott, Deni. 2002. Afterword to *Moral Engagement in Public Life: Theorists for Contemporary Ethics*, ed. Sharon L. Bracci and Clifford G. Christians, 277–80. New York: Peter Lang.

Emerson, Thomas I. 1970. *The System of Freedom of Expression*. New York: Vintage Books.

Entman, Robert. 1989. *Democracy without Citizens: Mass Media and the Decay of American Politics*. New York: Oxford University Press.

———. 2005. "The Nature and Sources of News." In *The Press*, ed. Geneva Overholser and Kathleen Hall Jamieson, 48–65. New York: Oxford University Press.

Enzenberger, Hans Magnus. 1970. "Constituents of a Theory of the Media." *New Left Review* 64: 13–36.

Ettema, James S., and Theodore L. Glasser. 1998. *Custodians of Conscience: Investigative Journalism and Public Virtue*. New York: Columbia University Press.

Fallows, James. 1995. *Breaking the News: How the Media Undermine American Democracy*. New York: Pantheon.

Fierlbeck, Katherine. 1998. *Globalizing Democracy: Power, Legitimacy and the Interpretation of Democratic Ideas*. Manchester, UK: Manchester University Press.

———. 2006. *Political Thought in Canada: An Intellectual History*. Petersborough, Ontario: Broadview Press.

Fishkin, James. 1992. *Democracy and Deliberation: New Directions for Democratic Reform*. New Haven, CT: Yale University Press.

———. 2007. *The Voice of the People: Public Opinion and Democracy*. New Haven, CT: Yale University Press.

Fishkin, James, and Peter Laslett. 2003. *Debating Deliberative Democracy*. Oxford, UK: Blackwell.

Fiss, Owen. 1996. *The Irony of Free Speech*. Cambridge, MA: Harvard University Press.

Fitzsimmons, M., and L. T. McGill. 1995. "The Citizen as Media Critic." *Media Studies Journal* (spring): 91–102.

Fjaestad, B., and P. G. Holmlov. 1976. "The Journalist's View." *Journal of Communication* 2: 108–14.

Fortunati, Leopoldina. 2005. "Mediatization of the Net and Internetization of the Media." *Gazette* 67 (1): 27–44.

Foucault, Michel. 1982. "The Subject and Power." Afterword to *Michel Foucault: Beyond Structuralism and Hermeneutics,* ed. Hubert Dreyfus and Paul Rabinow, 208–28. Chicago: University of Chicago Press.

Fourie, Pieter J. 2008. "Moral Philosophy as the Foundation of Moral Media Theory: Questioning African *Ubuntuism as a Framework.*" In *Media Ethics beyond Borders: A Global Perspective,* ed. Stephen J. A. Ward and Herman Wasserman, 105–22. Johannesburg, South Africa: Heinemann.

Fowler, W. W. 1893/2003. *The City-State of the Greeks and Romans.* Honolulu: University Press of the Pacific.

Fox, Elizabeth. 1988. "Media Policies in Latin America: An Overview." In *Media and Politics in Latin America: The Struggle for Democracy,* ed. Elizabeth Fox, 6-35. London: Sage.

Fraser, Nancy. 1989. *Unruly Practices: Power, Discourse, and Gender in Contemporary Social Theory.* Minneapolis: University of Minnesota Press.

———. 1992. "Rethinking the Public Sphere: A Contribution to the Critique of Actually Existing Democracy." In *Habermas and the Public Sphere,* ed. Craig Calhoun, 109–42. Cambridge, MA: MIT Press.

———. 1997. *Justus Interruptus.* New York: Routledge.

Friedland, Lewis. 2003. *Public Journalism: Past and Future.* Dayton, OH: Kettering Foundation Press.

———. 2004. "Public Journalism and Communities." *National Civic Review,* 93(3) (fall): 36–42.

Friedland, Lewis, Mira Sotirovic, and Katie Daily. 1998. "Public Journalism and Social Capital." In *Assessing Public Journalism,* ed. Edmund B. Lambeth, Philip E. Meyer, and Esther Thorson, 191–220. Columbia: University of Missouri Press.

Fuller, Linda K., ed. 2007. *Community Media: International Perspectives.* New York: Palgrave Macmillan.

Furisch, Elfriede, and Melinda B. Robins. 2002. "Africa.com: The Self-Representation of Sub-Saharan Nations on the World Wide Web." *Critical Studies in Media Communication* 19(2): 190–211.

Gadamer, Hans-Georg. 1980. *Dialogue and Dialectic: Eight Hermeneutical Studies on Plato.* Translated by P. Christopher Smith. New Haven, CT: Yale University Press.

Gallup, George. 1935. "A Study in the Selection of Salespeople for Killian's Department Store, Cedar Rapids, Iowa." Master's thesis, State University of Iowa, Iowa City.

———. 1938. "An Objective Method for Determining Reader Interest in the Content of a Newspaper." Ph.D. diss., State University of Iowa, Iowa City.

Galtung, John, and Richard Vincent. 1992. *Global Glasnost: Toward a New World Information and Information Order?* Cresskill, NJ: Hampton.

Gans, Herbert J. 2003. *Democracy and the News.* New York: Oxford University Press.

Garnham, Nicholas. 1995. "Comments on John Keane's *Structural Transformations of the Public Sphere.*" *Communication Review* 1(1): 23–25.

Garver, Eugene. 1994. *Aristotle's Rhetoric: An Art of Character.* Chicago: University of Chicago Press.

George, Cherian. 2002a. "'Asian' Journalism: More Preached Than Prized?" Paper presented to the winter meeting of the Association for Education in Journalism and Mass Communication, Palo Alto, California, December 6, 2002.

———. 2002b. "Singapore: Media at the Mainstream and the Margins." In *Media Fortunes, Changing Times: ASEAN States in Transition,* ed. Russell H. K. Heng, 173–200. Singapore: Institute of Southeast Asian Studies.

———. 2005, September. "Calibrated Coercion in the Maintenance of Hegemony in Singapore." Working paper series 48. Asia Research Institute, National University of Singapore.

Gerbner, George. 1983. "The Importance of Being Critical—In One's Own Fashion." *Journal of Communication* 33(3): 355–62.

Gerbner, George, Hamid Mowlana, and Kaarle Nordenstreng, eds. 1993. *The Global Media Debate: Its Rise, Fall and Renewal.* Cresskill, NJ: Hampton.

Giddens, Anthony. 1991. *Modernity and Self-Identity.* Oxford, UK: Polity.

———. 1994. "The Consequences of Modernity." In *Colonial Discourse and Postcolonial Theory,* ed. P. Williams and L. Chrisman, 181–89. New York: Columbia University Press.

Gillmor, Donald, Everette E. Dennis, and Theodore L. Glasser. 1989. *Media Freedom and Accountability.* New York: Greenwood.

Giroux, Henry. 2004. *The Terror of Neo Liberalism: The New Authoritarianism and the Attack on Democracy.* Boulder, CO: Paradigm.

Glasser, Theodore L. 1989. "Three Views on Accountability." In *Media Freedom and Accountability,* ed. Everette E. Dennis, Donald M. Gillmor, and Theodore L. Glasser, 179–88. Westport, CN: Greenwood.

———. 1991. "Communication and the Cultivation of Citizenship." *Communication* 12(4): 235–48.

———. 1995. "Press Should Tell Unabomber 'No.'" *San Francisco Chronicle,* July 4, 1995, p. A19.

———, ed. 1999a. *The Idea of Public Journalism.* New York: Guilford.

———. 1999b. "The Idea of Public Journalism." In *The Idea of Public Journalism,* ed. Theodore L Glasser, 2–18. New York: Guilford.

Glasser, Theodore L., and Marc Gunther. 2005. "The Legacy of Autonomy in American Journalism." In *The Press,* ed. Geneva Overholser and Kathleen Hall Jamieson, 384–99. New York: Oxford University Press.

Glasser, Theodore L., and Francis L. F. Lee. 2002. "Repositioning the Newsroom: The American Experience with Public Journalism." In *Political Journalism: New Challenges, New Practices,* ed. Raymond Kuhn and Erik Neveu, 203–4. London: Routledge.

Glasser, Theodore L., and Tamar Liebes. 1996. "Freedom of Censorship among Israeli Journalists." Paper presented to the annual meeting of the International Communication Association, Chicago, May 25, 1996.

Gleason, Timothy. 1990. *The Watchdog Concept.* Ames: Iowa State University Press.

Goh, Chok Tong. 1995. "The Singapore Press: Part of the Virtuous Cycle of Good Government and Good Society." Speech at *Straits Times* 150th anniversary gala dinner, Singapore International Convention and Exhibition Centre, July 15,1995. Press release, Public Affairs Directorate, Singapore.

Golding, Peter, and Phillip Elliott. 1979. *Making the News*. New York: Longman.

Gouldner, Alvin W. 1976. *The Dialectic of Ideology and Technology*. New York: Seabury Press.

Graber, Doris. 2001. *Processing Politics: Learning from Television in the Internet Age*. Chicago: University of Chicago Press.

———. 2003. "The Rocky Road to New Paradigms: Modernizing News and Citizenship Standards." *Political Communication* 20: 145–48.

———, ed. 2006. *Media Power in Politics*. 5th ed. Washington, DC: QC Press.

Graves, Michael A. R. 2001. *The Parliaments of Early Modern Europe*. London: Longman.

Grossberg, Lawrence. 1992. *We Gotta Get out of This Place: Popular Conservatism and Postmodern Culture*. New York: Routledge.

Gunaratne, Shelton A. 1995. "Books on Global Communication: A Philosophical Treatise." *Media Development* 42(2): 44–47.

———. 1998. "Old Wine in a New Bottle: Public Journalism, Developmental Journalism, and Social Responsibility." In *Communication Yearbook* 21, ed. Michael E. Roloff, 277–322. Thousand Oaks, CA: Sage.

———. 2005. *The Dao of the Press: A Humanocentric Theory*. Cresskill, NJ: Hampton.

Gunther, Richard, and Anthony Mughan, eds. 2000. *Democracy and the Media: A Comparative Perspective*. Cambridge: Cambridge University Press.

Gutmann, Amy, and Dennis Thompson. 1996. *Democracy and Disagreement*. Cambridge, MA: Harvard University Press.

———. 2004. *Why Deliberative Democracy?* Princeton, NJ: Princeton University Press.

Habermas, Jürgen. 1989. *The Structural Transformation of the Public Sphere*. Cambridge, MA: MIT Press. (Original German ed. 1962.)

———. 1990. *Moral Consciousness and Communicative Action*. Translated by Christian Lenhardt and Shierry Weber Nicholsen. Cambridge, MA: MIT Press.

———. 1994. *Justification and Application: Remarks on Discourse Ethics*. Translated by Ciaran P. Cronin. Cambridge, MA: MIT Press.

———. 1995. "Reconciliation through the Public Use of Reason: Remarks on John Rawls' Political Liberalism." *Journal of Philosophy* 52: 109–31.

———. 1996a. *Between Facts and Norms*. Translated by W. Rehg. Cambridge, MA: MIT Press.

———. 1996b. "Three Normative Models of Democracy." In *Democracy and Difference*, ed. Seyla Benhabib, 21–30. Princeton, NJ: Princeton University Press.

———. 2006. "Political Communication in Media Society: Does Democracy Still Enjoy an Epistemic Dimension? The Impact of Normative Theory on Empirical Research." *Communication Theory* 16(4): 411–26.

Hachten, William. 1981. *The World News Prism: Changing Media, Clashing Ideologies*. Ames: Iowa State University Press.

Hachten, William A., and James F. Scotton. 2007. *The World News Prism: Global Information in a Satellite Age*. 7th ed. Malden, MA: Blackwell.

Hackett, Robert A. 1984. "Decline of a Paradigm? Bias and Objectivity in News Media Studies." *Critical Studies in Mass Communication* 4(1): 229–59.

Hakker, Kenneth L., and Jan van Dijk, eds. 2000. *Digital Democracy*. London: Sage.

Hallin, Daniel C. 1997. "The Media and War." In *International Media Research: A Critical Survey,* ed. John Corner et al., 206–31. London: Routledge.

———. 1996. *Keeping America on Top of the World: Television Journalism and the Public Sphere.* New York: Routledge.

Hallin, Daniel C., and Paolo Mancini. 2004. *Comparing Media Systems: Three Models of Media and Politics.* Cambridge, UK: Cambridge University Press.

Hallin, Daniel C., and Todd Gitlin. 1993. "Agon and Ritual: The Gulf War as Popular Culture and as Television Drama." *Political Communication* 10: 411–24.

Hamelink, Cees. 1994. *The Politics of World Communication.* London: Sage.

———. 2000. *The Ethics of Cyberspace.* Thousand Oaks, CA: Sage.

———. 2008. "On Being Critical." *Communication, Culture and Critique* 1(1): 3–7.

Hamelink, Cees, and Kaarle Nordenstreng. 2007. "Towards Democratic Media Governance." In *Media between Culture and Commerce,* ed. Els de Bens, 225–40. Bristol, UK: Intellect.

Hanitzsch, Thomas. 2007. "Deconstructing Journalism Culture: Toward a Universal Theory." *Communication Theory* 17: 367–85.

Hanson, Ralph E. 2008. *Mass Communication: Living in a Media World.* 2nd ed. Washington, DC: CQ Press.

Hardt, Hanno. 1992. *Critical Communication Studies.* London: Sage.

———. 1995. "Without the Rank and File: Journalism History, Media Workers, and Problems of Representation." In *Newsworkers: Toward a History of the Rank and File,* ed. Hanno Hardt and Bonnie Brennen, 1–29. Minneapolis: University of Minnesota Press.

———. 2001. *Social Theories of the Press: Constituents of Communication Research, 1940s to 1920s.* 2nd ed. Lanham, MD: Rowman and Littlefield.

Hartley, John, and Alan McKee. 2000. *The Indigenous Public Sphere. The Reporting and Reception of Aboriginal Issues in the Australian Media.* Oxford, UK: Oxford University Press.

Harwood, Richard. 1995. "Some Criticism a Species of Poppycock." *Journal of Mass Media Ethics* 10(4): 251–53.

Hayner, Priscilla B. 2002. *Unspeakable Truths: Facing the Challenge of Truth Commissions.* New York: Routledge.

Held, David. 1992. "Democracy: From City-States to a Cosmopolitan Order?" *Political Studies* 40: 10–39.

———. 1995. *Democracy and the Global Order: From the Modern State to Cosmopolitan Governance.* Padstow, Cornwall, UK: Polity.

———. 2004. *Global Covenant: The Social Democratic Alternative to the Washington Consensus.* Cambridge, UK: Polity.

———. 2006. *Models of Democracy.* 3rd ed. Cambridge, UK: Polity.

Herbst, Susan. 1993. "The Meaning of Public Opinion: Citizens' Constructions of Political Reality." *Media, Culture and Society* 15: 437–54.

Herfkens, Eveline. 2001. "Communication Must Strengthen Civil Society." *Media Development* 48(4): 6–7.

Hilde, Thomas C. 2004. "The Cosmopolitan Project: Does the Internet Have a Global Public Face?" *Philosophy and Public Policy Quarterly* 24(1–2) (winter–spring): 19–26.

Hobbes, Thomas. 1985. *Leviathan*. London: Penguin Books. Originally published 1651.

Hocking, William Ernest. 1947. *Freedom of the Press: A Framework of Principle*. Chicago: University of Chicago Press.

Hodges, Lou. 1995. "Cases and Commentaries: The Unabomber." *Journal of Mass Media Ethics* 10(4): 248–49.

Hoffmann-Riem, Wolfgang. 1996. *Regulating Media: The Licensing and Supervision of Broadcasting in Six Countries*. New York: Guilford.

Horwitz, Robert Brit. 1989. *The Irony of Regulatory Reform*. Oxford, UK: Oxford University Press.

Howley, Kevin. 2005. *Community Media. People, Places and Communication Technologies*. Cambridge, UK: Cambridge University Press.

Hutchins, Robert 1947. *A Free and Responsible Press: Report of the Commission on Freedom of the Press*. Chicago: University of Chicago Press.

Immerwahr, John, and J. Doble. 1982. "Public Attitudes towards Freedom of the Press." *Public Opinion Quarterly* 46(2): 177–94.

Irwin, T. H. 1992. "Plato: The Intellectual Background." In *The Cambridge Companion to Plato,* ed. Richard Kraut, 51–89. Cambridge, UK: Cambridge University Press.

Isaac, Jeffrey. 1993. "Civil Society and the Spirit of Revolt." *Dissent* 40(3): 356–61.

Jakubowicz, Karol. 1990. "Between Communism and Post-Communism: How Many Varieties of Glasnost?" In *Democratization and the Media: An East-West Dialogue,* ed. Slavko Splichal, John Hochheimer, and Karol Jakubowicz, 40–55. Ljubljana, Yugoslavia: Communication and Culture Colloquia.

———. 1995. "Lovebirds? The Media, the State and Politics in Central and Eastern Europe." *Javnost—The Public* 2(1): 75–93.

———. 1996. "Civil Society and Public Sphere in Central and Eastern Europe: A Polish Case Study." *Nordicom Review* 2(96): 39–50.

———. 2007. *Rude Awakening: Social and Media Change in Central and Eastern Europe.* Cresskill, NJ: Hampton.

Jankowski, Nicholas, with Ole Prehn, eds. 2002. *Community Media in the Information Age.* Cresskill, NJ: Hampton.

Janowitz, Morris. 1975. "Professional Models in Journalism: The Gatekeeper and Advocate." *Journalism Quarterly* 52(4): 618–26.

Jenks, Rod. 2001. *The Contribution of Socratic Method and Plato's Theory of Truth to Plato Scholarship.* Lampeter, Wales: Edwin Mellen Press.

Johnstone, Christopher Lyle. 2002. "Aristotle's Ethical Theory in the Contemporary World: *Logos, Phronesis,* and the Moral Life." In *Moral Engagement in Public Life: Theorists for Contemporary Ethics,* ed. Sharon L. Bracci and Clifford G. Christians, 16–34. New York: Peter Lang.

Johnstone, J. W. L., E. J. Slawski, and W. W. Bowman. 1976. *The News People.* Urbana: University of Illinois Press.

Jones, Philip. 1997. *The Italian City-State: From Commune to Signoria.* Oxford, UK: Clarendon.

Kamilipour, Yahya, and Nancy Snow, eds. 2004. *War, Media and Propaganda: A Global Perspective.* Lanham, MD: Rowman and Littlefield.

Kaviraj, Sudipta, and Sunil Khilnani, eds. 2001. *Civil Society: History and Possibilities.* Cambridge, UK: Cambridge University Press.

Keane, John. 1995. "Structural Transformations of the Public Sphere." *Communication Review* 1(1): 1–22.

Keller, Bill. 2005. "N. Y. Times Statement Defends NSA Reporting." CNN.com. www.cnn.com/2005/US/2/6/nytimes.statement.

Kennedy, George A. 1994. *A New History of Classical Rhetoric.* Princeton, NJ: Princeton University Press.

———. 1999. *Classical Rhetoric and Its Christian and Secular Tradition from Ancient to Modern Times.* 2nd ed. Chapel Hill: University of North Carolina Press.

Kirtley, Jane. 1995. "The End of an Era of Independence." *Journal of Mass Media Ethics* 10(4): 249–51.

Kiss, Elizabeth. 2000. "Moral Ambition within and beyond Political Constraints: Reflections on Restorative Justice." In *Truth v. Justice: The Morality of Truth Commissions,* ed. Robert I. Rotberg and Dennis Thompson, 68–98. Princeton, NJ: Princeton University Press.

Koehn, Daryl. 1998. *Rethinking Feminist Ethics.* New York: Routledge.

Kohlberg, Lawrence. 1981. *Essays on Moral Development.* Vol. 1., *The Philosophy of Moral Development.* San Francisco: Harper and Row.

Kovach, Bill, and M. Rosenstiel. 2001. *The Elements of Journalism: What Journalists Should Know and the Public Should Expect.* New York: Three Rivers Press.

Kymlicka, Will. 1989. *Liberalism, Community and Culture.* New York: Oxford University Press.

———. 2001. *Politics and the Vernacular: Nationalism, Multiculturalism, and Citizenship.* New York: Oxford University Press.

Laclau, Ernesto, and Chantal Mouffe. 1985. *Hegemony and Socialist Strategy: Towards a Radical Democratic Politics.* London: Verso.

Lahav, Pnina. 1985. "Israel's Press Law." *In Press Law in Modern Democracies,* ed. Pnina Lahav, 265–313. New York: Longman.

———. 1993. "The Press and National Security." In *National Security and Democracy in Israel,* ed. Avner Yaniv, 173–95. Boulder, CO: Lynne Rienner.

Laitila, Tiina 1995. "Journalistic Codes of Ethics in Europe." *European Journal of Communication* 10(4): 513–26.

Lambeth, Edmund B. 1995. "Global Media Philosophies." In *Global Journalism: Survey of International Communication,* 3rd ed., ed. John C. Merrill, 3–18. New York: Longman.

———. 1998. "Public Journalism as a Democratic Practice." In *Assessing Public Journalism,* ed. Edmund B. Lambeth, Philip E. Meyer, and Esther Thorson, 15–35. Columbia: University of Missouri Press.

Lambeth, Edmund B., Philip E. Meyer, and Esther Thorson, eds. 1998. *Assessing Public Journalism.* Columbia: University of Missouri Press.

Lasswell, Harold. 1948. "The Structure and Function of Communication in Society." In *The Communication of Ideas,* ed. L. Bryson, 37–51. New York: Institute for Religious and Social Studies.

Lee, Kuan Yew. 2000. "From Third World to First: The Singapore Story from 1965–2000." In *Memoirs of Lee Kuan Yew*, 212–25. Singapore: Times Publishing and Singapore Press Holdings.

Lessig, Lawrence. 1999. *Code and Other Laws of Cyberspace*. New York: Basic Books.

Levinas, Emmanuel. 1981. *Otherwise Than Being or Essence*. The Hague: Martinus Nijhoff.

Levy, Leonard W. 1999. *The Palladium of Justice: Origins of Trial by Jury*. Chicago: Ivan R. Dee.

Limor, Yehiel, and Hillel Nossek. 1995. "Military Censorship in Israel: Anachronism in a Changing World or Modern Model of Coexistence between Press and Government in a Democracy." *Leipziger Jarhbuch zur Buchgeschichte* 5: 281–302.

Lippman, Matthew. 2007. "Darfur: The Politics of Genocide Denial Syndrome." *Journal of Genocide Research* 9(2): 193–213.

Lippmann, Walter. 1922. *Public Opinion*. New York: Free Press.

Locke, John. 1960. *Two Treatises on Government*. Edited by Peter Laslett. Cambridge, UK: Cambridge University Press.

Lowenstein, Ralph L., and John C. Merrill. 1990. *Macromedia: Mission, Message, and Morality*. New York: Longman.

Luscombe, D. E., and G. R. Evans. 1988. "The Twelfth-Century Renaissance." In *The Cambridge History of Medieval Political Thought*, ed. J. H. Burns, 306–40. Cambridge, UK: Cambridge University Press.

Lyon, David, ed. 2006. *Theorizing Surveillance: The Panopticon and Beyond*. Devon: Willan.

Lyotard, Jean-Francois. 1988. *The Differend: Phrases in Dispute*. Minneapolis: University of Minnesota Press.

MacCullum, Gerald. 1967. "Negative and Positive Freedom." *Philosophical Review* 76 (July): 314.

Macedo, Stephen, ed. 1999. *Deliberative Politics: Essays on Democracy and Disagreement*. New York: Oxford University Press.

——. 2003. *Diversity and Distrust: Civic Education in a Multicultural Democracy*. Cambridge, MA: Harvard University Press.

Mancini, Paolo. 1996. "Do We Need Normative Theories of Journalism?" Paper presented at the Joan Shorenstein Center on the Press, Politics and Public Policy, J. F. Kennedy School of Government, Harvard University.

Manheim, Jarol B. 2007. "The News Shapers: Strategic Communication as a Third Force in Newsmaking." In *The Politics of News: News of Politics*, ed. Doris Graber, Denis McQuail, and Pippa Norris, 98–116.Washington, DC: CQ Press.

Mansell, Robin, and Kaarle Nordenstreng. 2006. "Great Media and Communication Debates: WSIS and the MacBride Report." *Information Technologies and International Development* 3(4): 15–36.

Marongiu, Antonio. 1968. *Medieval Parliaments: A Comparative Study*. Translated and adapted by S. J. Woolf. London: Eyre and Spottiswoode.

Martin, John L., and Anju G. Chadbury. 1983. *Comparative Media Systems*. New York: Longman.

Martin-Barbero, Jesus. 1993. *Communication, Culture and Hegemony: From the Media to Mediations.* London: Sage.

Marx, Karl. 1970. *The Civil War in France.* Peking: Foreign Language Press.

Marzolf, Marion Tuttle. 1991. *Civilizing Voices: American Press Criticism 1850–1950.* New York: Longman.

Massey, Brian L., and Li-jing Arthur Chang. 2002. "Locating Asian Values in Asian Journalism: A Content Analysis of Web Newspapers." *Journal of Communication* 52 (December): 987–1003.

Masterton, Murray, ed. 1996. *Asian Values in Journalism.* Singapore: AMIC.

McCarthy, Cameron. 1998. *The Uses of Culture: Education and the Limits of Ethnic Affiliation.* New York: Routledge.

McCarthy, Cameron, Michael Giardina, Susan Harewood, and Jin-Kyung Park. 2003. "Contesting Culture: Identity and Curriculum Dilemmas in the Age of Globalization, Postmodernism, and Multiplicity." *Harvard Educational Review* 73(3): 449–65.

McChesney, Robert. 1999. *Rich Media, Poor Democracy: Communication Politics in Dubious Times.* Urbana: University of Illinois Press.

———. 2007. *Communication Revolution: Critical Junctures and the Future of Media.* New York: New Press.

McChesney, Robert W., and John Nichols. 2002. *Our Media, Not Theirs.* New York: Seven Stories Press.

McChesney, Robert, and Ben Scott, eds. 2004. *Our Unfree Press: 100 Years of Radical Media Criticism.* New York: Free Press.

McLaren, Peter, and Compañeras y Compañeros. 2005. *Red Seminars. Radical Excursions into Educational Theory, Cultural Politics, and Pedagogy.* Cresskill, NJ: Hampton.

McLaren, Peter, and Joe Kincheloe, eds. 2007. *Critical Pedagogy: Where Are We Now?* New York: Peter Lang.

McManus, John H. 1994. *Market-Driven Journalism: Let the Citizen Beware.* Thousand Oaks, CA: Sage.

McQuail, Denis. 1983. *Mass Communication Theory: An Introduction.* Beverly Hills, CA: Sage.

———. 1992. "Media Performance: Mass Communication and the Public Interest." London: Sage. 2nd ed. 1987; 3rd ed. 1994.

———. 1994. *Mass Communication Theory: An Introduction.* 3rd ed. Thousand Oaks, CA: Sage.

———. 2000. *McQuail's Mass Communication Theory.* 4th ed. London: Sage. 5th ed. 2005.

———. 2003. *Media Accountability and Freedom of Publication.* Oxford: Oxford University Press.

———. 2005. *McQuail's Mass Communication Theory.* 5th ed. London: Sage.

Media and Gender Monitor. 2005. "Promoting Gender Equality in News Media: GMMP 2005." *WACC Publications,* no. 16 (March). www.globalmediamonitoring.org.

Mehra, Achal, ed. 1989. *Press Systems in ASEAN States.* Singapore: AMIC.

Meiklejohn, Alexander. 1960. *Political Freedom: The Constitutional Powers of the People.* New York: Harper.

Merrill, John C. 1974. *The Imperative of Freedom: A Philosophy of Journalistic Autonomy.* New York: Hastings House.

———. 1977. *Existential Journalism.* New York: Hastings House.

———. 1989. "The Marketplace: A Court of First Resort." In *Media Freedom and Accountability,* ed. Everette E. Dennis, Donald M. Gillmor, and Theodore L. Glasser, 11–23. Westport, CT: Greenwood.

———. 2002. "The *Four Theories of the Press* Four and a Half Decades Later: A Retrospective." *Journalism Studies* 3(1): 133–34.

Merrill, John C., John Lee, and Edward Jay Friedlander. 1994. *Modern Mass Media.* 2nd ed. New York: Harper Collins.

Merrill, John C., and Ralph L. Lowenstein. 1979. *Media, Messages, and Men: New Perspectives in Communication.* 2nd ed. New York: Longman.

———. 1991. *Media, Messages, and Men: New Perspectives in Communication.* New York: David McKay.

Merritt, Davis. 1995. *Public Journalism and Public Life: Why Telling the News Is Not Enough.* Hillsdale, NJ: Erlbaum.

Merritt, Davis, and Maxwell McCombs. 2004. *The Two W's of Journalism: The Why and What of Public Affairs Reporting.* Mahwah, NJ: Erlbaum.

Merton, Robert K. 1949. "Patterns of Influence." In *Social Theory and Social Structure,* 387–470. Glencoe, IL: Free Press.

Meyer, Philip. 1987. *Ethical Journalism.* New York: Longman.

Meyer, Thomas. 2002. *Media Democracy.* Cambridge, UK: Polity.

Mill, John Stuart. 1951. "Essay on Liberty." In *Essential Works of John Stuart Mill,* ed. Max Lerner, 249–360. New York: Bantam. Originally published 1859.

Miller, David, and Michael Walzer. 2007. *Thinking Politically: Essays in Political Theory.* New Haven, CT: Yale University Press.

Milton, John. 1951. *Areopagitica: A Speech for the Liberty of Unlicensed Printing.* Boston: Beacon Press. Originally published 1644.

Mindich, David T. Z. 1998. *Just the Facts: How "Objectivity" Came to Define American Journalism.* New York: New York University Press.

Mnookin, Seth. 2004. *Hard News: The Scandals at the New York Times and Their Meaning for American Media.* New York: Random House.

Moemeka, Andrew Azukaego. 1997. "Communalisic Societies: Community and Self-Respect as African Values." In *Communication Ethics and Universal Values,* ed. Clifford Christians and Michael Traber, 170–93. London: Sage.

———. 2000. *Development Communication in Action: Building Understanding and Creating Participation.* Lanham, MD: University Press of America.

Mosco, Vincent. 1996. *The Political Economy of Communication: Rethinking and Renewal.* London: Sage.

Mouffe, Chantal, ed. 1992. *Dimensions of Radical Democracy: Pluralism, Citizenship, Community.* London: Verso.

Mowlana, Hamid. 1989. "Communication, Ethics, and the Islamic Tradition." In *Communication Ethics and Global Change,* ed. Thomas W. Cooper, 137–46. New York: Longman.

Mulhall, Stephen, and Adam Swift. 1996. *Liberals and Communitarians.* 2nd ed. Oxford, UK: Blackwell.

Mundt, Whitney R. 1991. "Global Media Philosophies." In *Global Journalism: Survey of International Communication,* 2nd ed., ed. John C. Merrill, 11–27. New York: Longman.

Murdock, Graham, and Peter Golding. 1974. "For a Political Economy of Mass Communications." In *Socialist Register,* ed. R. Miliband and J. Saville, 205–34. London: Merlin Press.

Mwangi, Sam Chege. 2001. "International Public Journalism." *Kettering Foundation Connections* 12(1): 23–27.

———. 2007. "The International Media and Democracy Project." www.centralstate.edu/imdp/Survey/c_studies.html.

Napoli, Philip M. 2001. *Foundations of Communications Policy: Principles and Process in the Regulation of Electronic Media.* Cresskill, NJ: Hampton.

Nederman, Cary J., and John Christian Laursen. 1996. "Difference and Dissent." In *Difference and Dissent: Theories of Tolerance In Medieval and Early Modern Europe,* ed. Cary J. Nederman and John Christian Laursen, 1–16. Lanham, MD: Rowman and Littlefield.

Negt, Oskar, and Alexander Kluge. 1993. *The Public Sphere and Experience: Toward an Analysis of the Bourgeois and Proletarian Public Sphere.* Minneapolis: University of Minnesota Press.

Nerone, John, ed. 1995. *Last Rights: Revisiting Four Theories of the Press.* Urbana: University of Illinois Press.

———. 2002. "The *Four Theories of the Press* Four and a Half Decades Later: A Retrospective." *Journalism Studies* 3(1): 134–36.

———. 2004. "Four Theories of the Press in Hindsight: Reflections on a Popular Model." In *New Frontiers in International Communication Theory,* ed. Medhi Semati, 21–32. Lanham, MD: Rowman and Littlefield.

Nichols, Mary P. 1992. *Citizens and Statesmen: A Study of Aristotle's Politics.* Lanham, MD: Rowman and Littlefield.

Nordenstreng, Kaarle. 1968. "Communication Research in the United States: A Critical Perspective." *Gazette* 14(3): 207–16.

———, ed. 1973. *Informational Mass Communication.* Helsinki: Tammi.

———. 1984. *The Mass Media Declaration of UNESCO.* Norwood, NJ: Ablex.

———. 1997. "Beyond the Four Theories of the Press." In *Media and Politics in Transition: Cultural Identity in the Age of Globalization,* ed. Jan Servaes and Rico Lie, 97–109. Leuven, Belgium: Acco.

———. 1999. "The Context: Great Media Debate." In *Towards Equity in Global Communication: MacBride Update,* ed. Richard Vincent, Kaarle Nordenstreng, and Michael Traber, 235–68. Cresskill, NJ: Hampton.

———. 2000. "The Structural Context of Media Ethics." In *Media Ethics: Opening Social Dialogue,* ed. Bart Pattyn, 81–98. Leuven, Belgium: Peeters.

———. 2004. "Ferment in the Field: Notes on the Evolution of Communication Studies and Its Disciplinary Nature." *Javnost—The Public* 11(3): 5–18.

Nordenstreng, Kaarle, and H. Topuz. 1989. *Journalist: Status, Rights and Responsibilities*. Prague: IOJ.

Norris, Pippa. 2001. *The Digital Divide*. Cambridge, UK: Cambridge University Press.

Nossek, Hillel, and Yehiel Limor. 2001. "Fifty Years in a 'Marriage of Convenience': News Media and Censorship in Israel." *Communication Law and Policy* 6 (winter): 1–35.

Nozick, Robert. 1974. *Anarchy, State and Utopia*. New York: Basic Books.

Nussbaum, Martha. 2001. *Women and Human Development: The Capabilities Approach*. Cambridge, UK: Cambridge University Press.

Nyamnjoh, Francis. 2005. *Africa's Media, Democracy and the Politics of Belonging*. London: Zed Books.

Ober, Josiah. 1989. *Mass and Elite in Democratic Athens: Rhetoric, Ideology and the Power of the People*. Princeton, NJ: Princeton University Press.

———. 1996. *The Athenian Revolution: Essays on Ancient Greek Democracy and Political Theory*. Princeton, NJ: Princeton University Press.

———. 1998. *Political Dissent in Democratic Athens*. Princeton, NJ: Princeton University Press.

Pacey, Arnold. 1992. *The Culture of Technology*. Cambridge, MA: MIT Press.

———. 2001. *Meaning in Technology*. Cambridge, MA: MIT Press.

Page, Benjamin I., and Robert Y. Shapiro. 1992. *The Rational Public*. Chicago: University of Chicago Press.

Pasquali, Antonio. 1997. "The Moral Dimension of Communicating." In *Communication Ethics and Universal Values*, ed. C. Christians and M. Traber, 24–45. Thousand Oaks, CA: Sage.

Patterson, Thomas E. 1994. *Out of Order: An Incisive and Boldly Original Critique of the News Media's Dominance of American Political Process*. New York: Vintage.

———. 1998. "Political Roles of the Journalist." In *The Politics of News, The News of Politics*, ed. Doris Graber, Denis McQuail, and Pippa Norris, 17–32. Washington, DC: CQ Press.

Paulu, Burton. 1981. *Television and Radio in the United Kingdom*. London: Macmillan Press.

Peri, Yoram. 2004. *Telepopulism: Media and Politics in Israel*. Stanford, CA: Stanford University Press.

Peters, John Durham. 1999. *Speaking into the Air: A History of the Idea of Communication*. Chicago: University of Chicago Press.

Peterson, Theodore. 1965. "The Social Responsibility Theory of the Press." In Fred S. Siebert, Theodore Peterson, and Wilbur Schramm, *Four Theories of the Press*, 73–103. Urbana: University of Illinois Press.

Picard, Robert. 1985. *The Press and the Decline of Democracy: The Democratic Socialist Response in Public Policy*. Westport, CT: Greenwood.

Pietilä, Veikko. 2005. *On the Highway of Mass Communication Studies*. Cresskill, NJ: Hampton.

Pietilä, Veikko, Tarmo Malmberg, and Kaarle Nordenstreng. 1990. "Theoretical Convergences and Contrasts: A View from Finland." *European Journal of Communication* 5(2–3): 165–85.

Plaisance, Patrick L. 2000. "The Concept of Media Accountability Reconsidered." *Journal of Mass Media Ethics* 15(4): 257–68.

Platon, Sara, and Mark Deuze. 2003. "Indymedia Journalism: A Radical Way of Making, Selecting and Sharing News." *Journalism* 4(3): 336–55.

Poster, Mark. 2001. *The Information Subject.* Amsterdam: G + B Arts International.

Poulakas, John. 1995. *Sophistical Rhetoric in Classical Greece.* Columbia: University of South Carolina Press.

Powell, J. G. F. 1995. *Cicero the Philosopher.* New York: Oxford University Press.

Pritchard, David. 2001. *Holding the Media Accountable.* Bloomington: University of Indiana Press.

Protess, David L., et al. 1991. *The Journalism of Outrage: Investigative Reporting and Agenda Building in America.* New York: Guilford.

Pulkkinen, Tuija. 2000. *The Postmodern and Political Agency.* Jyväskylä, Finland: University of Jyväskylä.

Ramonet, Ignacio. 2003. "Set the Media Free." *Le Monde diplomatique,* October. English ed.: http://mondediplo.com/2003/10/01media.

Rawls, John. 1993. *Political Liberalism.* New York: Columbia University Press.

Raymond, Joel, ed. 1999. *News, Newspapers and Society in Early Modern Britain.* London: Cass.

Reaume, Denise G. 2000. "Official-Language Rights: Intrinsic Values and the Protection of Difference." In *Citizenship in Diverse Societies,* ed. Will Kymlicka, and Wayne Norman, 245–72. Oxford, UK: Oxford University Press.

Reed, C. M., 2003. *Maritime Traders in the Ancient Greek World.* Cambridge, UK: Cambridge University Press.

Rennie, Ellie. 2006. *Community Media: A Global Introduction.* Lanham, MD: Rowman and Littlefield.

Riedel, Manfred. 1984. *Between Tradition and Revolution: The Hegelian Transformation of Political Philosophy.* Cambridge, UK: Cambridge University Press.

Riesenberg, Peter. 1992. *Citizenship in the Western Tradition: From Plato to Rousseau.* Chapel Hill: University of North Carolina Press.

Risen, James, and Eric Lichtblau. 2005. "Bush Lets U.S. Spy on Callers without Courts." *New York Times,* December 16, 2005, A1, A22.

Rivers, William L., and M. J. Nyhan. 1973. *Aspen Notebooks on Government and the Media.* New York: Praeger.

Robinson, John P., and Michael Levy. 1986. *The Main Source.* Beverly Hills, CA: Sage.

Rodriguez, Clemencia. 2001. *Fissures in the Mediascape: An International Study of Citizens' Media.* Cresskill, NJ: Hampton.

Rodriguez, Ileana, ed. 2001. *The Latin American Subaltern Studies Reader.* Durham, NC: Duke University Press.

Rosen, Jay. 1999a. "The Action of the Idea: Public Journalism in Built Form." In *The Idea of Public Journalism,* ed. Theodore Glasser, 21–48. New York: Guilford.

———. 1999b. *What Are Journalists For?* New Haven, CT: Yale University Press.

Rotberg, Robert, and Dennis Thompson, eds. 2000. *Truth v. Justice: The Morality of Truth Commissions.* Princeton, NJ: Princeton University Press.

———. 2000. "Truth Commissions and the Provision of Truth, Justice and Reconciliation." In *Truth v. Justice: The Morality of Truth Commissions,* ed. Robert Rotberg and Dennis Thompson, 3–21. Princeton, NJ: Princeton University Press.

Royal Commission on the Press.1949. *Report.* Command 7700. London: His Majesty's Stationery Office.

Sabine, Gordon H. 1952. "The Two Democratic Traditions." *Philosophical Review* 61: 451–74.

Salmon, Charles T., and Theodore L. Glasser. 1995. "The Politics of Polling and the Limits of Consent." In *Public Opinion and the Communication of Consent,* ed. Theodore L. Glasser and Charles T. Salmon, 437–58. New York: Guilford.

Sandbach, F. H. 1989. *The Stoics.* Bristol, UK: Bristol Classical Press.

Sandel, Michael. 1982. *Liberalism and the Limits of Justice.* New York: Cambridge University Press.

———. 1984. "The Procedural Republic and the Unencumbered Self." *Political Theory* 12: 93.

———. 1998. *Democracy's Discontents.* Cambridge, MA: Belknap Press.

———. 2005. *Public Philosophy: Essays on Morality and Politics.* Cambridge, MA: Harvard University Press.

Schiappa, Edward. 1991. *Protagoras and Logos: A Study in Greek Philosophy and Rhetoric.* Columbia: University of South Carolina Press.

Schiller, Dan. 1996. *Theorizing Communication: A History.* New York: Oxford University Press.

———. 2000. *Digital Capitalism: Networking the Global Market System.* Cambridge, MA: MIT Press.

———. 2007. *How to Think about Information.* Urbana: University of Illinois Press.

Schirato, Tony. 2000. *Communication and Culture. An Introduction.* London: Sage.

Schirato, Tony, and Jen Webb. 2003. *Understanding Globalization.* London: Sage.

Schouls, Peter. 1992. *Reasoned Freedom: John Locke and Enlightenment.* Ithaca, NY: Cornell University Press.

Schramm, Wilbur. 1957. *Responsibility in Mass Communication.* New York: Harper.

Schudson, Michael. 1998. *The Good Citizen.* New York: Free Press.

———. 1999. "What Public Journalism Knows about Journalism but Does Not Know about the Public." In *The Idea of Public Journalism,* ed. Theodore L. Glasser, 118–35. New York: Guilford.

———. 2003. *The Sociology of News.* New York: Norton.

Schulz, Julienne. 1998. *Reviving the Fourth Estate.* Cambridge, UK: Cambridge University Press.

Schulz, Winfried. 1997. "Changes in the Mass Media and the Public Sphere." *Public* 4(2): 57–70.

Schumpeter, Joseph A. 1942. *Capitalism, Socialism, and Democracy.* New York: Harper.

Seldes, George. 1938. *Lords of the Press.* New York: Julian Messner.

Servaes, Jan. 2001. "Participatory Communication Research for Democracy and Social Change." In *Communication and Development: The Freirean Connection,* ed. Michael Richards, Pradip Thomas, and Zaharom Nain, 13–32. Cresskill, NJ: Hampton.

———. 2007. *Communication for Development and Social Change.* Thousand Oaks, CA: Sage.

Servaes, Jan, and Rico Lie, eds. 1997. *Media and Politics in Transition: Cultural Identity in the Age of Globalization.* Leuven, Belgium: Acco.

Shah, Hemant. 1996. "Modernization, Marginalization, and Emancipation: Toward a Normative Model of Journalism and National Development." *Communication Theory* 6 (May): 143–66.

Shamir, Jacob. 1988. "Israeli Elite Journalists: Views on Freedom and Responsibility." *Journalism Quarterly* 65 (fall): 589–94, 647.

Sherman, Nancy. 1989. *The Fabric of Character: Aristotle's Theory of Virtue.* Oxford: Clarendon.

Sherwin-White, A. N. 1996. *The Roman Citizenship.* Oxford, UK: Clarendon.

Siebert, Frederick S. 1965. *Freedom of the Press in England 1476–1776.* Urbana: University of Illinois Press.

Siebert, Fred S., Theodore Peterson, and Wilbur Schramm. 1956. *Four Theories of the Press: The Authoritarian, Libertarian, Social Responsibility and Soviet Communist Concepts of What the Press Should Be and Do.* Urbana: University of Illinois Press.

Simmons, A. John. 1992. *The Lockean Theory of Rights.* Princeton: Princeton University Press.

Singer, Jane B. 2005. "The Political J-Blogger: 'Normalizing' a New Media Form to Fit Old Norms and Practices." *Journalism* 6(2): 173–98.

Sirianni, Carmen, and Lewis Friedland. 2005. *The Civic Renewal Movement: Community Building and Democracy in the United States.* Dayton, OH: Kettering Foundation Press.

Smith, Jeffrey A. 1988. *Printers and Press Freedom: The Ideology of Early American Journalism.* New York: Oxford University Press.

Solomon, William, and Robert McChesney, eds. 1993. *Ruthless Criticism. New Perspectives in U.S. Communication History.* Minneapolis: University of Minnesota Press.

Sparks, Colin. 1993. "Raymond Williams and the Theory of Democratic Communication." In *Communication and Democracy,* ed. Slavko Splichal and Janet Wasko, 69–86. Norwood, NJ: Ablex.

Spears, George, Kasia Seydegart, and Margaret Gallagher. 2000. *Who Makes the News? Global Monitoring Project 2000.* London: World Association of Christian Communication.

Splichal, Slavko. 2008. "Why Be Critical?" *Communication, Culture and Critique* 1(1): 20–30.

Stevenson, Nick. 1999. *Transformation of the Media: Globalization, Morality and Ethics.* London: Longman Pearson.

Suoranta, Juha, and Vadén, Tere. 2007. "From Social to Socialist Media: The Critical Potential of the Wikiworld." In *Critical Pedagogy: Where Are We Now?* ed. Peter McLaren and Joe Kincheloe, 143–62. New York: Peter Lang.

Sussman, Gerald, and Galizio, Lawrence. 2003. "The Global Reproduction of American Politics." *Political Communication* 20(3): 309–28.

Swanson, David, and Paolo Mancini. 1996. *Politics, Media and Modern Democracy.* Westport, CT: Praeger.

Swartz, Omar. 1998. *The Rise of Rhetoric and Its Intersections with Contemporary Critical Thought.* Boulder, CO: Westview Press.

Sylvester, Judith, and Suzanne Huffman. 2005. *Reporting from the Front: the Media and Military.* Lanham, MD: Rowman and Littlefield.

Tan, Yew Soon, and Soh Yew Peng. 1994. *The Development of Singapore's Modern Media Industry.* Singapore: Times Academic Press.

Taylor, Charles. 1989. *Sources of the Self: The Making of the Modern Identity.* Cambridge, MA: Harvard University Press.

———. 1992a. "Civil Society in the Western Tradition." In *The Notion of Tolerance in Human Rights,* ed. E. Groffier and M. Paradis, 117–36. Ottawa: Carleton University Press.

———. 1992b. *The Ethics of Authenticity.* Cambridge, MA: Harvard University Press.

———. 2007. *A Secular Age.* Cambridge, MA: Harvard University Belknap Press.

Taylor, Charles, et al. 1994. *Multiculturalism: Examining the Politics of Recognition.* Princeton, NJ: Princeton University Press.

Tessitore, Aristide. 1996. *Reading Aristotle's Ethics: Virtue, Rhetoric and Political Philosophy.* Albany: State University of New York Press.

Thomas, Pradip N. 1994. "Participatory Development Communication: Philosophical Premises." In *Participatory Communication: Working for Change and Development,* ed. Shirley A. White, 49–59. Delhi: Sage India.

Thompson, John B. 1995. *The Media and Modernity: A Social Theory of the Media.* Stanford, CA: Stanford University Press.

Traber, Michael, and Kaarle Nordenstreng. 2002. *Few Voices, Many Worlds: Towards a Media Reform Movement.* London: World Association for Christian Communication.

Truth and Reconciliation Commission. 2006. *Truth and Reconciliation Commission of South Africa Report.* New York: Palgrave Macmillan. (Originally published March 21, 2003.)

Tully, James. 1995. *Strange Multiplicity.* Cambridge, UK: Cambridge University Press.

Turley, Anna. 2004. "Global Media Monitoring Project." *Media and Gender Monitor* 15 (September): 3–12.

Turner, Bryan S. 1992. "Preface to the Second Edition." In *Professional Ethics and Civic Morals,* ed. Emile Durkheim, xiii–xliii. London: Routledge.

———, ed. 1993. *Citizenship and Social Theory.* London: Sage.

Weaver, David. 1999. *The Global Journalist.* Cresskill, NJ: Hampton.

Williams, Raymond. 1962. *Communications.* London: Penguin.

Van Cuilenburg, Jan J., and Denis McQuail. 2003. "Media Policy Paradigm Shifts." *European Journal of Communication* 18(2): 181–208.

van der Wurff, Richard. 2005. "Impacts of the Internet on Newspapers in Europe." *Gazette* 67(1): 107–20.

Van Zoonen, Liesbet. 1994. *Feminist Media Studies.* London: Sage.

Vasterman, Peter. 2005. "Media Hype: Self-Reinforcing News Waves, Journalistic Standards and the Construction of Social Problems." *European Journal of Communication* 20(4): 508–30.

Villa-Vicencio, Charles. 2001. "Communicating Reconciliation: In Pursuit of Humanity." *Media Development* 48(4): 31–37.

Vincent, Richard, Kaarle Nordenstreng, and Michael Traber, eds. 1999. *Towards Equity in Global Communication: MacBride Update.* Cresskill, NJ: Hampton.

Vittachi, Anuradha. 2001. "Can the Media Save the World?" *Media Development* 48(4): 50–52.

von Heyking, John. 2001. *Augustine and Politics as Longing in the World.* Columbia: University of Missouri Press.

Waldron, Jeremy. 1987. "Theoretical Foundations of Liberalism." *Philosophical Quarterly* 37: 135.

Walzer, Michael, ed. 1995. *Toward a Global Civil Society.* New York: Berghahn Books.

———. 2004. *Politics and Passion: Toward a More Egalitarian Liberalism.* New Haven, CT: Yale University Press.

Washburn, Patrick S. 1990, April. "The Office of Censorship's Attempt to Control Press Coverage of the Atomic Bomb during World War II." *Journalism Monographs* 120.

Weaver, David, ed. 1999. *The Global Journalist.* Cresskill, NJ: Hampton.

Weaver, David H., and G. Cleveland Wilhoit. 1986. *The American Journalist: A Portrait of U.S. News People and Their Work.* Bloomington: Indiana University Press.

———. 1996. *The American Journalist in the 1990s: US News People at the End of an Era.* Mawhah, NJ: Erlbaum.

Weber, Max. 1978. *Economy and Society.* 2 vols. Berkeley: University of California Press.

Webster, Frank. 2006. *Theories of the Information Society.* 3rd ed. London: Routledge.

Webster, James, and Patricia W. Phalen. 1997. *The Mass Audience: Rediscovering the Dominant Model.* Mahwah, NJ: Erlbaum.

Westley, Bruce, and Malcolm MacLean. 1957. "A Conceptual Model for Mass Communication Research." *Journalism Quarterly* 34: 31–38.

White, Gordon. 1994. "Civil Society, Democratization, and Development: Clearing the Analytical Ground." *Democratization* 1(3): 375–90.

White, Robert A. 1989. "Social and Political Factors in the Development of Communication Ethics." In *Communication Ethics and Global Change,* ed. Thomas Cooper, Clifford Christians, Frances Forde Plude, and Robert A. White, 40–66. New York: Longman.

———. 1994. "Participatory Development Communications as a Socio-Cultural Practice." In *Participatory Communication: Working for Change and Development,* ed. Shirley A. White, 95–116. New Delhi: Sage India.

Williams, Raymond. 1962. *Communications.* Harmondsworth, UK: Penguin.

Wood, Neal. 1988. *Cicero's Social and Political Thought.* Berkeley: University of California Press.

Wu, Wei, David Weaver, and Owen V. Johnson. 1996. "Professional Roles of Russian and U.S. Journalists: A Comparative Study." *Journalism and Mass Communication Quarterly* 73(3): 534–48.

Wuthnow, Robert. 1989. *Communities of Discourse: Ideology and Social Structure in the Reformation, the Enlightenment and European Socialism.* Cambridge, MA: Harvard University Press.

———, ed. 1992. *Vocabularies of Public Life.* London: Routledge.

Wyatt, Robert O. 1991. *Free Expression and the American Public, a Survey.* Washington, DC: ASNE.

Wyatt, Wendy. 2007. *Critical Conversation: A Theory of Press Criticism.* Cresskill, NJ: Hampton Press.

Wyschogrod, Edith. 1974. *Emmanuel Levinas: The Problem of Ethical Metaphysics.* The Hague: Martinus Nyhoff.

———. 1990. *Saints and Postmodernism: Revisioning Moral Philosophy.* Chicago: University of Chicago Press.

Xiaoge, Xu. 2005. *Demystifying Asian Values in Journalism.* Singapore: Marshall Cavendish International.

Yin, Jiafei. 2008. "Beyond Four Theories of the Press: A New Model for the Asian and the World Press." *Journalism and Communication Monographs* 10(1): 5–62.

Young, Iris Marion. 2000. *Inclusion and Democracy.* New York: Oxford University Press.

Zaller, John. 2003. "A New Standard of News Quality: Burglar Alarms for the Monitorial Citizen." *Political Communication* 20: 109–30.

Zassoursky, Ivan. 2004. *Media and Power in Post-Soviet Russia.* Armonk, NY: W. E. Sharpe.

Zassoursky, Yassen. 2001. "Media and the Public Interest: Balancing Between the State, Business and the Public Sphere." In *Russian Media Challenge,* ed. Kaarle Nordenstreng, Elena Vartanova, and Yassen Zassoursky, 155–88. Helsinki: Aleksanteri Institute.

Index

CLIFFORD G. CHRISTIANS is research professor of communications and director of the Institute of Communications Research at the University of Illinois at Urbana-Champaign. www.media.illinois.edu/faculty/christians.html

THEODORE L. GLASSER is professor in the Department of Communication at Stanford University, where he is also affiliated with the Program in Modern Thought and Literature. http://communication.stanford.edu/faculty/glasser .html

DENIS McQUAIL is emeritus professor of the School of Communication Research at the University of Amsterdam (the Netherlands), where he held the chair of Mass Communication from 1977 until 1997 and is currently an Honorary Research Fellow. www2.fmg.uva.nl/ascor/staff.html

KAARLE NORDENSTRENG is professor of the Faculty of Social Sciences at the University of Tampere (Finland), where he holds the chair of Journalism and Mass Communication. www.uta.fi/jour/english/contact/nordenstreng_eng .html

ROBERT A. WHITE is professor in the Faculty of Social Sciences and Communication at St. Augustine University of Tanzania, where he is also director of Postgraduate Studies and Research. www.saut.ac.tz/

THE HISTORY OF COMMUNICATION

The University of Illinois Press
is a founding member of the
Association of American University Presses.

———————————————————

Composed in 10.5/13 Adobe Minion Pro
with Meta display
by Jim Proefrock
at the University of Illinois Press
Manufactured by Thomson-Shore, Inc.

University of Illinois Press
1325 South Oak Street
Champaign, IL 61820-6903
www.press.uillinois.edu